THE SUENENS DOSSIER

The Case for Collegiality

THE SUENENS DOSSIER

The Case for Collegiality

José de Broucker

FIDES PUBLISHERS, INC.
NOTRE DAME, INDIANA

© COPYRIGHT 1970: FIDES PUBLISHERS, INC.
NOTRE DAME, INDIANA
LIBRARY OF CONGRESS CATALOG CARD NUMBER: 79-120475
ISBN: 0-8190-0515-0

THIS BOOK IS TRANSLATED FROM A FRENCH ORIGINAL
ENTITLED LE DOSSIER SUENENS
PUBLISHED BY EDITIONS UNIVERSITAIRES, PARIS 1970

Preface

One of the most important events in the life of the Church since the Second Vatican Council has been the interview Cardinal Suenens gave to *Informations catholiques internationales* of Paris on the unity of the Church in the logic of Vatican II.

The date was May 15, 1969, at the height of a crisis which many consider one of the most serious the Church has experienced in a long time. It came after the shock caused by the encyclical *Humanae vitae* on birth control and six months before the special Synod of Bishops called by Pope Paul VI to help him restore the authority and unity threatened by the outburst of experimentation and the explosion of debate which followed the Council.

Published simultaneously in twelve languages,* the interview shed a hard light on the sharp edges of the "credibility gap" which had reached into the very bosom of the Church and was steadily widening the breach between the Church and the world. The crisis became obvious to everybody. Cardinal Suenens forced each of us, at every level of responsibility, to take a stand on the diagnosis and on the remedies to be applied.

The Synod was to reveal that the vision of the primate of Belgium was shared by a large majority of the cardinals and bishops, to the surprise of most observers, for the impression

---

*French, English, German, Italian, Spanish, Dutch, Portugese, Czech, Hungarian, Polish, Croat and Catalan.

prevailed up to then that the cardinal represented scarcely anyone but himself, or at most, a small group of dissidents.

From the opening of the Synod, on the contrary, it was clear that favorable reactions to the interview of May 15 were far more numerous than the unfavorable ones. That was this writer's first impression when he began to collect, analyze and classify the voluminous file of commentaries which poured in during the summer and fall of 1969.

Although fewer in number, the critical reactions, often including personal attacks on the Cardinal, constituted an element of the diagnosis. This book takes them into account, but it is mainly concerned with the positions and proposals expressed by the cardinal and those who subsequently had the courage to speak out. The reason is not because they formed the majority, but because they are richer in hopes for the Church. While giving due consideration to the objections and difficulties raised, this report deliberately orients reflection toward the search for positive and constructive solutions.

The first part recalls the debates beginning with the interview of May 15 and going up to the Synod, including the discussions at the symposium of European bishops at Chur, Switzerland. A review of the reactions of world opinion enables one to put one's finger on the pulse of the Church. This section also treats the problem caused by the way in which the Cardinal made his statement: the rights and duties involved in the expression of public opinion in the Church.

Looking at the issue from another angle, with more perspective and detachment, the second part treats other key problems in depth. Is Cardinal Suenens' formulation of the logic of Vatican II the only acceptable one? How should the relationship between collegiality and primacy be understood and lived? Are ecclesiastical institutions subject to criticism and can they be reformed? Can Christian morality open up to pluralism without destroying itself?

These questions are answered by theologians who are specialists in their subjects and who have carefully examined the positions of both Cardinal Suenens and his critics in the light of the accepted theological principles.

After a survey of the ecumenical implications of the debate, a final chapter is devoted to the Synod. The results of the Synod, however positive, do not provide definite answers. But they mark a stage. They help us to see the goal.

Some may think that it is all quite "ecclesiastical," "ecclesiocentric," that it has little bearing on the more urgent problems of the world to which and for which Christ gave his Church its mission. On the contrary, the questions raised by Cardinal Suenens did not arise by the spontaneous generation of "a storm in a tea-cup." They are specific questions which a growing number of Christians are forced to ask by reason of the life they lead among people in the world. On the answers which are given depends not only the credibility of the Church for the entire world, but also more immediately, the possibility of its most elementary and direct Christian witness, especially toward the poor.

At stake in this debate is nothing less than the missionary responsibility of the Church. That is what places it on such a high level and makes it so important. This makes for both its grandeur and its gravity.

Contents

Introduction

To understand the Suenens "dossier," one must know the man, the cardinal himself, and see him in the context of the Church of today.

Cardinal Suenens was born in Brussels on July 16, 1904. His parents had a small brewery. He was ordained a priest in 1927. Doctor of philosophy and of theology, he was Vice-Rector and later interim Rector of the University of Louvain; auxiliary bishop of Malines in 1945, archbishop of Malines-Brussels in 1961, made cardinal by John XXIII in 1962.

From that time, his name and personality began to have a world-wide resonance. John XXIII honored him with his friendship. He selected him as a special emissary to the United Nations to present the great peace encyclical *Pacem in terris*. He also requested him to elaborate the plan of the Council.

The day following his election, Paul VI invited Suenens to his side on the balcony as he gave his first public blessing. He named him one of the four moderators of the Council, and asked him to preach the sermon at the memorial service for the late pope in St. Peter's in the presence of all the conciliar Fathers.

At the Council itself, besides his intervention of December 4, 1963, which was decisive for the choice of the conciliary theme centered on the Church *ad intra* and *ad extra,* the press made headlines of several of his proposals: an obligatory age limit for all bishops and cardinals; acknowledgment

1

of the charisms of the laity; permanent deacons; revisions of the procedure of canonizations; study of the birth-control problem ("One Galileo case is enough").

In the Commission of Coordination Cardinal Suenens was charged by John XXIII with the two schemas which were to become *Lumen Gentium* (on the Church) and *Gaudium et Spes* (on the Church in today's world). He was at the origin of that famous inversion—the "Copernican Revolution"—which put the chapter on the People of God before that on the hierarchy. He also succeeded in getting *Gaudium et Spes* over the hurdle of strong curial opposition both public and behind the scenes.

These aspects of the personality of Cardinal Suenens are public and belong to history. Other aspects, as a man and as a bishop, are less known. The daily and periodical press present a broad spectrum of evaluations.

The Catholic bishop of Leeds, Gordon Wheeler, described him in the *Ampleforth Journal* (Summer 1969) as

> . . . one of the giants of the second Vatican Council. He was regarded by some as a sign to be contradicted. This in no way distressed him or surprised him since he clearly thought of himself as possessing a kind of charisma for contradiction and he always undertook the role with humility and with a readiness to pay the price of misunderstanding. In the postconciliar period he has shown himself entirely faithful to this particular charisma, and hence we have *Coresponsibility in the Church* and the supplementary interview.

The sign-of-contradiction aspect has been grasped also outside the Roman Catholic Church. Bishop Chadwich, president of the Anglo-Catholic Commission, reviewing *Coresponsibility in the Church,* wrote:

> Cardinal Suenens is by any account an impressive figure in the ecumenical life of the Church today. For the Church of Rome he is a portent of real significance and, in some quarters, a sign to be spoken against. For those not of his Communion the humanity and charity of his outlook is an immediate challenge to rise above denominational barriers (*One in the Church*, No. 3, 1969).

As a sign of contradiction, on the negative side, is the bitter criticism of *l'Homme Nouveau* (6-15-69): "all those who acclaim him are at one in calling insubordination at the highest level 'courage,' and in describing a text which undermines tradition in its foundation as 'frankness.' "

Others carried insinuations and personal attacks even further. "The Roman Curia reactions are unanimous: all are openly relieved that Cardinal Suenens was not named Secretary of State. Certain here go so far as to say that these declarations of the cardinal are perhaps precisely due to his disappointment at not having got that post" (*L'Aurore*, 8-19-69).

A frequent criticism of the cardinal is that while he advocates democracy for the Church at large, in his own diocese he acts as a dictator. His close collaborators are of a very different opinion.

In an article which draws a portrait of the cardinal as a man of the Church and then as pastor of an important diocese, the well-known Belgian author Franz Weyergans, sums up:

Perhaps one could define the whole activity of Cardinal Suenens as coresponsibility at every level. In acting thus, he does not lessen leadership, nor the personality of his collaborators. He remains in the Church, but he opens the Church to the world. He leaves each one in his place, but each one can play his full role in that place. In reading his books, in hearing him speak, in seeing him at work, in contacting his immediate collaborators, it is evident that this spirit passes into everyday reality. By allying liberty and authority, by accepting collegiality at every level, Cardinal Suenens is very probably providing the most precious contribution he will bring in the immediate future to the universal Church (*Ecclesia*, August 1967).

Daniel Polet, a Belgian journalist, wrote in the weekly *Special* (7-2-69): "Archbishop Suenens at Malines does not at all act as a potentate. When a pastoral council was recently constituted in Brussels, all the members were freely elected."

Referring to this pastoral council, which was elected as seriously and democratically as could be, another Belgian journalist, George DeMaitre, wrote:

Few people have yet grasped the wide range, the originality, the import of innovations launched in his diocese by Cardinal Suenens. Since the Council, the transformation of the Catholic Church is well on its way, though stronger and more apparent at the periphery than at the center. Perhaps finally one day this renovated Church will recognize that Cardinal Suenens has not only shown himself to be a great cardinal and an intrepid bishop, but also a worthy prophet (*Phare-Dimanche*, 5-25-69).

In a letter to the Paris newspaper *Le Monde* (6-23-69), Marc Delepeleire of *La Revue Nouvelle* of Brussels wrote, under the title, "Cardinal Suenens, the Mote and the Beam":

Those who follow closely the life of the Catholic Church will not be surprised at the reactions of the Roman Curia to the interview of Cardinal Suenens.

The more liberal prelates regret the maladroitness—understand frankness—of the archbishop of Malines-Brussels. Others, and more numerous, refuse to meet the arguments of Cardinal Suenens and affirm their disagreement with his basic principle. According to tried techniques, they attack the person of the Primate of Belgium by subtle insinuations and half-veiled accusations. These remarks of "caustic commentators" quoted by the correspondent of *le Monde* were repeated to me with evident satisfaction during a recent visit to Rome, at the end of May.

All that is distressing but, after all, traditional and well in keeping with the judges of Ivan Illich. If it were not for the piquant detail: that of the Mote and the Beam. According to these zealous defenders of the Curia, Cardinal Suenens, a false progressive, is in his own diocese an autocratic conservative. And they quote the differences the cardinal has had and continues to have with some in his diocese, using criticisms addressed to him by groups or publications like ours.

If there is unrest in the archdiocese of Malines-Brussels—what about Florence or Rome?—it certainly does not spring from the traditionalism or the authoritarianism of the cardinal. To make such insinuations shows how little one knows him. The unrest was due to the fact that the cardinal delayed so long in speaking. His temperament led him to seek for solutions and compromise. His natural bent is towards diplomacy and discretion. It is true that he has difficulty, like all pastors of today, in dialoguing with certain spontaneous groups. But he has at least the merit of trying. In such a context, his clear and courageous declarations are a real liberation for many in his diocese.

Cardinal Suenens is aware of these contradictory interpretations of his thoughts and deeds. As he said after his interview: "I know I will be attacked. But I love the Church and the Pope, and I am ready to pay the price" (*Paris-Match*, 7-5-69).

The attacks are not only from those who reproach him unreasonably for not practicing what he preaches. Others ask if the cardinal should not be counted among those priests whom Pope Paul described as having "made a martyr of the Church." Under the cover of a challenge to the structures and the ecclesiastical institutions, are not the very foundations of the faith being all unconsciously sapped, if not by the cardinal himself, at least by those who acclaim him?

Such is not the judgment of Theodore Hesburgh, president of the University of Notre Dame. In a statement to the press (8-8-69), he sums him up: "He is a person with great courage saying what I think are very rational things. You can't say things like this without ruffling a little fur."

In the view of *Time* (8-1-69): "Suenens maintains a careful orthodoxy of language and purpose. He has little patience with ultraliberal Catholics who challenge basic Church doctrines." And in an interview with Robert Kroon, *Time* correspondent in Brussels, the cardinal said: "If you don't believe in the Holy Spirit or in the resurrection, or in life after death, leave the Church. The Church is not a sort of spiritual Red Cross organization . . . but something must be done and soon.

Under the title "Cardinal of the New Wave," the *New York Times* (7-24-69) wrote: "Cardinal Suenens is described by many as the strongest progressive voice in the Church's hierarchy; he is said to display a more marked interest in the power of the Gospel than in the routine of canon law."

Le Soir (Brussels, 1-15-69) once asked him where he would place himself. The Cardinal's reply is significant:

I would answer as did a well-known American theologian expert at the Council: "I am at the extreme center." In my opinion the two extreme conflicting tendencies, paradoxical as it may seem, suffer from a real lack of faith. But for different reasons.

The extreme left risks losing the purity of doctrinal faith. One is not or one is no longer a Christian if there is not belief in a personal and transcendant God, in the divinity of Christ, in his resurrection, in life everlasting, in the real presence, as in all that implies the life of Christ in us today. There can be no ambiguity here. But, at the extreme right, I see a lack of faith also, not on the doctrinal but on the existential level. They have no true real faith in the active presence of the Holy Spirit in the Church today.

A strong faith demands not only fidelity to the past but also openness to and acceptance of the future. Authentic faith flows into hope. All legitimate aspirations in the Church and in the world must be taken into account, for the Church and the world are linked together.

The Council forced the Church to launch out into the deep; it is not all plain sailing, for she must face stormy waters and yet maintain her balance. Christians today, no matter what their natural tendencies may be, must be receptive to one another, refuse all sectarianism, be full of charity for their opponents, be armed with a certain dose of patience and impatience at the same time; but over and above, they must be conscious of what is vital and essential and common to all. Their hope in the future must be based, not on a naturally optimistic temperament, but on the certitude that Christ is living among us.

Such is the spirit in which the "dossier" has been compiled. It should be read with the same dispositions.

1

The Suenens Interview

"For those interested in history-making dates in the life of the Church, I suggest May 15, 1969, as a candidate for the most select list. That was the day on which *Informations catholiques internationales* published this interview" (Gary Mac-Eoin, in *St. Louis Review,* 6-20-69).

The reference is to the interview given by Cardinal Suenens to José de Broucker, editor of *Informations catholiques internationales.* History-making though it might be, this interview was only the prolongation, development and clarification of the cardinal's book published a year earlier, *Coresponsibility in the Church.*

"The fact that the book is enormously important and satisfactory," Rosemary Haughton commented when the English translation appeared, "is partly due to its inherent virtues of honesty, charity, farsightedness and vigorous hope. But this is also and to a far greater extent a historic event due to the assessment it demands from the other point of view, of coresponsibility in the Church as an event in Christian history. Many Catholics are rightly worried and shamed by the mean and poor-spirited, as well as the logically unsound, behavior and attitudes of some of their spiritual leaders.

"Here is a man whose ideals and aims are clear and explicit, but who, because he intends to make them a reality, is going to take people along with him whenever possible. If he can avoid antagonizing he will, not only for tactical reasons but because he sees others in the Church as coresponsible with himself in the work of Christ. He avoids even valid polemic" (*New Christian*, February 1969).

Months went by. The development of the crisis in the Church showed that the urgency of the cardinal's appeal had not been sufficiently recognized. Then José de Broucker reread *Coresponsibility in the Church.* "I noticed," he wrote in an explanatory note prefixed to the interview, "that the book contained not only a substantive thesis, but also a number of observations, of question marks and hypothetical suggestions that left the reader asking for further clarification. These were the questions I formulated for the archbishop of Malines-Brussels and which he graciously answered."

In your book, Coresponsibility in the Church, *you make a special study of coresponsibility at the level of the Holy See. It cannot be denied that there is at present a tension between the center and the periphery. May one ask where precisely you consider the tension to lie?*

I will gladly answer your question, but only in terms of tendencies, functions and institutions as such, rather than of personalities; in any case the intentions of individuals are not under question, and to classify them *en bloc* would be an oversimplification.

There is genuine tension, and it is producing serious uneasiness. I believe that the basic problem dividing us, whether consciously or otherwise, is one of theology; we are starting from differing visions of the Church, especially in the matter of its necessary unity.

There is nothing especially surprising about that: even Proudhon—whom no one could accuse of clericalism—said in his day that at the root of every problem there is a theological one. How much more so when it comes to the politics of religion!

Therefore, at the inevitable risk of oversimplifying, I will try to analyze this conflict of tendencies.

At the center the prevailing tendency, even since Vatican II, is still strongly marked by a formalist, juridical vision of things.

Seeing the Church as a "perfect" society, with a clearly defined supreme authority with universally applicable laws, there is a tendency to think of the universal Church before considering the individual Churches; the latter are seen as part of a whole which must be unified as closely as possible in relation to the center, through a close network of detailed rules and regulations.

Of its nature, then, this is an essentialist, bureaucratic, static, juridical, centralizing tendency; it is characteristic of men more aware of the established order and of the past than of the demands of the future, closer in spirit to Vatican I than to the year 2000, more anxious to repress abuses than to understand and foster the new values and aspirations which are coming to the fore in the Church as in the rest of the world.

The tendency of such men, perhaps even in spite of themselves, will be to think of local Churches as administrative departments, of the bishops as merely the delegates who carry out the wishes of the central authority, and of any decentralizing of powers as the dangerous prelude to a latent schism.

This is, in general, how the center sees the periphery.

But when the perspective is reversed, the view is quite different. Then the Church is perceived first and foremost as an evangelical reality, in its deepest spiritual and sacramental mystery.

I use the term "mystery" advisedly, for we must never forget that the Church is a supernatural reality far beyond our inadequate human categories and transcending all juridicism.

Any dialogue about the Church or in the Church is doomed to failure as long as we do not see the Church as, above all, a people made up of brothers in communion with the divine life of the Trinity, Father, Son and Holy Spirit.

We must look first not to any code of canon law, however venerable it may be, but to the Gospel and the Acts of the Apostles which immerse us directly in the mystery of Pentecost. Any worthwhile discussion we have can only begin from there. It was no mere pious gesture that opened every day's session of the Council with the solemn enthronement of the Bible.

From this viewpoint, at once evangelical and historical, the first thing one sees is the local Churches—the Church of God in Paris, in London or New York; and one goes on from there to see the structure of the Church as a communion of individual Churches linked to the Church of Rome and its head as their center of unity.

You will have noticed that I say *the Church* of God in Paris or London. I do not speak of *the Churches* of Paris or London. It is an important difference. St. Paul did not speak of the Churches of Corinth or Ephesus, but of the Church of God at Corinth or Ephesus. Such an expression excludes any possibility of thinking in terms of bits and pieces, or of a mosaic. At the very core of the diversity is already the unity; it does not result from a later grouping together. That rules out, from the very start, any conception of a national Church which would compromise the nature of the One Church.

Such, too, is the standpoint of Eastern ecclesiology, of historical development, of the only theology which allows of genuinely ecumenical dialogue. In my view it is the only true vision.

But it is not a vision familiar to the Romans we have become through our historical inheritance. We are inclined to begin by seeing the Church as a universal society made up of individuals put together like a collection of cells directly linked with the head. But it is not: it is a body made up of variously constituted organs, a communion of Churches which together make up the *Catholica*.

The local Churches contain, make present, reveal within themselves the mystery of the one and only Church of

Christ; they are its incarnation in reality, in time and in space.

These two differing viewpoints determine two different ideas of unity, two opposing sets of reactions. Both perspectives involve unity, but each understands it differently. In reality, there is a genuine and Christian concept of unity which includes legitimate diversity, and also an inadequate concept of that unity which inhibits or excludes legitimate diversity. We must begin by making clear what the truly Catholic notion of unity is. It in no way implies the greatest possible uniformity, nor the concentration of everything in the center. Essentially it allows of a far deeper diversity than some accepted but merely superficial differences; it includes the areas of the spiritual, the liturgical, the theological, the canonical, the pastoral. The very fact that within the one Catholic Church there exist the Eastern Churches with their rich diversity should be enough to remind us of this. And it seems to me that this is what the controversy is really about.

PRIMACY AND COLLEGIALITY

You say in your book: "It is most important to understand to what degree primacy and collegiality are bound together, and to situate them in a mutual context." Might I ask you to say a little more precisely how you would define their relationship?

The Council defined the collegiality of the bishops, with the pope and under his leadership, in terms which usefully fill in the gaps left by Vatican I. As you know, the war of 1870 cut short the work of that Council, with the result that it never said anything about the complementary role of the bishops and their place in the Church. Nor did Vatican II say the last word on the subject. In particular, nothing was said of the consequences of collegiality for the pope in his relationship to the other bishops. This is a major omission, and it is causing us serious problems at the present time.

Let me explain what I mean: for ecumenical as well as theological reasons, it is important to avoid presenting the role of the pope in such a way as to isolate him from the college of bishops whose leader he is. While we emphasize that the pope has a right to act or speak alone, the word "alone" never means "separately" or "in isolation." Even when the pope acts without the formal collaboration of the bishops—as he has a legal right to do— he is still acting as their leader. Christ entrusted his Church to Peter and the Eleven, who are diversely but indissolubly linked in a twofold way: there was the link between the Eleven and Peter, and the link between Peter and both the Eleven and the people of God.

I am struck by this text from the Acts: "Peter, *standing with the eleven,* lifted up his voice and addressed them" (2: 14). And equally by this one, which it would be very interesting to transpose into the present day: "Now when the apostles at Jerusalem heard that Samaria had received the word of God, they sent to them Peter and John" (Acts 8:14).

It is impossible to over-emphasize the vital unity of the apostolic college. The divine help promised to Peter and his successors does not take the form of a personal inspiration from God, but of special help in the normal working out of collegiality. It is difficult to make an exact juridical statement of "the rules of the game," but they certainly do not depend merely on law and the literal force of any one text.

It follows the logic of Vatican II that the individual Churches—through their bishops gathered in episcopal conferences—should be consulted publicly and collectively, and enabled to collaborate in documents that vitally affect the whole Church. And that, not merely by associating their strictly theological commissions in the work, but also by including lay people qualified to speak on the matter at issue.

This corresponds both with the spirit of the Council and with the aspirations of our most active Christians, who are intensely aware of being full members of the Church which is "all of us together."

I think, further, that it is of very great importance psychologically, in order to ensure the acceptance and internal loyalty of the people of God, that encyclicals and important documents from the Holy See should be seen by everyone to be the result of a wide collaboration between Rome and the individual Churches. Once this had been agreed in principle, then we should of course have to consider what are the best ways and means of putting it into effect. To bring about such coresponsibility, it goes without saying, we should have to respect the charism proper to each group, and the supreme authority must preserve its supremacy intact. But we should in this way have overcome the "credibility gap" to which our American friends so often refer.

Doing this could only serve to strengthen our bonds with the pope, whose authority is an incomparable advantage to the Church. But his rôle, in all its aspects, can only be understood in relation to the Church, in it, and for it—never apart from it or above it. I do not mean that the pope is merely a spokesman for the Church, nor that he needs its legal consent to validate his actions. Certainly not. But the pope is never outside or apart from the people of God: the head is never cut off from the body. To those who spoke at Vatican I in favor of isolating the pope from the Church in order to make his rôle more important, one bishop cried out: "We refuse to have Peter beheaded again!"

One must be careful to avoid any extrinsicism or isolationism. L'Osservatore Romano does not always escape this danger: it does a disservice to the cause of the papacy, not merely through the one-sidedness of its news, and its triumphalism (denounced by the Council), but also by opening its columns only to the least collegial type of theology. One would prefer the reader to be able to find in it other forms of theology as well, of equal value, and witnessing to the same one faith. If you only hear one bell, you are only hearing one sound; there are times when one prefers to hear a carillon.

The thought of music recalls another art form—the film. The Shoes of the Fisherman presents us with an image of the papacy in which there is no hint of collegiality—the pope is shown as solitary, alone responsible for the Church, bearing it in his arms as Atlas carries the world, and saving it from all comers. The image has a certain splendor about it, but, despite a modernized façade, it makes the papacy still appear basically preconciliar in its isolation.

BISHOPS AND THE PEOPLE OF GOD

You rightly stress the unity between pope and bishops. But is it not also important to stress the unity between the bishops and the people of God? You make some mention of it in your book, but would it not be useful to give more details about just what it means?

Yes, undoubtedly; this too follows the logic of the Council. At Vatican II a major change in theological perspective was made when the Fathers of the Council decided to put the chapter on the people of God *before* the chapter on the hierarchy in *Lumen Gentium*. I think it will take us many years to bring out fully all the pastoral consequences of their having done so. Ever since the Counter Reformation, all our textbooks on the Church have hinged on the hierarchy, as a defense reaction against Protestantism with its stress on the priesthood of the people. By bringing the idea of the people of God into the foreground, the Council made clear at one stroke what all the faithful—pope, bishops, clergy, laity— have in common: the same baptism that makes them all sons of God, brothers in Christ, sanctified in the Holy Spirit. Simply by doing this, the hierarchy were establishing the fact that their authority is a service at the center of the Church community, closely in union with its life.

This improved arrangement of subject matter was enormously fruitful. The Church, seen from the starting point of baptism rather than that of the hierarchy, thus appeared as a sacramental and mystical reality first and foremost, rather than—which it also is—a juridical society. It rested on its base, the people of God, rather than on its summit, the hierarchy. The pyramid of the old manuals was reversed; one Roman prelate described it as a truly "Copernican" revolution.

As a result—and here I come more directly to the point of your question—the bishop also must take a fresh look at his position among the people of God under his care; he must come closer to his clergy and faithful; he must live as they do—even down to the kind of clothes he wears—while yet preserving in its totality the authority he receives from God by virtue of his consecration.

This kind of union between bishop and people will make new demands upon us, and the changes are only beginning. It is fairly clear that in future clergy and laity will take a more active part in the choice of bishops—as indeed they did in the past. This must make the bonds uniting them still stronger, and also make it easier to live out a collaborative obedience.

Even now, the post-Vatican II bishop finds himself facing new obligations: he must learn to enter into dialogue with his priests and people in the context of the new priests' councils and pastoral councils. He too must get rid of a certain paternalist isolation and accept a new method of exercising his authority—though the authority itself does not change—by making use of the more democratic methods explicitly demanded by the Council.

Over the years, authority has been exercised in many different ways. It is high time for us to realise that the old régime is no more—but this does not mean a sudden change to parliamentarianism. Decisions will not be made in our councils as a result of party pressure, or of the majority outvoting the minority. It would be helpful to reread together St. Paul's first epistle to the Corinthians, with its warnings against the kind of partisanship which championed Paul over against Apollos or Cephas. No *credo* will ever be established by majority vote. We come together to find an answer to just one question: what does the Lord want of each of us that the world may be saved? The opinion that must have the greatest weight in the gathering must be that of the informed Christian who is closest to the Lord Jesus, the most receptive to his wisdom, the most humbly ready to be led by his light.

The bishop must recognize, in theory and in practice, that many problems today cannot be simply resolved by the decree of authority without also having the support of priests and people.

Authority, if it is to be effective, must gain consent, and consent can only be gained where those involved have been able to take part—and their part is a very real one, though it requires careful definition—if not in the final decision, at least in the steps leading up to it. Their rôle is not necessarily to share in the "decision-taking," but in the "decision-making," and we must be ready to accept that rôle loyally and with sincerity. The same holds good for the head of a family or of a firm, or for the rector of a university. One need only study a few newspaper and television reports to be convinced of this. In the declaration of the French bishops (6-20-68), I was especially struck by this statement:

> We have reached a point of no return. From now on the exercise of authority demands dialogue and a certain measure of responsibility for every one. The authority needed for the life of any society can only be strengthened as a result.

A closer and more active collaboration between bishops, priests and people is bound to involve difficulties as soon as one reaches the stage of actual decisions. That must be recognized. On the one hand, you find a priests' council or a pastoral council filled with concern to help the church community to develop and flourish, proposing to the bishop a collection of steps designed in varying ways to intensify local religious life and the part it plays in the world. These priests and laymen have now moved from what was all too often an automatic passivity to a lively awareness of their coresponsibility, and of the charisms of the Holy Spirit which they have received. They belong to a world from which the authoritarian legalism of the past has vanished: for them a law is a reasonable regulation worthy of obedience precisely because it is reasonable—and where they no longer see a reason for it, then the demands of life itself must take priority over the law. This point of view is simply a fact—as respectable as a lord mayor—and we must take account of it.

On the other hand, let us take the case of the bishop who will accept the general conclusions as long as he, too, judges them reasonable.

What is to happen when he has to say that the conclusions reached cannot be put into effect because present canonical legislation stands in the way? He will be asked to remove the obstacles, and he will be obliged to reply that universal laws cannot be altered just like that; that the experiments which might make it easier to make the laws more flexible have not been allowed by authority; and that, until a change is made in the law, it must take priority over the actual demands of the moment. Such a situation produces serious unrest. The tension between the local Church and the Curia will continue to increase if the latter jealously clings to its powers and hampers the freedom of action of local authorities in areas which they are best equipped to understand.

The bishop, in this situation, will be quite unable to guide, to direct, to canalise initiative which he should be able to assess and make good use of. He appears in the guise of the custodian of an outmoded law, the victim of a structure so rigid that it cannot accept the shape of reality, so paralyzed that it cannot develop according to the rhythm of the age, so universalist that it cannot possibly be true all the time and everywhere.

Though I am talking about the individual bishop, I am not forgetting—as he himself will be the first to realize—that there are some major measures of change or flexibility that cannot be taken by any individual without regard to their possible effects on other dioceses or other areas. The problem becomes the more acute when the episcopal conference of a whole country has its proposals rejected. This inevitably creates the impression that the center is blocking development, that it does not believe in the genuine coresponsibility of the bishops, and that Vatican II has not yet been translated into life on the level of collegiality.

This is a tragic situation which is holding back the pastoral advance of the postconciliar period, and intensifying the tendency of protesters to extol an unlimited policy of the *fait accompli*. On the one hand, there must be order in the Church, and laws, and, in cases of systematic transgression, adequate sanctions (revised in common consultation), as is the case in every self-respecting society. On the other hand, life does not stand still, and customs which go against the laws take root, undermining authority at every level. It is impossible for the Curia to maintain the thousands of prescriptions of canon law. The canonically obligatory demand for innumerable permissions which the Curia used to grant for one, two or sometimes five years, as the case might be, has luckily been reduced under pressure from the Council. But there is still a long way to go before the bishop can fully affirm his own responsibilities in his own diocese.

All this juridical formalism, that is still pointlessly preserved, handicaps and falsifies his pastoral activity. On my desk I have a clock which tells me the precise time at any moment in all the capitals of the world. Most ingenious. But I cannot imagine what kind of machine would be needed on the desks of the Curia to keep them in touch with the precise situation everywhere, so that the same law could be adapted to fit every longitude and latitude in the world.

I am, of course, referring to the things in the Church which belong not to faith but to the local situation, the evolution of customs, the development of cultures. And it must be admitted, too, that bureaucracy, with its weighty machinery, exists in every country, and must inevitably exist where jurisdiction is being applied to the whole world; we are all dependent on the minor officials who handle the documents, and the inevitable slowness of dealing with things at a distance.

But this seems to me to indicate how essential it is to give scope in current practice to a theology of the Church which combines unity with a respect for diversity—the sort of theology I spoke of in answer to your first question. It would also respond to the requirements of true realism. In short, it seems to me to be the path we must follow if we are to emerge from a centralizing legalism which is stifling the present, and endangering the future.

LAWS AND THE LESSONS OF LIFE

You quote among other things these words of Paul VI: "The seeds of life planted by the Council in the soil of the Church must grow and achieve full maturity."

How would you apply this to the development of a canon law for the future?

We are at present in a difficult situation. The Council was like a sun which produced a sudden melting of glaciers so that great torrents poured down the side of the mountain, bearing along with them masses of stones, huge trees, and so on; they are trying to break through and find an outlet. The chaos is inevitable, and one may hope it is merely temporary; but it must be faced, without leading us to any abandonment of authority.

Today, as always, we need rules and laws. The Church, like every other society, needs laws, or it will have anarchy. Indeed, to abdicate religious authority would go against the Gospel itself.

But the way in which authority is exercised must evolve with time.

The problem, then, is what attitude one should adopt. There are, *a priori*, two possible attitudes: either one tries to hold back each torrent by damming it along the way, or one tries to control the water, guiding it and canalizing it between wider banks. In my opinion this latter is the only possible solution: it calls for great discernment, for the situation is a fluctuating and ambiguous one; and above all, we must not err in our diagnosis of what is causing the phenomenon.

There are some people who see the Council as the root of all our present problems. To some extent they are right. The Council did undoubtedly start the unfreezing process. But where there is melting, there has been freezing, and we must not forget that. A glacier stops plants from growing: its very immobility is oppression. Our legislation was—and still is— alarmingly behind the development of life.

The Gospel teaches us that the Sabbath was made for man, not man for the Sabbath. But for far too long we have forgotten that man is a living being, and it was with some surprise that we suddenly found out that the man of today is not the same as the man of yesterday, any more than the society in which he lives is the same.

In a world of ultra-quick change, where every decade seems like a new century, there is a great risk of psychological dislocation—especially since we must try to catch up with lost time by leaps and bounds, time which can itself perhaps be reckoned in centuries. It is this that is causing our present confusion, and it is largely due to the suppression of problems which still remain as unsolved as ever.

We are dealing with contemporary man, whose idea of human nature, whose scale of values, whose whole outlook is quite new. Conscious of his dignity as an individual, his rights as a human being, his inalienable freedom of conscience, the man and the Christian of 1969 rejects certain procedures (or absences of procedure), and, in case of dispute, demands to be judged openly by his equals. One need only think of the unanimous indignation with which the press all over the world greeted the publication of the Illich questionnaire, with its antedeluvian approach, to realize this.

This single example pinpoints the oppressive nature of the old canon law in judicial matters. How many "Talmudic" prescriptions and casuistical solutions, barely believable nowadays, were imposed, and sometimes for centuries, under the Roman Curia's direction!

It is precisely this kind of pressure we must recognize if we want to understand the reason for and the force of, the present reaction. Otherwise, the most we can have is one deaf man talking to another.

It is not possible to understand anything about the French Revolution or the Russian Revolution without a knowledge of the former regimes which they destroyed. Of course, this does not justify every method they used. It does not justify, for example, the beheading of the King of France.

Similarly, in the Church, a reaction can only be judged in relation to the state of affairs which preceded it.

To understand this fact is a great help towards moving forward faster, towards sympathising with young people's longing for authenticity—and they are the future of our world. This is another thing we must not forget, unless we want another conversation between the deaf—one between the different generations.

If we are to understand the present tremendous aspiration towards greater truth, flexibility, openness, adaptation—towards the freedom of the children of God spoken of in the Gospel—we must become keenly aware of the weight of those far too numerous laws, supported by the threat *sub gravi* (that is, that it is a mortal sin to infringe one of them). I am thinking of the many prescriptions in canon law which impose the threat of grave sin on the consciences of priests and people.

When the legislator adds such a sanction to the rule he is giving, it means either that the words are meaningless, or that deliberately to break this particular law dooms the culprit to eternal damnation. It is worth considering this, and then looking carefully at the kind of thing to which it was so often attached.

Sub gravi, reading a book on the Index (Descartes, Flaubert, Rosmini . . .);

Sub gravi, omitting to say one of the little hours of the Office;

Sub gravi, not observing the Friday abstinence;

Sub gravi . . . one could go on and on.

And how often were these sanctions applied abusively to protect not the law of God, but arrangements of discipline made by the Curia!

One could make quite a catalogue of mortal sins that were declared to be such over the centuries, and which have gradually vanished as we have gained a greater understanding of man, of psychology and of real life.

One can hardly help contrasting this with Our Lord's words: "My yoke is sweet, and my burden light."

We are only just emerging from a centuries-old immobility in liturgical matters, too. As long as the Latin language, like Noah's cloak, covered all the anachronisms and failures of adaptation, they could pass unnoticed. Now we have discovered that it is not enough just to translate a text into a living language to make it accessible to the Christian of 1969. We have to transpose, translate in relation to varying cultures, and so on. All this calls for time, for creativeness, for scope for research.

That does not mean anarchy or lack of all control. Rather, it demands an understanding of genuine human life, grassroots of sincere and worthwhile aspirations, directed towards producing a language every man can understand, as happened at the first Pentecost.

Our priests still suffer as they say their Office—under pain of mortal sin—over the rigidity that this prayer reflects.

We have sinned through passivity, through laziness, and also through lack of imagination. It is late, but we have at last realized this; we must take care the lesson is not lost upon us.

It is hardly necessary to say anything more about the countless rubrics—now being simplified at last—in which the liturgy was shrouded like Lazarus in his tomb, to preserve it from the living participation of the people. But what is one to say about the minor orders which are still obligatory as gradual steps which the candidate to the priesthood must climb? They are, in their flagrant anachronism, as great a trial for the bishop as for the young men themselves. Acolytes today, as everyone knows, are altar boys. Porters or doorkeepers are sacristans. A lector is any layman who volunteers for the job, and the exorcist is forbidden to exercise his functions.

As in the liturgy, so in the organization of the religious life, what a collection of rigid, outmoded and stifling rules and customs! I discussed this subject in my book, *The Nun in the World*. The entire purpose of that work was to free the apostolic religious life from its anachronistic and sometimes positively inhuman bonds.

Another whole book could be written on the practice still current in the Church of treating women as though they were children—indeed I see that there are authors who are trying to point this out; there is certainly no lack of illustrative material.

Consider too the enormous area of canonical legislation about marriage, in which the juridical mentality has had, and still has, far too free a scope. The Canon Law Society of America recently initiated an important work with the object of correcting such abuses, and opening the door to the pastoral adaptations needed to ensure respect for the individual's conscience and its priority over certain presumptions of the law in areas of conflict. But there still remains much to be done.

This is not meant to be a historical survey, or a complete study of the problem, but simply an attempt to give some idea of the *status quo ante* and the reasons for the reaction now taking place against the center from which such laws came—and are still coming.

Believe me, I am not multiplying various examples just for the fun of it; my one wish is to provide an explanation for those torrents of melting glacier water to which I have likened what is now going on.

Honesty demands that I also say something of the theological oppression that has put a stop to some projects of research, an oppression emanating from those who consider themselves as having the monopoly of orthodoxy (which is to them synonymous with that fixed and scholastic philosophy which they tried—generally, however, in vain—to impose at the Council). Quite an impressive list could be made of theological positions taught in Rome in the recent and more distant past as the only true ones, which were simply done away with by the Council Fathers.

We all know the prolonged sufferings of our finest theologians, held suspect, if not positively condemned, in the name of that theology: Rahner, Congar, Murray, de Lubac; to say nothing of those men who were the "heroes" of my young days: Cardinal Mercier, whom the Curia of his time suspected of Modernism; Dom Lambert Beauduin, whose heresy was ecumenism; and Père Lebbe, whose crime was to defend the ideal of a native Chinese clergy, including bishops and cardinals.

One might also run through the list of decrees issued by the Biblical Commission as authoritative, which no one nowadays would support, to say nothing of works put on the Index which had to be removed subsequently—such as Rosmini's book *The Five Wounds of the Church*, some of which remains relevant even today. What is significant is not the fact that mistakes were made—*errare humanum est*—but the whole working of a system designed to prevent freedom in scientific research, and deny people's right to defend themselves. This is not to say that there is no case for being watchful, but simply that we must today find other and more suitable ways of being so.

Each point could be developed to show that this "tale of woe" still needs to be remembered, especially in order to prevent yesterday's mistakes from happening again tomorrow. I am thinking now of our present-day theologians, uneasy over their freedom in scientific research, who have recently put out a statement (not every word of which I would agree with) of their anxieties—which are far from imaginary ones.

The history of the Council, though it is now over, is still alive in all our memories: it was, in large part, the history of a tenacious and skillful struggle by the Curial minority against the striving of the majority of the Council Fathers towards greater openness. The first episode in that history was the intervention of Cardinal Liénart, in the name of the French hierarchy, and Cardinal Frings, in the name of the German hierarchy. Both rejected from the beginning the documents pre-fabricated by the commissions presented to the bishops to vote on. And I would add, as a symbol, the intervention of one leader of the Curia, who attempted to hamper the freedom of our discussions by declaring that the schemas, prepared before the Council began, must be accepted in substance and could only be changed in minor detail . . . because the pope had given them his approval; what he omitted to say was that the pope had indeed approved them, but *only* as material for the freest possible discussion. How many later episodes were similar to this in nature, and were indeed—I do not exaggerate—a real way of the Cross in our fight for freedom in the Council!

But all this is now in the past: your question relates to the future of the new canon law.

Let me say at once: there is good cause to think that the new code now being formulated will avoid a number of the old pitfalls. Will it in fact get to the theological and pastoral roots of our problems? I do not know: we cannot yet be sure of that.

Among the questions that need to be reconsidered is the position of the Curia itself in the Church.

Canonists are in fact questioning whether, after Vatican II, the Curia should still be considered solely as the executive body of the papacy, or whether we must not widen our vision, and see the Curia in the context of the development of episcopal collegiality as a whole, together with the pope and under his direction.

It would look as though a move was being made in that direction by the introduction of seven residential bishops into each congregation—an interesting straw in the wind. But we still have to rethink the working out of this collaboration, if the measure is to have any real effect. I recently said something about this in an article in the review *Concilium*.

But the problem remains: how are we to prevent this new canon law being a stillbirth, overtaken by the movement of life by the time it actually sees the light of day? Drafted by specialists, it can only respond to the needs of the Church and the world if it also receives the continual, living agreement of the whole people of God for whom it is intended.

We suffer at present from a manifest dislocation between life and our juridical rules which are no longer in accord with it. Our Code of Canon Law dates from 1917; how can we make sure such immobility does not recur in the future? I believe a commission is to be set up to review it periodically. Let us hope so. But how maintain that continual contact with the people of God who must translate its laws into their life? This, it seems to me, should also be given the most serious consideration.

If law and life are to go forward at the same pace, and offer support to one another—for the law is *for* life, and life needs to develop in a context of order—the key to any solution would seem to me to be that of subsidiarity: that a higher authority should never, at any level, take over what a lower authority could normally decide for itself: that general laws should provide a framework rather than a mass of detail, and unity never be mistaken for the constraint of uniformity.

The more individual Churches are in a position to interpret the framework of law into concrete measures, the stronger and more effective will authority be.

As I was saying, we suffer at present from the impossibility of getting people to respect some of our universal laws, which have failed to keep pace with life, or are no longer in tune with the state of religious and cultural development of a given society.

It is not hard to foresee that the future of the new canon law will depend on how we apply the principle of subsidiarity—a principle, after all, which applies to all good social management. Pius XI stressed it strongly as long ago as *Quadragesimo Anno*, and John XXIII in *Mater et Magistra*. The principle was recalled again at the first Synod of Bishops, and accepted as valid—at least in theory.

The success of the new code will depend on the extent to which, animated by the spirit of Vatican II, it translates into legislation the theology of the Church which we already discussed, and which is essentially based upon subsidiarity.

ON ELECTING THE POPE

You write: "Given the determining rôle of the Sacred College in the election of a pope, it is desirable that a matter so fraught with consequence for the whole people of God be studied by the world Synod of Bishops, and by consultation with the various episcopal conferences."

Will not the experience of coresponsibility in the end lead to a new method of electing the pope?

That is a delicate question, but one which must certainly be faced if we are to analyze all the consequences of Vatican II.

I believe, in fact, that there may well be occasion one day to reconsider papal elections in the light of episcopal collegiality. In his remarkable book, *The Theology of Vatican II*, the eminent English theologian, Bishop Butler, who was a member of the theological commission of the Council, asks the question: To whom in the Church does authority rightfully belong when a pope dies? And his reply is: to the body of bishops as such. In his view, the monopoly reserved to the college of cardinals at the death of a pope can only be justified by reference to a kind of implicit delegation from the worldwide episcopal body. Theologians will have to look more deeply into this problem. As everyone knows, the composition and duties of the college of cardinals have varied greatly over the course of history.

Then, too, it is only in recent years, since the Council in fact, that all the cardinals have been bishops, which would seem to be a step towards overcoming the dualism between the episcopal body and the college of cardinals.

It seems to me that change must continue along the same collegial lines. This would require, for instance, that the electoral body should be, in the first place, the whole body of bishops, and then, as a second step, a narrower college of bishops; or should application be made directly to the Synod of Bishops, and if so, what form should that synod take? I do not know. But the matter calls for attention and study. A question of such tremendous importance for the good of the whole Church needs to be studied by priests and faithful as well; the whole concept of the Church would be falsified if one declared that this question concerned the pope alone, and not the members of the Church. It would be precisely the kind of juridicism that has done so much harm in the past. And there is the further problem that simply by the fact of a pope's dying, his directing will as such no longer exists, while yet authority in the Church cannot die.

Hence the very way in which cardinals are chosen itself poses a theological problem. You see how right Proudhon was. There is no getting away from it.

In the past, kings administered the state in their absolute discretion. Without going so far as saying "I am the state," as Louis XIV is supposed to have said, they raised armies, minted money, levied taxes by decree, and conferred benefices and titles on anyone they pleased.

All this is over, and such things are decided now with the help of a mandate given by popular elections. In the Church we have not yet completed the change of *regime*. I speak of regime rather than of authority, for the latter remains immutable in essence, fixed by the law of God; but it is something that can and must develop in inessential detail in accord with the changing ways of society. To look back for a moment at the example of titles bestowed at the whim of the monarch, can we not see a vestige of this in "ecclesiastical honors" of all kinds, from those conferred on Knights of the Holy Sepulchre or of Malta, to the "princes" of the Church, to give cardinals their official designation?

We witness an uneasiness, a sense of dislocation from our age, every time a "promotion" to the cardinalate is announced. People at once start gossiping: who is in favor—or who is not? Why is so-and-so left out or such-and-such an unexpected name put forward? It is a form of solitary decision whose objective criteria cannot be known and about which dialogue is not possible. No one denies the legality of this procedure. The only question is whether this age-old custom is in line with collegiality, in the spirit of Vatican II, or not. We are all heirs of the past, and it would be wrong to see anything positively anticollegial in something that is simply the result of a tradition once taken for granted: all one can hope is that, one day, this problem may be studied in harmony with the views of the people of God.

In *Informations catholiques internationales* of April 1969, I read this from one correspondent, in regard to the nomination of bishops: "How are such nominations made, by what commission are they put forward, on what criteria, and who provides the information?"

We wonder the same things about the nominations of cardinals, and we all hope that the advice of the episcopal conference of the country concerned will be taken into account. Anything that arouses a suspicion of favoritism, of the "good pleasure of the Prince," is a harking-back to the days of absolute monarchies and a source of uneasiness. Our age is especially sensitive to the need for objective criteria.

The question of these choices is all the more important since, in the present state of the law, it is the college of cardinals who, in their turn, elect the pope. If, then, the law is to coincide with the realities of the situation and the demands of distributive justice, the Church must have in that college a faithful image of its true diversity: which brings us back to the theology of the individual Churches—something else we cannot get away from.

The Churches should be represented in the running of the universal Church, not according to the numbers of the baptised, but of genuinely practicing members—allowances being made for the diversity of rites. There must be a representation which respects, as far as possible, the balance between nations and continents, in the light of what each actually contributes to the whole.

The Sacred College must be an image of the Church not just as it was in the past but as it is now and will be in the future; we need a balance among the generations, or the Church will become fixed in its structures and closed to the future. The experience of the old is valuable but equally so is the initiative and enthusiasm of the young, if we are to combine the *nova et vetera* recommended in the Gospel. With all these requirements in mind, we must look at the actual situation we are now in. The pyramid of age—the average age of promotion recently was 59; the imbalance of countries—41 Italians out of 83 European cardinals, virtually half: these things give rise to problems and demand serious study in the light of a complex situation inherited from a past which is no longer adapted to the good of the Church. Such a reform must not be held in check by our anxiety to preserve "promotions of honor" in the Church. They have no place in it. One can hardly imagine Peter and Paul addressing each other as "Your Eminence"! For further discussion of this subject, I recommend P. Winninger's excellent little book, *La vanité dans l'Eglise* (Vanity in the Church). It hits the nail right on the head.

Let me add one further comment. Various publications are currently promoting the idea that the laity should also play a part in the election of a pope. Apart from the fact that it seems hard to see how such a thing could be practicable, it seems to me that the solution which would come closest to this legitimate desire would be to associate the laity more closely with the election of bishops. The bishops would then be, not just theologically, but psychologically, more recognizable as spokesmen for the people, while still remaining their leaders.

THE STYLE OF THE PONTIFICATE

You say in your book: "After Vatican I, the papacy appeared to the non-Catholic world as an absolute monarchy, incompatible with any form of collegiality." May I ask you how the function of the pope appears after Vatican II, allowing for such collegiality? And would it be indiscreet to ask what you think of the wish felt by so many to have a non-Italian pope? Would that promote collegiality?

To take your last question first—Italian or not, what matters is the function itself, seen in the light of Vatican II and the new circumstances prevailing in the Church and the world. The question of the pope's nationality seems to me completely secondary.

I then come to your question on the function itself, apart from anything that may characterize it in any individual possessor.

Look at the *Annuario Pontificio:* the first thing that strikes one is the number of functions a pope combines in his person. He is at once Bishop of Rome, Archbishop and Metropolitan of the Roman province, Primate of Italy, Patriarch of the West, Head of the universal Church, and Head of Vatican State.

The essential question is this: out of all these, which are of divine law, which merely historical accident?

It is important to stress the two essential, divinely established functions: every pope is of necessity Bishop of Rome, and supreme pastor of the universal Church.

As Bishop of the Church of Rome, every pope has to make that Church the mother and leader of all the Churches in the world—*mater et caput omnium Ecclesiarum*—as it is expressed on the front of the basilica of the Lateran, his cathedral as Bishop of Rome. We must recognize that the Church of Rome has that primacy in faith and in charity which belonged from the first to "the Church of God which is at Rome," founded by Peter and Paul, its life enriched by their blood and by so many martyrs and saints. The religious and pastoral excellence of Rome should be visible and attractive to all; it should be the light of the Christian life, the lamp set on the lampstand.

The supernatural prestige of the Church of Rome is an important element if one wants the pope, its bishop, to be seen as, in the fullest sense, the Church's center of gravity. Therefore anything in Rome itself that smacks of human imperfection or injustice is more of a scandal to the Church than it would be anywhere else. The utmost must be done to increase vocations there, and to make parish life and worship models for the world, so that all other Churches will want to imitate them.

It is obvious to what extent anything that frees the center from the weight of bureaucracy and administration, in order to live the Gospel more fully, is a blessing not just for the world, but first of all for Rome itself. It is in this spirit that recent popes have urged all the members of the curia to devote part of their time to practical apostolic work.

Let us glance quickly at the functions that have simply arisen during the course of history. As the Head of Vatican City, the pope becomes the ruler of the old Papal States; these were in no sense divinely appointed such, whatever the ultramontane Cardinal Manning may have thought (and he actually wanted it inscribed in the Syllabus), or, later, Father Capello of the Gregorianum, whose idea was substantially the same.

The pope is also Archbishop and Metropolitan of the Roman province and Primate of Italy. Here there is a new element: the recent creation of the Italian episcopal conference.

This step is part of the process of decentralization, and will have repercussions on the whole life and organization of the Church in Italy.

As Patriarch of the West, the pope also has special links with the Latin Church. He is in charge of some things in connection with the Latin Church which are determined for the Eastern Churches not by him but by their own Patriarch. As we know, the patriarchate has a role of great importance in the East. This form of decentralization seems a steppingstone, a source of future riches for the Church, especially from the ecumencial point of view.

I next come to the role of every pope as head of the Universal Church. The first thing to note about this title is that it is inalienable. Every successor of Peter personally possesses it, by divine right. This does not mean that he exercises his mandate from outside the Church or its collegiality, but simply that it is a function which he cannot, as such, delegate to anyone else.

We must not confuse the papacy with the services which depend upon it. One of my friends, a layman involved in the world apostolate, told me how, for a long time, his correspondence with some of the Curial offices had been disappointing, with almost every response a negative one. Up to the day, he said, when he rewrote his letters in a different language, with the result that they were answered from another department which gave him full satisfaction. It is just one story, but it indicates that there is a difference between the papacy itself and the apparatus of administration.

The Roman Curia is an indispensable human organization, but it exists for the sake of supernatural realities which transcend it. To criticize the Curia as a "system" is not to criticize either the Church or the papacy. That must be clearly understood. Every page of history makes the distinction abundantly clear.

At the First Vatican Council, the bishops put forward a long list of complaints against the Curia, which have not even yet been wholly satisfied. Even in modern times, we all know that John XXIII deplored its hegemony, and that one of the things which determined him in convoking the Council—which was, by theological definition, above the Curia—was to reduce the rôle of the latter to a more reasonable size.

We too, at our own diocesan level, must get rid of everything that makes bishops the prisoners of their own bureaucratic, juridical, administrative apparatus. We must do this if we are to respond as we should to our major task, which is that of preaching the Gospel to the whole world, in all the purity and freshness of the resurrection.

This liberation at the summit, this restructuring of the governmental "system," really requires an immense study conducted on an international scale.

Not merely distinguished theologians, but specialists in the massive techniques of organizing international concerns, such as the UN, for instance, could all contribute fruitfully to it; as also could the heads of large firms, "managers," sociologists, people involved in communications, in human relations, in forward planning.

A large-scale, interdisciplinary study should be set on foot without delay. From a positive point of view, it would, I think, answer a major need; negatively, it would help to give confidence to those people all over the world who now criticise the present structures and their failings precisely because they love the Church.

I should imagine that it would also be useful to learn what has been done in the way of this kind of practical readaptation of government, of decentralization, in the great religious orders and congregations which have modified their statutes in line with the modern world since the Council. The Jesuits, I believe, have given lengthy consideration to the relation between center and periphery in their own organization, and the same thing has been done, I think, with the statutes of the Brothers of the Christian Schools.

Obviously all these conclusions can only be applied to the Church itself and its forms of government *mutatis mutandis*, but there are certain universal political laws—laws, that is, of "political science"—which one cannot ignore with impunity.

When I say this, I am thinking of the work of an unbelieving friend of mine, the director of the review *Res Publica*, Leo Moulin, whose publications are absolute mines of information about how the religious orders in the Middle Ages contributed towards the secular democratization of Europe. In a curious way, the world might thus return something of what the Church has given it.

The papacy, freer from the overcentralized system which at present envelops it, will then be in a much better position to carry out its incomparable universal mission. The inalienable and unique charism of the pope is surely the charism of unity, of communion.

It is this charism which is at the heart of the communion between all the individual Churches, in the unity of our faith in the Gospel and the resurrection, transcending all schools of theology, all the varying and legitimate liturgical or pastoral expressions of that faith.

It is not essential that the pope should personally make the rules for how we express our worship, but it is essential that he should watch over the integrity of our eucharistic faith and the reverence due to it, without having therefore to impose any particular mode of expressing it on this or that nation.

The pope is also at the heart of this communion between the local Churches in his rôle as animator and co-ordinator of the Church's worldwide missionary activity. Vatican II was insistent that we have no right to make the pope alone bear the burden of evangelizing the world, even to the ends of the earth. We must put into effect what Paul VI called "the coresponsibility of the bishops on a worldwide scale."

This communion between the individual Churches and Rome will be made easier by the internationalizing of the Curia which is now taking place, but only to the extent that the latter process goes hand in hand with the internationalizing of ideas and pastoral exchanges between different countries. Without that it is merely a pretense.

Rome could be, not merely in law, but in fact, a most valuable center of meeting. A place like the UN in New York is enormously valuable for world peace, because it makes possible dialogue which would be impossible, or at best difficult, to achieve anywhere else.

Rome has a sense of the universal, and a worldwide vision, which it is good to know at first hand, and which, more than once, will show up the complexity of a problem which appears quite simple at the local level. For its part, the Curia must be accessible to genuine dialogue; it must not be presented to the bishops as having the sole monopoly of solving problems on the spot. Collegiality is an art which must be learned in common, or not at all. "When it comes to the Council," John XXIII used to say, "we are all novices." The same can be said of collegiality.

Nothing constructive can be achieved if every honest criticism, every desire to question, is seen as arising out of pride or ill will. Real truthfulness, in full deference, but without servility, remains an essential condition of all collaboration in renewal.

At present, if any group of bishops decide to confer together, they are seen as conspirators. During the Council we suffered from this, for it made it impossible to have meetings which the rules did not allow for: the "Bar Jonah," despite all the noise, did to some extent make up for this, but it was not the best place for organizing open discussions on matters under consideration. Yet what an ideal meeting place Rome could be, if one could have places in the environs of St. Peter's to exchange and share ideas, without continually having to justify not all being in total agreement about everything; where we could talk without fear about what needs to be done to help the Church in its mission. There is no substitute for personal contacts: they can, in a matter of minutes, remove all misunderstandings, and they are so much more effective than written communications, even if these be models of objectivity and not, as can happen at times, concave or convex mirrors.

While on this subject, we might also rethink the quinquennial reports bishops are obliged to send to Rome, as also the *ad limina* visits which the law requires every diocesan bishop to make at regular intervals. Every bishop wants to carry out such a visit not as a matter of more or less sheer formality, but in a spirit of faith, with open dialogue and complete accessibility.

The more our lines of communication with Rome are varied and free of juridical formality, the more will the Church be enriched by the tremendous mixture of varying pastoral experiences; the more, then, it can direct its common energies to the major problems of the contemporary world.

The pope is also at the heart of the communion between the Christian Churches, following the splendid beginnings already made—Jerusalem yesterday, Geneva tomorrow.

And also of communion outside Christianity itself, with all mankind, whether religious or not, beyond all conflicts of race, of war, of national barriers.

It was magnificent to see Paul VI at the UN, pleading so eloquently the cause of disarmament and peace, and embodying in a unique way a Church which is at the heart of the great human family, closely in touch with its sufferings and its hopes, *Gaudium et Spes* incarnate: this the whole world could see.

In *The Times* (London) for 5 April last, I read these striking words of the English thinker and agnostic, Arnold Toynbee:

"The change of the heart is the heart of the matter," he said. ". . . The union of hearts is primary." Going on to speak of the pope, he continued: "When Pope Paul VI landed at Amman airport in the course of his pilgrimage to the Christian Holy Places in Jerusalem, he was met and greeted by a welcoming crowd which must have been about 90 percent Moslem. When, on a later journey, he arrived at Bombay, to take part in a

Catholic Christian Eucharistic Congress, he received another warm-hearted welcome from a crowd that must have been about 99 percent Hindu. The reason, we may guess, why the pope touched the hearts of crowds whose religion was not his own was that they recognized that the pope's concern was not limited to the members of his own flock, but embraced all human beings of all religions—as Pope Paul had shown and has continued to show in his untiring labors on behalf of world peace."

These words from Toynbee's new book, *Experiences*, are a noble homage to the papacy. They put a finger on the unique evangelical mission of the head of a Church called to be, as Vatican II says, "the sacrament of the unity of the world."

PAPAL NUNCIOS

I must thank you for being so frank in your answers. Might I once again ask you to enlarge on one sentence that specially struck me: "The theology of a papal nuncio is more important than his nationality."

Is this perhaps a suggestion that we should review the status of nuncios in the post conciliar Church?

I suppose I could have evaded your questions to some extent, but I am convinced that there is a great liberating force in the honest expression of what one profoundly believes to be true. "The truth," said Jesus, "will make you free." Truth can best be seen in the open air. I know that it may seem more diplomatic to deal with problems behind closed doors, but though I do appreciate the value of secret diplomacy in some cases, I do not believe in secrecy over pastoral matters, and secrecy in itself serves only to maintain the *status quo*. The Church is either a family or it is nothing; and in any family there must be open dialogue if misunderstandings are to be got rid of, and the air cleared.

The question of the status of nuncios is, in fact, under discussion in a number of countries. It is important, for it concerns the working out of relations, day by day, between the center and the periphery. Anything that reinforces that supernatural bond is of vital importance to the Catholic and Roman Church.

To clarify the problem, one must distinguish between the two functions of a nuncio. One is diplomatic: he is the ambassador of the State of the Vatican, and in every country he is of right the doyen of the diplomatic corps.

The other is religious. In effect, he is a decentralized member of the Curia, whose task is to watch over, on the spot, the carrying out of canonical regulations, and to supervise the bishops.

The problem really consists in the combining of these two functions, and it was one that was raised several times during the Council. The theology of Vatican II leads us to look deeply at the basic purpose of these functions. And this would seem to call for a profound restructuring.

The ambassadorial function has its own problems. Why give it to a priest, to a bishop—a bishop with no flock, no pastoral duties? Would it not be better to confer it on laymen, as the Fathers of the Council suggested more than once?

To this is added a further problem. The diplomatic function of nuncios is often out of balance. It establishes a dialogue with Rome only at the level of political powers, and the voice of the poor is not heard at all.

The religious function poses even more radical problems, in terms of the conciliar theology of collegiality. If the Synod really—as its plan proposes—establishes genuine and direct communications, honest and brotherly links between the pope and the episcopal conferences, should there be any need to keep a permanent inspector watching over the episcopate of each country? Would it not be adequate to have temporary delegates where there are special or complex problems? Would not our pastoral work be more dynamic, more effective and more in tune with our society, if the episcopal conferences shouldered their own responsibilities in direct liaison with Rome, and not under this kind of sometimes dubious supervision?

Changes along these lines seem to me highly desirable and urgent. Until a fundamental reform takes place, some immediate steps could be taken which would do much to improve both the quality and effectiveness of the links between Rome and the local Churches. A nuncio's day-to-day work has certain analogies with that of a government secret service. He holds a kind of watching brief to see that the established order is preserved—in other words, the order fixed for the whole world by the Roman Curia. The more detailed that order becomes, the more manifold must be his vigilance; the more that order is in a state of evolution, the more delicate is his task. His function makes him the man people complain to, the "letter box" for denunciations—and God knows these are still taking place! As the confidant of malcontents, he may well, if he is not careful, be imposed upon by individuals hostile to the bishops—for many different kinds of reasons. All this applies everywhere, and varies according to individual temperament.

It is vital that every nuncio be penetrated by the theology of the Council. All too often he judges people and situations in the light of a Curialist theology which is generally the kind he has been trained in.

That is why I wrote in my book the words you refer to: "The theology of a papal nuncio is more important than his nationality."

The future of the Church in every country is determined by the choice he makes of those put forward for the episcopate.

Therefore it should be natural for a nuncio to be a native of the country, who knows its customs and its language; this would avoid many misunderstandings.

A native nuncio, of the Vatican II kind, could have a merely temporary mandate. This would avoid the problem of finding a job for him at the end of his "career"—that horrible word!—which is almost automatically solved nowadays by "promotion to the cardinalate." Hence, in fact, we find the preponderance of Italian cardinals, a situation which needs reviewing, and that aspect of the cardinalate as a "recompense of honor" which is, rightly, so criticized at every level in the Church.

A native nuncio need not be limited to the spheres of diplomacy or legalism. At present, a nuncio only occasionally acts as a bishop, and then it is a fringe activity, not a part of the pastoral work of the country. He would not seem to be a kind of "foreign body," but would become a living link with Rome. His rôle as inspector from outside would cease, but he would remain the chargé d'affaires, expected to inspect what needs inspection, and far better equipped for the job pastorally. He would emerge from too exclusively bureaucratic a rôle, and could, if need be, become the spokesman of the episcopal conference to the government, as well as in all those international relationships that are extending further afield all the time.

It still remains to consider the inevitable objection: would such a nuncio, being so close to the bishops, still preserve the trust of the center?

It is a real and most understandable difficulty; for obviously a nuncio will always have a somewhat delicate part to play. The bishops are quite ready for some degree of supervision to be exercised in the name of the pope; the problem is just how it is done.

By definition, it is ultimately the Holy See that makes the choice: surely it should not be impossible to find a man on the spot who could carry out this function of liaison officer between the center and the periphery, the periphery and the center, and could thus genuinely be a religious ambassador.

THE CRISIS IN THE CHURCH

You say in your book: "We must recognize that the Church lives right now in troubled times." This is even more evident now than it was a year ago. Everyone can see the signs of the trouble. It is harder to see its causes. What, in your opinion, are they? What is the reason for all these defections in so many different countries? Why are so many priests leaving the priesthood, so many monks and nuns leaving their communities; why this virtually world-wide crisis in vocations and why do so many young people hesitate to commit themselves to solving it?

This is in fact a question everyone is asking. The answer is certainly not a simple one; there are too many elements involved in the phenomenon. It seems to me that the most useful thing, for our present purpose, is to discover which causes are due to ourselves, to our own failings and weaknesses.

Wherever we find a case of error, deviation, violence, the most important thing is to understand the elements of truth involved, which make it attractive, formidable and contagious, and then to isolate these from all the distortions which disfigure them.

The opponents are of several kinds. There are those who have turned away in revolt: it would be wrong to call them just "protestors." They have broken with the Church and criticize it from outside.

Then there are those who are unhappy with the juridical forms of the institution, and who slip quietly out of it.

There are those who "protest" in the etymological Latin and traditional sense of giving evidence. In other words, Christians who give evidence, within the Church, and in the name of the Gospel and our common inheritance, in order that it become "without spot or wrinkle."

Even though their objections may sound the same as those who have left in revolt, they are very different. Like them, but *within* the Church, they battle against juridicism, but not against justice; against authoritarianism, but not against authority; against legalism, but not against law; against rigidity, but not against order; against uniformity, but not against unity.

The sharpest dissatisfaction is felt against the Roman

Curia, but it touches on all authority. The people at the top will diminish or increase the objections, accorā…ıg to the extent of their openness to conciliar renewal; but beyond individuals, it is the "system" itself that is being objected to, the institutional and sociological "mechanism" of the Church in our day.

It is not the authority of the pope which is in doubt among faithful sons of the Church, but the "system" which holds him prisoner, and involves him in the smallest decision made by the Roman congregations, whether or not he has actually signed a given decree. What is wanted is to liberate everyone, even the Holy Father himself, from the system—which has been the subject of complaint for several centuries, and yet we have not succeeded in really loosening its grip or reshaping it.

For while popes come and go, the Curia remains. During the Council, one Curial prelate was quoted as saying: "Let the bishops have their say—they'll go home in the end; we shall stay and put right all the damage they may do." The story may be apocryphal, but it does reflect a certain mentality.

More generally, the variety of recriminations and complaints faces us all with the basic objection which is one form of the accusation the world so often brings against the Church: of betraying the purity of the Gospel instead of living by it, of not showing forth the Lord and his Spirit.

That is certainly the heart of the matter. We are not attacked for being Christian, but for not being Christian enough. The protest is, first and foremost, an agonized call to us to free ourselves from everything which, in our structures and in ourselves, does not reflect Christian brotherhood, freedom, and simplicity.

For a good many of those who leave the priesthood—though of course not all—the problem of celibacy, however important in itself, is not primarily the crucial one; what is involved is the credibility of the Church as it actually behaves, as witness to a Gospel of truth and love.

The Church of Rome has sometimes been contrasted with

the Reformed and the Orthodox Churches, describing them as the Churches respectively of Peter, of Paul and of John. Peter, the firm guarantor of unity and supreme authority; Paul, the indefatigable promoter of the liberty of the children of God and of welcome to all nations, beyond the law and the legalists of his day; John, the apostle of contemplation and love.

I will not accept any such antithesis. We all want to be, together and inseparably, the Church of Peter, of Paul and of John.

We are the heirs of the Apostles—not just of one of them. It is up to us to accept the necessary authority of Peter, as also the indispensable liberty of the children of God, and, like Paul, to reject any legalism that belongs to the slavery of the Old Law and stifles life; just as we must also recognize with John the primacy of prayer and love, without which there can be no Christian life. We must be more than ever united with Peter, to help him to free the Church from all the things that hamper its life, and to reaffirm our links with him.

Rome is like an oak tree full grown. The oak has spread its branches, and the birds nest in them. But there are parasite creepers clinging to the trunk, and drawing off the sap. The tragedy is that some people confuse the creepers with the bark of the tree. The bark is part of the tree, and must be strong and solid to protect the sap.

The creepers are quite different—they are a mass of archaic customs, procedures, and prohibitions, which both damage the tree and hide it from view.

Must we despair of ever seeing its life triumph over all this?

No. A Christian is a man of faith, and faith develops outwards into hope, as also into charity. This by no means is to say that we can have the ready-made optimism of the after-dinner speaker. The history of the Church is a long pascal triduum, living over again Good Friday, Holy Saturday and Easter morning. Good Friday is too real to permit of any naïve optimism; we believe in the reality of sin and the forces of evil. But the presence of him who rose at Easter enables us to go forward in tranquil faith: "I know him in whom I have believed."

We travel along a rocky path, amid dust, setbacks, weariness—but the Master is there, with us, on our own road to Emmaus.

I may add, in conclusion, that though our interview has dealt exclusively with dialogue within the Church, I do not forget, any more than you do, that the Church is for the world, and that it must overcome its own inner tensions as soon as possible, in order the better to take up its task in relation to all men, and the vast problems they face.

The Council's schema *Lumen Gentium* cannot be taken in isolation from *Gaudium et Spes*.

"Home," said Eliot, "is where one starts from." This is really what underlies what I have been saying. To make our home more spacious, more airy, more habitable does not mean just putting in such amenities as central heating, but providing a family security which enables us to start out with the rest of mankind along the great highways of the world.

2

The Impact on World Opinion

The Suenens interview had a considerable repercussion on public opinion: an immediate, prolonged, widespread and profound echo. Published on May 15, it was widely quoted and commented upon the next day by the principal international news media: The *Times* (London), *Le Monde* and *La Croix* (Paris), *La Libre Belgique, Le Soir* and the *Standaard* (Brussels), *La Stampa* and *Il Messaggero* (Italy), the *Tijd* and the *Volkskrant* (Holland) the *New York Times*, and many others.

The *ICI* had arranged things well, finding in the world market publications interested in having the complete text exclusively in their respective tongues. The interview appeared almost simultaneously in Paris (*ICI*); in Dutch at Bruges (*Internationale Katholieke Informatie*); in Spanish in Mexico (*Informaciones Católicas Internacionales*) then at Lima (*Noticias Aliadas*) and at Barcelona (*El Ciervo*); in Italian at Milan (*Famiglia Mese* and *Aggiornamenti Sociali*), then at Bologna (*Il Regno*); in English at London (*Tablet*) and at Kansas City (*National Catholic Reporter*), in German at Zurich (*Orientierung*), in Portuguese at Petropolis, Brazil (*Vozes*) in Croat at Zagreb (*Glas Concilia*), in Czech at Prague (*Catholicke Noviny*, but its serialized publication was later interrupted), in Hungary at Budapest (*Vigilia*), in Polish at Cracow (*Tygodnik Powszechny*) and in Catalan at Montserrat.

Some saw in this a big maneuver of "the international pressure group IDOC" and "its world religious information trust." This is a convenient way to deny the evidence of a current of opinion which it had no need to mobilize because it was waiting.

While sending out the complete text, the *ICI* distributed large excerpts to the news agencies and to many religious editors throughout the world. The public everywhere thus learned of the existence and substance of the document even before the subscribers to the *ICI* had received it. Editorial reaction was immediate and widespread.

When the daily papers had finished reporting the story and saying what they thought of it, the weeklies took over at the end of May and early June, then the bimonthlies and the monthlies up through July, August and September.

Various circumstances helped to extend the fall-out time for what became known as the "Suenens bomb." In France, *Figaro* was on strike, so that Abbé René Laurentin could not discuss the event until the end of May. An even more important and widespread factor was the election campaign: the press was little interested in general news until after June 15. In Italy, a long postal strike slowed down considerably the arrival of the original French text at Curial offices, and many commentators were undoubtedly awaiting the Curia's reaction before deciding what importance to attach to the Suenens proposals.

It was only about June 20 that a letter of Cardinal Tisserant, dean of the Sacred College, to the Primate of Belgium was leaked to the press. The interview, filed by most religious editors, immediately became big news again. A second wave of comment surged from dailies to weeklies and from weeklies to monthlies.

The first two weeks of July marked the symposium of European bishops at Chur. More than 200 journalists saw and heard Cardinal Suenens put his ideas on the problem to the test and in an actual situation. Later, in September-October, comments on the interview gradually merged with the discussion of the upcoming meeting of the Synod of Bishops in Rome.

The debate at first was strongly centered on the person and action of Cardinal Suenens. During the five months it kept growing and becoming deeper, until finally it took on the dimensions of a fundamental debate on the Church.

The range of the response can be considered in both a geographical and socio-ecclesiastical sense. The interview provoked reactions at the "center," in Rome. These will be discussed later. It provoked them also at the "periphery," though apparently not everywhere in the same volume or of the same nature.

Without doubt Belgium reacted most quickly, most massively and most often positively. The proverb, "No man is a prophet in his own country," did not apply. Not that there were no reservations, or even bitter criticism, but one had to search for them amidst the flood of often enthusiastic support. If no Belgian bishop seems to have publicly expressed his views, numerous theologians, especially those of Louvain, commented on the proposals and developed them: Msgr. Philips in the *Nouvelle revue theologique* (July-August), Fathers Heylen, Delhaye, Janssens, Strottman, and Aubert in *De Maand* (Sept.).

France was slower to express interest, especially (as noted) because of the elections which followed the departure of General de Gaulle. Perhaps France's long tradition of being "the eldest daughter of the Church" had not prepared Frenchmen to believe and admit that something truly interesting could come from outside the country. Even the Dutch experience of recent years had not succeeded in breaking down the wall of skepticism, indulgent and amusing for some, blasé for others, probingly hostile for still others. Perhaps the memory of tensions with Rome during the 1950s over worker priests and biblical exegesis caused the more responsible French Catholics to think that the shock-treatment method is not always the best way to promote an idea or get action in the Church. Perhaps also some of the most committed French Catholics felt that the ecclesiological and ecclesiastical problems raised by Cardinal Suenens were neither the most important nor the most urgent, and that prior consideration should be given to the need for an evangelical presence of the Church in the world.

However true all this may be, French reactions to the interview, although very numerous, were somewhat divided. The first press comments in *Le Monde* and *La Croix* were rather cautious. Henri Fesquet wrote (*Le Monde*, 5-17-69): "The pope and Cardinal Suenens are, each in his own way, reformers. But the latter is apparently the more sensitive to what needs to be done rather than to what has been done." According to Pierre Gallay (*La Croix*, 7-5-69), the interview, in view of the date it was given, "does not take into consideration the changes which have occurred in the Roman Curia and in the liturgy. These changes are proof that the reforms desired by the Council continue to be carried out. . . . There are necessary transitions."

Marcel Clement, a French publicist, published in *L'Homme nouveau* of June 1 the most direct and most systematic criticism of the interview. Antoine Wenger, at a time when backstage rumors were circulating on what the Curia thought about it, reported to *La Croix* of May 29-30 the first echo and the most credible of the Roman reactions. Three French Curial cardinals, Tisserant, Villot and Garrone, it was leaked, were to be the spokesmen for the pain caused in Rome by the interview. Cardinal Daniélou (also French and a noted theologian) would become the most eloquent critic, if not directly of Cardinal Suenens, at least of the challenging viewpoints he defended. Another French theologian, Fr. Bouyer, would not be sparing in his criticism.

Such reactions, however, were not typical of those of France. The initial fence-straddling position of *Le Monde* was abandoned even before the Chur meeting at which Cardinal Suenens emerged as a "man of mediation." René Laurentin spoke his mind openly the moment the strike at *Figaro* had ended. "This frank and daring reflection," he wrote, "is above all a cry of faith" (6-28-69). Marie-Dominique Chenu, writing in *Le Monde* (6-21-29) was the first theologian with an international reputation to give an ecclesiological explanation and justification of the step taken by the Belgian primate. Another Dominican, Father Biot, followed in *Témoignage chrétien* (6-26-69). Hans Küng, the Tübingen theologian, sketched "a portrait of the pope" inspired by the article of Cardinal Suenens in *Le Monde* (8-12-69). And later in the same newspaper (9-19-69), Father Yves Congar added a positive ecclesiological reflection to the claims of collegiality and coresponsibility.

Few French bishops entered the debate. Bishop Gerard Huyghe, of Arras, was one of the first: "The temptation is great to refuse, in the name of the unity to be defended, to abandon a style of government which gives the illusion of security." And if, in an interview with *La Croix*, Cardinal François Marty expressed a noticeably different "temperament" from that of Cardinal Suenens, it was the same vision of things that his interventions in the synod subsequently showed.

As might be expected, Dutch opinion received the interview well. However, it did not seem to consider it as an "event" properly so-called. This was, no doubt, because in the Low Countries they no longer claim the rights of local Churches to diversity in unity: for these are already in effect there. That is why their journalists, theologians and bishops did not feel the need to mention, apropos the May 15 interview, what they had been saying, writing and putting into practice for several years.

Everybody could compare the Suenens proposal with that made by Cardinal Alfrink of Utrecht on June 22, for the pope's anniversary: "The primacy of the pope in the community of faith, is not in question. Nobody wants to harm it. On the one hand, the Second Vatican Council noted that the same theological and dogmatic value must not be attributed to the mission of the world episcopate in union with the pope as to the primacy of the pope." Cardinal Alfrink, a few days later in the United States, proposed two principles emphasized by the Council: "the legitimacy of pluriformity within the unity of the Church" and "a certain measure of democratization within the framework of the hierarchial structure of the Church."

All the Dutch bishops expressed the same sentiments even more clearly in a letter to their priests written after the Chur symposium. They said they were "deeply touched" by the reflections which Cardinal Suenens had developed.

The London *Times,* the most serious newspaper of phlegmatic England, departed from its customary reserve. "A theological blockbuster from the Cardinal" was the shattering title of a commentary prepared by Norman St. John-Stevas, Catholic member of Parliament (5-16-69):

Cardinal Suenens, Archbishop of Brussels and Primate of Belgium, one of the giants of the Second Vatican Council, and perhaps the greatest of the episcopal theologians, has published in today's *Tablet,* the Roman Catholic weekly, a ten thousand word theological blockbuster, which could constitute a major turning point in the life of the Church. Profound in its loyalty to the pope and the see of Rome, it is at the same time strongly critical of the existing structures of the Church, making a series of concrete suggestions for a root and branch reform, but calling, above all, for a spirit of openness and freedom within the Roman Catholic Church.

The cardinal's manifesto will encourage and strengthen the many Roman Catholics throughout the world, zealous for reform and renewal, but who have been losing faith in the episcopal hierarchy as an instrument by which these ends can be carried out. For them the significance of the article will lie as much in its authorship as in its content; if such views can be expressed with frankness by one who is both a leading pastoral prelate and a prince of the Church, there is hope for the ecclesiastical establishment yet. If the cardinal's views make headway the ecumenical movement, at the moment in the doldrums, could leap ahead to a new breakthrough. . . .

What is needed today is an ever closer association between the national episcopal conferences and the pope, so that he is not in practice isolated from the college of bishops. One practical consequence of closer collaboration would be "that the individual churches—through their bishops gathered in episcopal conferences—should be consulted publicly and collectively and enabled to collaborate in documents that vitally affect the whole Church. And that not merely by associating their strictly theological commissions in the work, but also by including lay people qualified to speak on the matter at issue. The cardinal is too tactful to say so, but it was precisely the ignoring of such a procedure that made the papal encyclical on birth control *Humanae Vitae* incredible to so many.

On the issue of how best to elect the pope in future, the cardinal is not dogmatic but he clearly feels the use of the college of cardinals has disadvantages and strongly disapproves of the present method of appointment to the college which is entirely at the disposition of the pope, thus opening the way to choice by whim or favoritism, and its use as a means for rewarding nuncios who have finished their diplomatic careers. We feel an uneasiness, a dislocation from our age, every time a "promotion" to the cardinalate is announced.

All these practical changes, recommended by Cardinal Suenens, flow from a profound analysis of the nature of authority in the church today. To give up religious authority, he declares, would be contrary to the gospel, but the way in which authority is mediated must be in tune with the age in which it is exercised. For the priests and laity of today the old authoritarian legalism of the past has vanished, and a law commands obedience only insofar as it is reasonable. "The bishop must recognize", says the cardinal, "in theory and practice that no series of problems today can be simply resolved by the decree of authority without also having the support of priests and people."

And what of the authority of the pope? The cardinal finds two essentials in the pope, he must be Bishop of Rome and Supreme Pastor of the Universal Church. A principal role is a simple but vital one: To watch over the integrity of our faith in the eucharist and the reverence due to it, without having therefore to impose any particular mode of expressing it on this or that society.

Cardinal Suenens will doubtless be accused of being disloyal to the pope in expressing himself as he has done but the truth of the matter is precisely the opposite. Not the least of the merits of what he has written is that he has rendered a signal service to the Holy See by pointing the way it must follow if it is to retain its position and prestige in the contemporary world.

This editorial, however, did not really set the tone for British reactions, at least for the Catholic press. If the *Tablet*, which published the full text of the interview, continued to follow the affair in a positive way, London's two other Catholic weeklies, the *Universe* and the *Catholic Herald*, remained very discreet.

Auxiliary bishop Butler of Westminster seems to have been the first to express explicitly his adherence to the views expressed by Cardinal Suenens:

The interview with Cardinal Suenens is one of the most important contributions to the contemporary discussion in the Catholic Church. . . . His frankness and prudence should serve to provide a rallying point for all those who share his own position "at the extreme center" of the postconciliar Church. His views should be of immense interest not only to all educated Catholics but to all who believe in Christian ecumenism and in the Christian dialogue with the modern world.

Germany reacted slowly. It was only in early June that one sees some news and substantial commentaries in such Catholic publications as *Publik* and *Herder Korrespondenz*, or in the secular *Der Spiegel* and the *Frankfurter Allgemeine Zietung*. The commentaries were sympathetic, but their major concern seemed to be with Rome's reaction rather than with the substance of the interview. *Herder Korrespondenz* regretted that the interview bore more on the problems of ecclesiastical structures than on problems of the faith which seemed to it more relevant and serious.

Cardinal Suenens received the clear and unequivocal support of several great German theologians. Karl Rahner published a long article in *Publik* (7-4). Then Hans Küng wrote an article in *Le Monde* in August, while in the United States Bernard Häring and John Baptiste Metz took positions on particular points analagous to those of Cardinal Suenens. Also noteworthy is the commentary of Professor Neumann of Tübingen on the *motu proprio* reforming the statute on nuncios, in the Jesuit review of Zurich, *Orientierung*.

The interview was published and diffused in several countries of Eastern Europe. However, only one commentary was reported from these countries, that of the weekly *Kierunki* (Warsaw), organ of Pax, the "progressist" Catholic movement:

> By rejecting the ever present sensational element, only the tenor of the interview justifies the interest of which it has become the object in Catholic circles, especially those interested in reform. Coresponsibility as regards the contemporary destiny of the Church . . . obliges us to observe attentively all the manifestations of renewal going on, to draw from the experience of other persons, and encourages us to observe different problems in a confrontation of attitudes and conceptions.

It is always hard to evaluate opinion in Italy. There are too many opinions which conflict or are nuanced to infinity within a province, from one city to another, within a Christian community, from one "spontaneous group" to another, from one political family to another. This is the way it was with the interview of Cardinal Suenens. The number of publications, both Catholic and general, which asked for the rights of translation and publication of the whole text was greater in Italy than in any other country. At the same time it was in Italy that the innuendoes and unfavorable interpretations of the article tending to discredit and disparage the Primate of Belgium first appeared.

Fabricio de Santis no doubt expressed the opinion of a whole Italian political and ecclesiastical "milieu" when he described the interview as "a speech which has, in a sense, the character of a personal effusion dictated by bitter frustration," when he denounced "a substantial divergence concerning the concept of collegiality (of Cardinal Suenens) from that sanctioned by the Council," and when he concluded: "The moral of the story is that the Church of Suenens and that of Paul VI appear to be two different Churches" (*Corriere della Sera*, 5-31-69).

The commentator of *Il Messaggero* (5-17-69) also voiced, no doubt, the interested but prudent expectation of another segment of opinion when he wrote: "The opposition is not limited to marginal and accessory questions, nor to a difference of form, style, intonation or accent. The difference is defined by the answers one gives these questions: Should the Church be a family or an army? a community of brothers or a bureaucratic organization?" The way questions are raised, it is true, is already an invitation to answer them in a certain way.

Raniero La Valle, whose reports on the Vatican Council were considered among the best, reflects the feeling of numerous groups of laymen and priests impatient to see the Church in Italy commit itself to the postconciliar *aggiornamento,* and to escape the suffocation of mental, administrative and political structures felt more burdensome in Italy than elsewhere. "Cardinal Suenens, by taking a frank position on the burning questions of the Church today," he wrote, "has a liberating and pacifying value; it shows indeed how possible it is in the Church to discuss institutions, with fidelity and full communion with the successor of Peter, while breaking with the sterile opposition between those who attack and those who defend the institutional Church. . . . It is clear that if the Cardinal decided to intervene it is because he felt the urgent need."

At least two Italian bishops took positive positions. The first was Archbishop Salvatore Baldassarri of Ravenna, who told *Sette Giorni* that he saw "specific proposals which must not be dropped. Episcopal collegiality should be enacted in at least two circumstances: first in the election of the pope, because it is a crying contradiction that the cardinals alone choose the person who ought to assure the unity of the whole episcopate; and secondly, in the elaboration of important documents."

Later, Cardinal Pellegrino, Archbishop of Turin, interviewed by *La Rocca* of Assisi, regretted that the majority of commentators did not pick up the "essential point" of the proposal of his Belgian colleague: "the observation that the principle of collegiality proclaimed by the Council has not yet found concrete and precise applications capable of effectively influencing the life of the Church. His objective is to obtain from the next synod, with the full agreement of pope and bishops, concrete ways to apply collegiality. This basic demand seems to me fully justified."

If it is difficult in Italy to identify any definite tendency of public opinion because of the prevailing confusion, in Spain it is practically impossible because of suppression. The press did report the Suenens interview, but it was through the shocked and indignant pens of Roman correspondents, an approach that gave the analyses and commentaries a one-sided coloration. It took several weeks for the whole text to be translated and made known. The comments in the publications of the Propaganda Popular Católica group (such as *Vida Nueva*), in such Jesuit journals as *Hechos y Dichos* and *Mundo Social*, and in independent publications like *El Ciervo*, suffice to show the favorable response of the most active segments of the laity, clergy and episcopate.

"For those interested in history-making dates in the life of the Church I suggest May 15, 1969, as a candidate for the most select list." For Gary MacEoin, well-known religious chronicler in the United States, the interview of Cardinal Suenens is therefore an historic act. American opinion made no mistake about it and gave great attention and interest to the event.

This can be explained by the generally recognized fact that it is in the United States that the crisis is most serious. Very well and very regularly informed about the accelerat-

ing evolution of this crisis in the American Church, Cardinal
Suenens certainly had it in mind when he decided on the
manner and content of his proposal.

An American sociologist, Andrew Greeley, has best defined the nature of the crisis and understood how much the
intervention of Cardinal Suenens can help overcome it:

> The present crisis in the Church is not one of schism, apostacy
> or infidelity, but of credibility, consensus and alienation. Large
> numbers of Catholics are not going to leave the Church, much
> less is anyone likely to start a new heretical Church. Rather the
> danger is that Church leadership will continue to lose its credi-
> bility; a substantial segment of the Catholic population will
> withdraw consensus from the leadership and will remain within
> the Church but substantially alienated from the Church as an
> organized institution.
>
> It is within the context of that very real possibility that one
> must read the remarkable interview that Cardinal Suenens gave
> recently to the world press. The program of 'coresponsibility' he
> describes is an obvious attempt to arrest the erosion of con-
> sensus which is going on within the Church (*Catholic Voice*,
> 7-2-69).

But has the "credibility gap" grown that wide already in
the United States? Did Suenens speak too late? That is the
precise issue discussed by an American Lutheran theologian,
Martin E. Marty, in the *National Catholic Reporter* (7-9-69),
and his conclusion is pessimistic.

> Suenens' comments probably have come too late. The broad
> renewal party has fragmented; some have given up and left
> leadership posts in the Church. Others have become embittered
> or enraged. There simply does not seem to be a large talent
> pool on which to draw for new leadership at the moment. . . . I
> do not mean to imply that the Curia is almost absolutely cor-
> rupt, as the American political system today appears to be. But
> it is equally unresponsive, self-protective, and oblivious to the

need for creative changes. Thereby it contributes to increasing polarization and disenchantment. In such circumstances, Cardinal Suenens seems to be all the more worthy of admiration.

Disenchantment approaches skepticism in a *National Catholic Reporter* editorial (5-28-69):

> The question now is whether the interview will be taken as seriously by the several publics to which it is addressed as it is by its principal author. That is not a sure thing. . . . Every Catholic whose faith came alive because of the Council will endorse these views—if he can be persuaded to read them. The reason he may be hard to persuade is that he also endorses, in advance, the Cardinal's admission that the same system "has been the subject of complaint for several centuries, and yet we have not succeeded in really loosening its grip or reshaping it."
>
> Even more pertinently, he will anticipate, correctly, that nothing he will read in the interview will provide an answer to the key question, once succinctly phrased by Lenin, "What is to be done?" Cardinal Suenens has boldly and eloquently reformulated the goals of renewal, but he has not talked about means. . . . The Church the Cardinal describes is attractive, but it doesn't exist and he does not show how it can be brought to being, or how a lay person or member of the lower clergy can work for its realization. For the power to complete the conciliar reform belongs to those who oppose reform; the prophets of gloom are in charge.

To keep things in the right perspective it must be borne in mind that these reservations stem from fundamental agreement with Cardinal Suenens and an appreciation of his initiative. This point was well formulated by the *Catholic Transcript* (6-23-69). It described the interview as "a performance remarkable in many respects: for its lucidity and fluency, for its strict order of priorities, its logic and incisiveness, for its comprehensiveness and balance," and especially for the "positive vision of the Church" which dominates the entire proposal. The same point was made by the *Catholic Messenger* (7-3-69) in a reply to a series of criticisms:

Alternatives to an institutional structure based on the political power model are not yet in sight. They will not be in sight until enough elements of the Church take the risk of striking out on new paths of Christ-following to build our experience of freedom in unity to the level where a newfound faith in evangelical freedom takes over the consciousness of the whole Church. We have an appalling lack of that faith at present. It is this that Cardinal Suenens is trying to push us toward.

And as Gregory Baum wrote in the Catholic World (December 1969):

While Catholic publications all over the world have applauded Cardinal Suenens' interview and praised his courage, a few persons in the Church have been highly critical of him. Needless to say, some of these were part of, or closely associated with, the Church's central administration in Rome. In the United States a few columnists known for extreme conservative views have found fault with the Belgian Cardinal.

Cardinal Suenens is not in need of a defense. Nonetheless, the objections raised against his interview deserve to be taken seriously.

Cardinal Léger, former archbishop of Montreal, is a Canadian. He was the first member of the Sacred College to publicly reproach Cardinal Suenens for his intervention. In an interview given to *Corriere della Sera* (Milan), he said: "I do not find it right that the archbishop of Malines-Brussels spread widely his opinions in the press." He criticized those who would reduce "the pope to a club president, and the Church to an immense Rotary . . . where people would meet to air their opinions and 'do a bit of good.'" All Canadian opinion was not like that of Cardinal Léger—far from it. Archbishop Alexander Carter of Sault Sainte Marie, president of the episcopal conference, publicly expressed his "fundamental agreement" on the essential points treated by Cardinal Suenens: "My own meagre offerings over the past few years ran in the same general direction." Archbishop

Henri Routhier of Grouard-McLennan, however, warned at the same time just as publicly against the dangers of a revolutionary spirit in the Church.

In Canada, as elsewhere, the interview provoked a movement of consternation and recoil. The Dominican theologian Bernard Lambert explains that it came "at a moment when a certain number of persons were asking if it were not better to stop the movement rather than to follow it, given the present crisis. They take cover behind the letter of the Council taken in a rigid sense."

Father Lambert knows well not only the letter but also the spirit of the Council to which he contributed analyses which attracted considerable attention:

> Vatican II defined the place of the bishops in relation to the pope in the episcopal college. It laid the foundations for the theology of the local Church, but everything is not clear as regards the relations of local Churches with the universal Church. Likewise, new relationships have been established between the episcopal conferences and the pope, and vice versa, just like those between the episcopal conferences themselves; but many points remain to be settled, for example, freedom of experimentation, the right of dissent, recognition of the Catholic legitimacy of the distinctive features the individual Churches will give themselves, the right of the pope to reserve to himself certain questions which in law belong to the bishops, the participation of episcopal conferences in the great decisions which concern the universal Church, the possibility for particular or national Churches to opt not to accept certain practical decisions taken elsewhere, etc. Now it is clear that in all this one can adopt either a maximalist or a minimalist position (*Le Devoir*, 7-28-69).

The survey is not exhaustive. It may suffice, nevertheless, to show the geographical extension of the reaction. It was very widespread, but at the same time, it did not cover the whole planet or even the whole Christian world.

One might anticipate that this interview would be well received by the Eastern Churches of the Near East and elsewhere. But the only public witness we have is a letter from Greek-Melchite Archbishop Elias Zoghby of Baalbek, Lebanon, to the *Informations catholiques internationales* (9-15-69).

The interview was likewise published throughout Latin America. But apart from a positive comment by the Argentine theologian and journalist Jorge Mejia in *Criterio,* the reactions were rather reserved, like that of the Urugayan layman Hector Borrat; frankly critical, like that of Cardinal Alfredo Sherer of Porto Alegre ("Paul VI did not deserve the criticisms which, according to the press, have been made by those from whom one could not expect them"); or even absolutely hostile, like that of the daily *O Estado de São Paulo* (5-20-69):

> This interview, by reason of the authority of the Cardinal himself and the magazine which published the text, constitutes a new pressure, a particularly important one, in favor of a "democratization of the Church". . . . If the moderate monarchy (which the Church is) should be destroyed, the very authority of the Church would be sapped and Western civilization would lose its center of crystalization. Then the barbarians will come and future generations will begin again from scratch with a church which will no longer be Christ's but the world's: a church which will no longer be the Church.

The extent of the reaction, as noted earlier, can also be taken in the socio-ecclesiastical sense. All levels of the Church have in fact been affected and shaken, from top to bottom.

The top is Rome. Its first reactions were anonymous, roundabout, informal. One guessed them rather than knew them through the rumors and gossip circulating in Curial corridors and waiting rooms and filtered to the outside through the more or less distorting lenses of Vatican diehards.

"Acute irritation" *(Paese Sera)*; "Like a Bomb" *(Le Soir)*; "Great Impression" *(Ya)*; "Real Uneasiness *(L'Aurore)*; "Surprise and Vexation" (*Ansa*): these are a few of the headlines given to the Roman reactions on the morrow of May 15.

"In the Curia," said the Italian news agency *Ansa,* "the interview is openly stigmatized as 'extravagant', or 'irresponsible.' But no one has tried to hide the embarrassment caused by assertions which, coming directly from a prince of the Church, cannot be officially denied nor refuted polemically. Nonetheless, the fact that the Cardinal made such a grave declaration with such frankness permits the supposition that he enjoyed the support of several bishops and cardinals."

The Rome correspondent of the Brussels *Soir* reported on May 16:

> In short, this is what they are saying: Why such a publication? Why didn't the cardinal send it directly to the Pope and the high authorities in the Church rather than question them through the rebound of public opinion? Hasn't the cardinal ever heard of hierarchical channels? Is he unaware of the reforms already put into effect in most of the areas discussed? They do not understand this "untimely outburst."

The correspondent of the Paris *Aurore* reported on May 19:

> The reaction of the Curia is unanimous: they are congratulating themselves that the Cardinal of Malines was not named Secretary of State. Some even go so far as to say that the declaration of Cardinal Suenens is due precisely to his vexation because he was not chosen for this position.

On his return to Paris from Rome at the end of May, Antoine Wenger expressed himself in *La Croix* (5-29-30) more irenically. "The general idea prevailing in Roman circles is that the points which were the objects of his criticisms or requests have not escaped the attention of Rome and are at present being subjected to a profound revision." Summing up his two articles, Father Wenger wrote: "An interview like that of Cardinal Suenens has something stimulating about it.

On the other hand, the way his intervention can affect the people responsible at the center of the government of the Church is that he does not recognize the efforts already undertaken, most frequently in the sense he advocates. This misunderstanding risks undermining the confidence of the laity."

But this was all vague rumor and insinuations. One had to wait until June 20 to learn that there had indeed been a reaction in Rome and what it was. A leak revealed that Cardinal Tisserant, dean of the Sacred College, Cardinal Villot, the new Secretary of State, and Cardinal Garrone, prefect of the Congregation for Catholic Education, had each written to Cardinal Suenens. Initially, Italian Curial cardinals had wanted to react. But, as *La Libre Belgique* reported, "according to well informed sources, the pope wished to forestall a polemic between Italian Curial cardinals and the primate of Belgium, since such a conflict might compromise the progressive internationalization of the Curia. This is likewise why only non-Italian Curial cardinals—the three French prelates, Tisserant, Villot and Garrone—expressed their disapproval in private letters to the cardinal." Those letters have not been published but some journalists have given what purports to be the substance. Thus, Henri Fesquet in *Le Monde* (6-24):

Three men, three different temperaments. The first, Cardinal Tisserant from Lorraine, was the most offensive and ironical. Writing in the name of his Curial colleagues, he claimed that their honor had been defamed, reproached the archbishop of Malines for having advanced slanderous proposals and asked him to retract. Cardinal Villot, younger and more diplomatic, regretted the lack of sobriety in the interview. He showed himself especially sensitive to criticisms—superficial and far-fetched to his mind—of the nuncios. Cardinal Garrone, also a flexible person, feared especially that the most troublesome Catholics would be encouraged. He expressed the shocked surprise of those close to Pope Paul who consider that the pope is carrying out the program of reform with as much speed as is feasible. He also thought that an attempt to mobilize public opinion through the press was incompatible with the correct conduct and delicacy due to the Sovereign Pontiff.

It is significant, Fesquet concluded, "that none of those involved tried to invalidate the theological viewpoint underlying the interview: the role of the pope, the election of the pope, ecclesiology, etc. This silence might implicitly express awareness of the validity of the theological arguments used by the primate of Belgium, arguments which in fact are accepted by outstanding experts esteemed by Paul VI."

Paul VI's reply to the wishes of the Sacred College expressed on June 23 by Cardinal Tisserant for the feast of St. John the Baptist, was generally understood as the papal reaction to the Suenens interview, although he did not refer to it explicitly.

We cannot remain insensitive to criticisms—they are not all exact, nor all just, nor always respectful and opportune—which come from different sides to this apostolic see, identified by a name that is more easily attacked, namely, the Roman Curia. . . .

We shall merely say that we reflect serenely on the protests addressed to this apostolic see from two viewpoints. The first is that of a humble and sincere objectivity, ready to take into account the valid reasons for these attitudes of challenge, and disposed to modify purely juridical positions whenever it appears reasonable to do so, desirous as we are to renew continually and interiorly the spirit of canonical legislation for the better service of the Church and for a beneficial and efficacious development of its mission in today's world. This goes hand in hand with a predisposition in favor of specific praiseworthy proposals in the direction of a legitimate pluralism in unity. . . .

The other sentiment is that of the great confidence we want to place in the very persons from whom these discussions and deviations we speak of come. We readily admit that there is present in these sons of the Holy Church a fundamental rightness of intention, and we want to recognize also that what depends on us has constant need to be corrected and perfected, a need made more urgent by the greatness of the present needs for continuing renewal of the Church. But obviously our greatest confidence for the defense and growth of the Church at this important hour is placed in the Church itself: in the episcopate, the clergy, religious, and the Catholic laity, in the innumerable good souls who pray, work and suffer in silence for the cause of the reign of Christ.

At the base, that is, among the Christian people, reactions have been numerous and multiple, as the press survey has already demonstrated. Two complementary observations can, however, be added.

The first is to note the support voted by groups for the Suenens' proposals, for example, the "Renewal" groups of Birmingham, England, the John XXIII brotherhoods of Belgium, the general Catholic Action of Belgium, a whole group of priests in Western Canada, and the participants in the annual symposium on sexology of Louvain gynecologists, psychiatrists, sociologists, theologians, and demographers from various countries of Europe. The executive board of the conference of priests of Western Canada, for example, sent the complete text of the interview to its 350 members along with a two-page resumé, asking each to sign a declaration expressing firm support for the essential positions of the Cardinal, "as well as the wish that the Canadian representatives at the Rome Synod express and promote this same principle forcibly." This document was signed by 240 priests.

Father Ora McManus, president of the group, summarized the comments and evaluations of the members as follows:

I add my vote to support Cardinal Suenens completely. I hope our bishops speak with as much force. I feel that hesitation will be paid for by the dropping out of the young clergy and people. As a priest, I pray that our bishops remain free vis-à-vis the present system and that they can assume their legitimate role as head of the presbyterial council.

The second thing to note is the feeling of revived hope and liberation which is expressed by many commentators.

"Your words have been truly liberating," wrote Jean Delfosse, editor of *La Revue Nouvelle*. "The cardinal has offered us his hand" is the title used by H. Buntrinx in *Kulturleven* of July: "What matters in the cardinal's interview is . . . the fact that he recognized publicly that there are faithful who no longer draw strength and give meaning to their lives from the traditional image of the Church." "The cardinal archbishop of Malines has put in a nutshell the things which weigh heavily on the minds of countless Catholics. It was high time that someone of status had the courage to say all this publicly and to back it up with his own authority. At last this has been done." (*Het Volk*, 5-17-69).

A. Collard wrote in *La Croix* of Belgium (5-21-69):

> In a courageous interview Cardinal Suenens has given faith and courage to all those who hoped in Vatican II. . . .
>
> In making this declaration, the most important in the Church since the calling of the Council, he knows that there will be voices of protest . . . He knows also that the majority of Christians will read his message with immense hope. He should know how comforting it is for his people that a bishop could take this risk.

"The majority of Christians?" Some would challenge such a statement and there exists in fact no way to verify it. But that is not the real issue. What does it really matter if, as Claude Roffat thinks with a good deal of justification, that the vision of the Church which is outlined by Cardinal Suenens, "remains very novel for the majority of the faithful." Claude Roffat answers this objection very well (*La Croix* 6-24-69):

> Every revolution starts from an active and convinced minority. And here we have a small platoon of Gideon's soldiers whose job is to renew the structures of the Christian army, mobilizing

it neither for defense nor for conquest, but in a search for communion. And what is the life of the Church but communion?

Is not the principal function of the movements of lay apostolate today to call all laymen to this awareness of their coresponsibility, with the bishops and priests, of the new face to be given to the Church of tomorrow, one of communion between the different degrees of the hierarchy and laity, between the different legitimate trends towards stability or movement, replying moreover to complementary charisms received from the same Holy Spirit, accepting each other without mutual condemnation, and affronting each other in all charity. We are all, before God and men, coresponsible for communion.

We said at the beginning of this chapter on public opinion that the effect of the interview of Cardinal Suenens had been immediate, prolonged and widespread. But also profound, for by this interview Cardinal Suenens provoked serious reflection not only among theologians, but also among all believers.

3

The Cardinal Replies to Criticisms

The interview Cardinal Suenens gave to the ICI resulted in a flood of reactions and also raised new questions. The most critical reactions might have inclined the cardinal to water down some of his most progressive ideas. He did not do so. The most enthusiastic reactions might, on the other hand, have led him to make more advanced proposals. But he did not do this either.

The cardinal might have been satisfied to refer to his interview or to his book. On the contrary, at the risk of repeating himself, he chose to constantly explain and clarify his proposals. Two important statements must be especially taken into account:

REPLY TO CRITICS IN THE ROMAN CURIA

The first statement was made June 23, 1969, as a result of the reaction of Cardinal Tisserant, dean of the Sacred College, to the interview. This was widely publicized by the press and most frequently *in extenso*. The text of the press release is as follows:

> The press has carried reports of a letter to me from Cardinal Tisserant, as from a few other Curial cardinals, disapproving my recent interview with *Informations catholiques internationales*.
>
> According to these reports, the interview was judged as being defamatory, disrespectful and even slanderous with regard to

officials of the Roman curia. There was even, the press relates, a suggestion that a public retraction was called for.

Difference of opinion is quite normal in the church. But I cannot accept that my intentions are questioned and that a discussion which was about ecclesiastical structures, should be considered as an attack on personalities.

I had attempted, at the beginning of the interview, to anticipate such criticisms emphasizing that I would only speak in terms of tendencies, functions and institutions as such, rather than of personalities; in any case the intentions of individuals are not under question, and to classify them 'en bloc' would be an over-simplification.

Furthermore, I mentioned in the interview that the problems of the administrative reorganization of the Church and the exercise of ecclesiastical authority have been already questioned for many centuries, and were even brought before Vatican I.

It is obvious, then, that I was not speaking of specific persons, but rather of structures and systems in the Church. Discussing the exercise of authority is not at all the equivalent of denying that same authority.

I, therefore, consider as being totally unacceptable the accusation made against the interview, saying it was defamatory and slanderous and I therefore also see no cause for a retraction.

I quite admit that there can be divergence of opinion about the adequacy of public discussion of these problems. Certain people want them to be treated in very private circles and others do not want them to be discussed at all.

Frank, open and constructive dialogue, inspired by a love of the church and its head, is a sign of vitality and strength. It is normal and healthy that there should be this open discussion about vital problems which concern the whole church, and all the more so, when these problems are felt in their acuity and urgency all over the world, and are being publicly discussed in the press, whether we like it or not. Intolerance of public discussion of these differences, under the pretext of preserving unity, seems to me to be harmful in the present day.

Furthermore, the numerous and positive reactions to the interview, coming from laity and priests of every rank, from at home and abroad, show that the suggestions made merely explicitated the feelings of many; and that, if implemented, they could help to surmount the tragic situation in which the church finds itself today and which impedes its mission in the world, in the service of humanity.

We are confident that a careful reading of the whole original text and not falsified extracts or fragments out of context will enable one to form an objective judgment.

And to conclude, it would perhaps be useful to reread these lines of Paul VI, by which he invited the members of the Roman Curia, on Sept. 21, 1963: "to receive criticism with humility, reflection and even gratefulness. Rome has no need to defend herself by turning a deaf ear to suggestions coming from honest voices, and all the more so, when they come from friendly and fraternal ones."

"UNFAILING ATTACHMENT TO PETER, OUR HEAD"

The second important statement was the address made by Cardinal Suenens on the evening of June 28, 1969, on the occasion of a Mass celebrating the anniversary of the coronation of Paul VI, and in the presence of Archbishop Cardinale, who had just been named the nuncio to Belgium.

"What an excellent occasion today for me to affirm publicly and forcefully my unshakable attachment to Peter, our leader, in the person he has just named as his representative to our country, the new nuncio to Belgium.

I am the more happy to be spokesman for the Belgian bishops, priests and people, because some—though fortunately few—seem to fear, in the wake of my recent interview and the repercussions in the press, that I am seeking to minimize the Holy Father's authority. I have already answered the distortions not only of my intentions but of my words. I think that a rereading of the text objectively and attentively would end the criticisms. I am happy, moreover, to use this occasion to thank all who showed their understanding through the innumerable letters I have received. They are here with me in a special way today to welcome the nuncio with joy, enthusiasm and respect.

To say that authority should today be exercised in the Church— as in society—in a different way to that in which it was formerly exercised is quite different from saying that it should be suppressed or lessened. To look facts in the face, one must see in a very striking manner that an irreversible trend has taken possession of the people of God, filling them with a longing for a renewal of life, for joy, change, progress and freedom within today's Church. Some thought they could block this trend by pretending to ignore its presence. The facts show, on the contrary, that there is a most urgent need to support it, meeting it fairly and taking it into account in order to direct it.

Rapid, numerous and constant changes characterize the condition of civil institutions today. How, then, can the Church do other than adjust to the life rhythm of its members? The principle of authority remains unshaken. Only the ways to exercise it are at issue.

This task of helping to change structures can be singularly advanced by the nuncios sent by the Holy See to represent it in the local Churches, if they study the reactions of the people of God and their desires, with a view to making them known in Rome. We are consequently in favor of everything that helps the exchange of information and encourages people to profit from the experiences of others.

In addition, Saint Peter described the Church as a living organism, with a multiplicity of organs in a single body. Pluriformity does not exclude unity, but rather gives new strength to unity, opening up all the dynamism of life and strength. Did not Our Lord say that there were many mansions in his Father's house?

You know that the relations between the center and periphery consitute the agenda of the upcoming Synod of Bishops, because the Church is today concerned about them. Let us pray together for this meeting. It will be a most important one because of the basic issues it will study with a view to implementing the decisions of the Council in the different countries. Let us ask God to make us fully open to the action of the Holy Spirit, so that we may the better guide and help the people of God in the whole world."

In his reply, Archbishop Cardinale said: "I salute your archbishop, Cardinal Suenens, with joy and sincere affection. I appreciate his profound love of the Church and his loyalty to the Vicar of Christ."

Further Suenens statements in subsequent months served less to explain the interview than to expound and explain his ideas in various specific contexts. At the Chur symposium, he discussed the problems of priests; at the Rome synod, the relations between the Holy See and episcopal conferences. These talks will be examined later.

THE INTERVIEWS

Among the many interviews he gave to radio and television networks and to newsmen, one is particularly important. It is an interview with René Laurentin, published in *Figaro* (6-26-69). It follows in full.

What was the purpose of the interview you gave to ICI?

I wanted to bring the essential issues into the open while we are preparing for the Synod of Bishops, the issues which —I believe—involve not only the interpretation of the Council but its intrinsic logic. The people around us are raising them, the people I meet for whom the Church seems remote and alien, as they ask themselves questions about the faith and the Gospel. Many such people have written to tell me that this interview renewed their confidence in the Church.

Did the interview accomplish its purpose?

The goal is a long-term one. It is a question of stimulating the work and research that will enable us to reach it. The research is under way.

In what respect do you think you were misunderstood?

The opening observations, which are essential, have too often been overlooked. They present the Church in the perspective of "an evangelical reality," and all the rest follows from that concept. Let me recall: "The basic problem dividing us, whether consciously or otherwise, is one of theology; we are starting from different visions of the Church. . . . Proudhon said in his day that at the root of every political problem there is a theological one. How much more so when it comes to the politics of religion!" The Church is not a uniformity, but unity in diversity, and diversity within unity. Collegiality involves not only consultation, but also coresponsibility. The first two questions of the interview are the important ones. They discuss the relation of the center to the periphery, of primacy and collegiality in the Church. The others are only illustrations or consequences.

Some are surprised that you launched your ideas through the press.

The ideas were already a matter of public knowledge. Now, since the time of Pius XII and even more since the Council, the existence of public opinion in the Church is recognized. No reform can be achieved without its participation. This is a relatively new fact in the Church. We must get used to it.

Some say that you are giving weapons to troublemakers.

I think rather that I am taking them away, for the discussion of real problems disarms criticisms. We must discover and accept the part of truth there is in every criticism.

Some are surprised that you did not stress the values of the reforms already instituted by Rome. What do you think of this?

The interview answers questions raised in my book *Co-responsibility in the Church*, a book which quotes Paul VI on almost every page. There was no need for me to summarize what has already been done by the Holy See. It is clear that I rejoice in the progress already made.

The NCR which praises your interview is surprised that you spoke of "objectives without discussing the means."

The author of the NCR article wonders if it is not too late. I do not think so. But the first thing is to ask the question. To phrase a question well is to give it a better chance of solution.

INOPPORTUNE?

In another interview, in the *Catholic Voice*, Oakland, California (7-2-69), Cardinal Suenens explained again what he meant by the opportuneness of his intervention:

Some have said that they agreed with 80% to 90% of what I said but that the moment was inopportune. Here is my reply to this reaction: I wonder, first of all, what day, month or year would be opportune for an open discussion of these problems. Then, I would point out that when there is tension, it is always better to admit it frankly. It is the first step towards the solution. I believe that now is an opportune time because we are living in a period of crisis; we are losing some of the best members of the Church. It is urgent that we open up a dialogue with them, in order to help them remain faithful. It is no longer possible for us to be like the ostrich with his head in the sand. Finally, I believe that the problems I have raised will require a long study in the Church. I am not speaking for tomorrow; I am thinking of the future, of the next generation. But we must begin discussion now.

THE CRISIS OF FAITH IN THE CHURCH

Some extracts from an interview with Robert Serrou published in *Paris Match* (7-5-69) are also pertinent.

*Why did you, in your interview, appeal to public opinion?
You have been widely criticized for short-circuiting the hierarchical lines of command in this way.*

May I answer with a recollection? As a young seminarist,
I was in the Brussels-Rome express when stifling smoke filled
the carriage. I pulled the alarm signal and opened the win-
dow to avoid total asphyxiation.

In our day thousands of Christians all over the world feel
that certain structures are smothering them. I spoke to set
them free, but also from a deep love for the Church and the
papacy. If some deplore the manner of my intervention, I
would say that an alarm signal is always to some extent
strident. What use would it be if it were otherwise? It is its
function.

*The Church is passing through a serious crisis. Is it a
blessing or an evil? Are the pope's anxieties justified?*

We are witnessing an extremely grave phenomenon. In
my view there are three superimposed crises which must
be singled out: First, what I would call a crisis of faith in
God; second, a crisis of faith in Christ and his divinity; and
third, a crisis of faith in the Church.

The crisis of faith in God is in a rather favorable state of
evolution. God is more alive than He ever was. If I am to
believe the publishers, literature on the "Death of God" is
perceptibly diminishing. The crisis of faith in Christ worries
me considerably.

It is very important to be precise on this subject. In order
to be a Christian there must be unequivocal belief in Christ,
the risen son of the living God. This is a problem, moreover,
which concerns all Churches.

I come now to the crisis of faith in the Church. The problem is to see Christ through the Church. Everything which
at the present moment is an obstacle is a matter of very
lively concern. Everything in the Church which is not suffi-

ciently evangelical and not open enough to the values of today is a stumbling block: the human values of dialogue, exchange, authenticity, simplicity.

Is this crisis leading to death or life?

I will say as Jesus did with Lazarus: this sickness is not mortal, but is directed to the glory of the Lord. We are passing through Good Friday, but afterwards there is the dawn of Easter.

In the meantime Christians must be fraternally open to each other and no one should consider his adversary as heretical. One sees people causing injury to others in the name of the Gospel. Not one of us possesses the fullness of truth. I believe that the present crisis is purifying, but I understand the anguish of the pope, an anguish which I share with him.

Do you not have the impression that Catholics, preoccupied primarily with their petty internal problems and even with parochial squabbles tend to ignore the big questions which men are asking the Church?

It is very important to clarify these internal problems of the Church, because on their solution depends the authentic proclamation of the Gospel to the world. "To love one another" said St. Exupéry, "does not mean to gaze at one another but to look together in the same direction." That is for all of us the basic goal. One of the ways to achieve this is to organize Christians who belong to the same Church, and then to join their efforts with those separated from us.

I believe we have an immense common task of resolving world problems. We must be at the service of the world and at the service of men. The entire social sphere falls within the purview of the Gospel, but the Gospel is not bounded by the social sphere.

A Gospel addressed in its fullness to mankind must be

applied in all domains, family, personal, social, national and international, and in all sectors of economic life. The entire Gospel—it is just that.

But the Christian must live it in all its dimensions. I would fight shy of a Christianity which was social only, a kind of spiritual Red Cross. We are those who proclaim the Lord's word and at the same time try to improve the human condition. We have to provide the alphabet *and* the catechism, the temporal *and* the eternal. The "and" is important.

4

Public Opinion in the Church

"God does not act like that."

This laconic expression of a Roman prelate, published in *Le Monde* (6-14-69), says a good deal about the "scandal" caused by the way Cardinal Suenens set forth his analysis and expressed his opinions in the public forum, through the press, without doing anything to limit its diffusion or muffle its echo.

It is an open question whether God, as this prelate seems to believe, systematically puts aside every appeal and recourse to public opinion when He wishes to wake up his people; the voice of the Old Testament prophets and of those of the early and modern Church could no doubt teach us a great deal about that. What is certain is that churchmen are not, or are no longer, accustomed to act this way.

A few weeks after the Suenens interview, a new group of cardinals created by Paul VI was called to swear a new oath: "I shall not divulge, in order to distort or discredit them, the *consilia* (instructions or information) entrusted to me either directly or indirectly, without the consent of the Holy See." Well-informed circles, commentators have added, think that this obligation of secrecy should logically be extended to bishops and prelates.

The news was hardly startling, because it fitted so well into the logic of Church practice. The same was true of Cardinal Felici's statement in the *Osservatore Romano* about the same time, that it was normal that the commission in charge of the reform of canon law, which regulates the life of all the members of the people of God in the Church should work in secret. It was equally true, even if the reactions of that occasion were more mixed, when the revised rules of procedure of the Synod of Bishops restored the rule of secrecy, after the experience of the council and of the first synod had shown its anachronistic and ineffective character.

The correspondent of the *Europe Magazine* (6-4-69) was not the only one to think and to write "that hard truths and incontestable evidence are to be found in the declaration of Cardinal Suenens." Neither was he the only one to add:

We would have willingly recognized that the whole Suenens document constituted a report addressed to the pope or to his close advisers. We think that the publication of this interview, far from restoring calm to the climate of Christendom and strengthening the prestige of the papacy, confronted it with a raft of difficulties and follies, striking a clumsy and unfortunate blow on the bark of Peter and its courageous pilot.

One point is clear. There are certain things which people who belong to the same club do not do to each other.

The strongest such reaction was that of Cardinal Léger, former archbishop of Montreal. He was one of the leaders most listened to by the majority at the Council, and his supporters increased in numbers when he resigned his see to become a missionary among the lepers in Cameroon. "I do not find it right," he said, "that the archbishop of Malines-Brussels spread widely his opinions in the press and public lectures on the government of the Church, on the best way to choose a pope, and on the legitimacy of apostolic nuncios. I would find it more respectful if these things were first discussed with other bishops and cardinals, so that they might all together present them to the pope. The Church is certainly in a state of grave uneasiness. Too much is said and written; there is no longer any time for prayer and mediation. A pact should be concluded on all ecclesiastical levels to limit talking and writing—better yet abolish them completely for at least a year. Afterwards we would see things more clearly" (*La Libre Belgique*, 6-24-69).

A CONFLICT OF DUTIES

There have probably always been cardinals, bishops and prelates who have liked to talk. However, the immediate and universal audience of the mass media is a very recent phenomenon. There has not always been a secular press as avid and interested, nor a Catholic press as "emancipated" as now. Hence the novelty of the situation and the problems raised.

At one time, a suggestion or counsel of a bishop or a nuncio would have decided the whole local Catholic press to refuse to publish a statement ruled inopportune. Today, one sees the very religious Italian Paulists ignore the pressing pleas made to them, and publish the Suenens interview in their widely circulated monthly, and then as a pamphlet. This incidentally brought them a discreet call to order from the Pope at an audience at St. Peter's. In only one country, Czechoslovakia (in exceptional circumstances) the publication of the interview by a Catholic weekly led to its suppression after two issues as a result of the intervention of the hierarchy. Everywhere else the press, and the Catholic press first of all, considered it a right and a normal duty to report and evaluate the declaration of Cardinal Suenens as it would a declaration of Cardinal Ottaviani or Daniélou.

Perhaps the Catholic press and Catholic journalists have an erroneous concept of their rights and duties, perhaps they lack a sense of responsibility. They are, in any case, frequently urged by the pope to examine their conscience on this point.

On Nov. 23, 1968, for example, Paul VI told the International Catholic Press Union:

> You have to select from the mass of news available; and in your selection, you must be inspired by the desire to give the most exact picture possible of the Church's life. To do this requires a

great concern for truth, and that assumes the ability to resist, when the need arises, the temptation to follow the popular trend, even when such a trend is overwhelmingly strong.

You have recently observed in several countries phenomena which showed varying degrees of disagreement in the minds of many in the Church, even on quite serious issues of doctrine or discipline. You properly judge it to be your professional duty to report such phenomena. But does it serve the Church to highlight the most questionable trends and experiments, the ones least in conformity with sound tradition and without a real fidelity to the texts of the recent Council and even to the truth of the Gospel? Does one serve the Church by becoming a constant and willing echo of those who challenge it, when that can mean disturbing and disorienting the great mass of the truly faithful?

Religious journalists, or at least those among them who know their business, are well aware of this "risk of troubling." Their knowledge does not simplify their responsibility to the Church, to the whole Church, to the Church in transition as well as the institutional Church. Commenting on Pope Paul's observations, José de Broucker (ICI, 12-15-68) wrote:

When the Catholic journalist selects and presents news, he is progressively more conscious not only of the good believers, but also of the good nonbelievers: of the enormous mass of the unchurched who—ever since John XXIII and the Council—have recovered an interest in the Church; and also of the growing number of believers, especially among the young, who are convinced that it is their duty to turn away from the Church in order to remain faithful to Christ. Members of all these groups are also readers of those Catholic newspapers which wish to be apostolic. The temptation, then, can be, in order to capture or retain the sympathetic attention of this new public, to give an agreeable, sweet and, finally, false image of the Church.

This temptation can be stronger, the more there is a passion to make Christ known and to encounter Him. This passion exists among religious news reporters as well as among others who suffer from ecclesiastical ways of living, thinking and speaking which seem to them an obstacle to the preaching of the faith.

The religious news reporter, who has known even one man—
and how many are there?—whom certain aspects of Church life
prevent from knowing and sensing Christ, cannot but pay
attention to the facts and acts which try to make Christ more
visible in the Church. He will often find himself in a grave conflict of duties, because he knows that the news most likely to
appeal, in an evangelical way, to the man in search of the Church
and of Christ, is often also the kind which risks shocking the man
who has already reached port, and vice-versa.

Professional Catholic reporters of religious news have
trouble making this conception and this situation understood
by pastors and teachers responsible for their flock, and even
more trouble getting them to share their attitude.

Such persons readily suspect them of prostituting their
talents, consciously or otherwise, for commercial reasons, or
of yielding to fashions and prevailing currents of opinion
from lack of personality and courage, or even of bowing to
pressure groups which aim at nothing less than spreading
subversion in the Church. Such at least were the reactions of
some to the press coverage of the Suenens interview.

An article signed with three asterisks on public opinion in
the Church was published in the Jesuit-edited semiofficial
Civiltà Cattolica (Rome, 7-19-69). It began with an excellent
summary of the basic rights of public opinion in the Church
as derived from the Church's nature and as expressed by Pius
XII and the Council. The author noted that these rights are
perhaps not adequately recognized and certainly not adequately applied in practice, so that ambiguities and uncer-
tainties still exist. The purpose of the right, he said, is not to
spread or promote any opinion whatever, but—as the Council decree *Inter mirifica* specifies—"to form and spread right
public opinions," and in this area as in others, to fulfill "the
duties of justice and charity."

"It is a fact," wrote the author, "that today many more or
less visible and evident factors (opinion as 'matrix') contribute to polarizing the judgments, attitudes and conduct of in-

dividuals and groups; and also that precise techniques of propaganda, even 'occult,' are extensively studied and applied in order to obtain determined results. This is not in itself necessarily wrong, provided that the 'manipulation' leaves a true freedom of choice commensurate with the moral, individual and social importance of the matter. But past and present experience have established, and the future may well confirm this situation even in the Church, that minority groups skilled in propaganda techniques and well organized, can create a climate of violence—at least psychological—to manipulate currents of opinion regarding doctrinal opinions and practical choices. One can today visualize an atmosphere of 'spiritual terrorism' in the Church, created by such pressure groups, so intense that those who do not conform will find themselves in a certain way 'excommunicated' or at least 'to be avoided.' "

Civiltà Cattolica agrees that people should not fear to express their views with courage and frankness, but also "with respect . . . for the Christian virtue of prudence." This is, of course, for laymen, but also for theologians so that they may not appear to be opposing the magisterium, "as if their competence . . . dispensed them from docility to the unique authentic magisterium" of the Church.

It is clear in this article, as in other analagous warnings against bad use of the rights of public opinion in the Church, how one passes quickly from the desire not to trouble the people of God, to a desire not to compromise authority. These two concerns are one, but not everyone understands this solidarity in the same way. To those who think that it is bad use of public opinion which risks compromising authority and troubling the faithful, others reply that it is the wrong use of authority not weighted by the free play of public opinion which risks compromising the growth of the people of God more and more avid for truth and conscious of responsibility.

The *Civiltà Cattolica* article was not aimed specifically at the Suenens interview. Neither was that of Cardinal Tisserant, dean of the Sacred College, in the *Osservatore romano* (6-23/24-69), but the allusion is clearer:

> Certain inexact doctrinal and historical perspectives, certain sweeping and false criticisms . . . sad phenomena which do not help orderly progress but even hinder the calm and responsible study of problems, especially because of the repercussions and disorientation they provoke in public opinion and because of the undue pressure they seek to exercise. . . . Attitudes which, in any case, should express themselves in another way, not to trouble but to edify the people of God, and for the growth of this organic and hierarchical communion in charity which is characteristic of the Holy Catholic Church.

This same view of pressure groups as manipulators of the press, bent on undermining the very foundations of authority and of the Church, is also found in the interview given by Cardinal Daniélou to the monthly *Famiglia Mese* (Sept. 1969):

> I repeat that we must be careful because certain press campaigns, on the pretext of denouncing or preventing abuses, in fact aim to impair the very exercise of this authority. Never before has the authority of the Church been attacked so violently, as a result of the initiative of small groups, easily identified, who try to make their particular points of view prevail. The inflammatory polemics about recent episodes—I am speaking of Msgr. Illich and of Isolotto, as well as of auxiliary Bishop Defregger of Munich—have convinced me of the existence of a massive offensive aiming to exploit certain facts in order to discredit dishonestly the authority of the pope and the bishops. . . . It is therefore improper for certain bishops to lend their voice to this quarrel and to the contentious press.

For Cardinal Daniélou things are clear: "If one goes to the root of all these challenges, we find the intention of bringing the class struggle into the Church, overturning the hierarchical relations and placing the accent on the base instead of the summit of Church organization. And that means applying a sort of Marxism to religion."

In the ecclesiastical world as in every society, when a storm threatens it is easier to blame the barometer, to put it out of order or break it, than to prepare oneself rationally to face the squall. Like every society which experiences difficulties and problems, the Church is tempted to find a scapegoat for all its misfortunes and to imagine a subversive plot. It is an understandable and normal human reaction, but an irresponsible and ineffective one. Since it involves the Church, it is very far from what the common faith in the same Spirit should inspire.

Commenting on the Suenens case, Fr. Sanchis, a Spanish Jesuit, wrote in *Mundo Social* (7-15-69):

> The heart of the problem in this case resides in the difficulty of accepting a necessary reality in the Church: public opinion. The transition from a customary silence on vital questions to the free expression of complaints and suggestions, displeases those who have become accustomed not to give any account to those who are under their orders. For contemporary Catholicism it is a new fact, and like every novelty, it can be upsetting.

Giuseppe Venturini, an Italian commentator, sees it as a difficult problem:

> All the speeches and all the efforts undertaken today in the Church to promote an awareness of community, and the consequent sense of responsibility among all the baptized will remain unfortunately paralyzed if one does not accept the necessity of promoting and encouraging a complete diffusion of news and opinions on the problems of the Church. These problems do not pertain exclusively to the hierarchy, but imply likewise the co-responsibility of all the baptized.

Why is the Church's practice not in agreement with her theoretical recognition of public opinion? "Why this fear in the Church"? F. J. Trost asks in the German Catholic weekly

Publik: "Why do they require sacred oaths and try to build a wall of silence? Why do they delay an announcement so that it cannot be modified, and so that the functionaries who advised the decision can hide behind it. Are they afraid of public discussion?"

We have seen that the answer the most frequently given to these questions is to invoke the argument of authority, or of concern for pastoral responsibility. This latter consideration is obviously very important, as is the difference between the nature of the Church and that of secular society. Many of the warmest partisans of a broader and freer exercise of public opinion in the Church agree with Jean Tordeur of *Le Soir* of Brussels:

> It is evident . . . that the spirit of participation urgently invoked today cannot transform the Church into a parliament and that discussion should be tempered and guided by what distinguishes the Church, a society both human and divine from other societies. But is this not precisely what those who want to replace secrecy with openness wish to demonstrate? Cardinal Suenens in his interview declared explicitly that unity in the person of the pope could not be better preserved than by dialogue.

This begging the question does not solve all the concrete problems. For example, it does not solve the case of conscience—examined by Gregory Baum in the *St. Louis Review*—of the churchman who finds himself in disagreement with the policy of his bishop or with canon law, or the moral teaching of the Church: should he remain silent or speak up? Should he leave or remain?

> If the priest has solid convictions, if his views of these questions have been tested through dialogue with others and have become a part of the way he sees the Gospel and his own life, then . . . I do not see how he can hide his views completely. What should he do? Is he obliged to quit? No. In this case, it seems to me, he can remain if he is able to state his own views to the community—and, therefore, remain an honest man—but not use the

pulpit or the liturgy as the place from which he defends his controversial views . . .

If it is impossible for someone to express his disagreement, then his moral position in the Church becomes problematical. It will seem to him that he is dishonest vis-à-vis the hierarchy which named him, and vis-à-vis the people who assume he is in agreement with the official attitude, and above all vis-à-vis himself. But if he is able to say it, even though it be in a humble and nonpublic way, he remains an honest man.

Some of those who agree with Fr. Baum in thinking that the pulpit and the liturgy are not places to express private opinions may still have difficulty in understanding how a churchman can present himself in all honesty to his community if he has to express himself in a "nonpublic" way. But agreement will easily be reached on the substance of Fr. Baum's position:

> Some disagreement in the Church is inevitable. A healthy community can exist despite conflicting opinions. It knows that disagreement is helpful to clarify its positions. A society is very sick if it does not allow free speech.
>
> A sick society, like a sick family, fears that this kind of disagreement may be disloyal and may break the link which holds the members together. A healthy family counts on the fact that the bond which unites the members is stronger than their disagreement. It hopes that conflict will lead to growth and development.

A "sick society" distrusts discordant voices and is suspicious of them. Another theologian, this one a German, Johannes Metz, said the same thing while lecturing in the United States. Speaking of the symptoms of a "new Counter-Reformation," he said: "Too often, in judging those who propose reforms, the hierarchy lacks confidence in the reformers and doubts their faith. . . . Much too frequently the appearance of free criticism in the Church is judged censoriously as a germ of disbelief."

Of course, no one went to the point of suspecting the faith of Cardinal Suenens, at least publicly. The indirect reference made by the pope, June 23, 1969 to the Suenens interview, left some, nevertheless, with a sense of "uneasiness." The pope seems automatically to see a sign of distrust in the recourse to publicity, while Cardinal Suenens sees in it a sign of vitality and of strength. While recognizing that some may question the opportuneness of a public discussion, Cardinal Suenens declared:

> To my mind, acceptance within the very heart of the Church of a rank, open, constructive judgment inspired by a love of the Church and its head, is a sign of vitality and of strength. It is normal and healthy, it seems to me, that there be open discussion of vital problems which concern the whole Church when these very problems are perceived in their acuteness and their urgency throughout the world. It is inevitable that they be discussed before public opinion; this must be accepted.

A Catholic Belgian journal (*Voix du Temps,* 6-8-69) wrote:

> Knowing Cardinal Suenens as we do, it was certainly only after having exhausted all diplomatic means, which ran into the inertia of the system that he, Suenens, decided to speak openly. Recourse to public opinion, even in this case, would be out of place on his part if the ideas he is trying to win support for were the ideas of a coterie, even a very numerous one, in the Church, the ideas of a party, the ideas of a faction. . . . But they are the ideas and the spirit of the Second Vatican Council, approved by practically all the Fathers of the Church.

This point is important. It shows to what world Cardinal Suenens wanted to lend his voice, namely, the world of the "almost-unanimous majority" at the Council; the world of those "thousands of men throughout the world" who suffer from "a growing uneasiness," to whom the John XXIII brotherhoods of Belgium refer. Of "these thousands of men" Cardinal Suenens is, along with all the bishops of the episcopal college, the shepherd. One shepherd among others. But if he remained silent, if Dom

Helder Camara was silenced, if the Dutch bishops were silenced and several theologians habitually persecuted, these thousands of men who criticize structures and denounce deficiencies out of love for the Church would find themselves without a shepherd—and, in the Church at least, without a voice.

"Some are afraid of the scandal these frank discussions are provoking in the Church," says Douglas J. Roche, editor of the *Western Catholic Reporter.* "But we think that Peter and Paul have given the example of a constructive dialogue which has contributed to the development of the Church . . . ."

This reference to the Acts of the Apostles often comes up in the theological affirmation of the rights of public opinion in the Church. In one of his Sunday talks over the Luxembourg radio-television station, Abbé Berthier drew the lesson of the confrontation between Peter and Paul as it affects the Suenens case:

How can we not recall the confrontation of Peter and Paul at this time when world public opinion is taken up with this quarrel between the Roman Curia and the cardinal? Have those who are scandalized by this open challenge forgotten the epistles of Paul? In the present organization of the Church the cardinals are charged with helping the pope in his responsibility as regards all the people of God. If Cardinal Suenens judged in conscience that he should spell out the improvements necessary to bring the Church more in line with the Gospel, who can blame him?

Do they protest because he did it before public opinion? Did not Paul say that he had resisted Peter "in front of everyone?" In some reactions I seem to hear an echo of those followers of James who had so much difficulty accepting Christian liberty. This liberty which shakes up habits and routine disguised as principles. Finally, we hope for only one thing: that Peter and Paul and every Christian profit from this incident in order to discover the freedom of the children of God, in respect for an authority which was never for a moment questioned.

Cardinal Suenens had emphasized that the basic problem dividing us, whether consciously or otherwise, is one of theology; we are starting from differing visions of the Church. That diagnosis is also valid for the difference of opinions on the subject of appealing to public opinion in the Church. As Francois Biot said in *Temoignage chrétien* (6-26-69):

> In a church conceived above all as an institutional pyramid, from the pope down to the faithful considered as passive members, it was normal for a cardinal-bishop to express his thought in the form of secret reports. On the contrary, in the Church of Jesus Christ, recognized clearly as a people in which different functions are fulfilled—within a constituted diversity of dynamic unity—it becomes normal, that such thought be publicly expressed. And this even when it differs from that of other cardinals, or even from that of the pope, in the many areas where papal infallibility is not involved. There is no reason for this to provoke "a sad astonishment," and it should not be considered "defamatory."

Two theologians of international stature, Karl Rahner and Marie-Dominique Chenu, O.P. also joined Cardinal Suenens in affirming the rights of public opinion in the Church and setting out the principles underlying it.

THE PRESSURE OF PUBLICITY

In the German Catholic weekly *Publik* (7-4-69), Rahner wrote:

> Of course, one can always quarrel over details, one can always discuss whether, in a concrete situation, should one emphasize more strongly the need for reform or the recognition of continuity? These are matters of judgment which can never be finally resolved. But in these matters, when the substance of the faith and the dogmatically founded basic structures of the Church are not affected, then there should be real freedom of opinion on both sides in the Church. Nobody can possibly say that Cardinal Suenens has offended in the slightest degree against the Church's

understanding of her own essential nature. But if that is so, one has to ask why there should be in certain quarters such a negative and hostile reaction to this interview.

Perhaps the explanation is that a Catholic or a cardinal should not discuss such matters in public? One can easily answer this objection. Those who say this should first of all ask themselves whether or not they use this objection, consciously or unconsciously, as a tactic for avoiding discussion and any serious treatment of the real questions raised. Anyone who has no other objection than this should as soon as possible go to work on the matter at hand and attempt to find with Cardinal Suenens common ways to the solution of the problems that he has raised. Alternatively, he will have to assert that these problems do not even exist. And then we would be once again discussing the subject matter of the interview itself.

Why are there so many complaints about these questions being discussed publicly? What has happened to public opinion, which Pius XII said was absolutely necessary in the Church? It is perfectly reasonable to concede that every public discussion in the Church leads to a certain amount of "pressure" on those who are ultimately competent and responsible for the changes that are proposed. But why should such a "pressure" not be exerted upon them? Are Church authorities not sufficiently sensible and courageous to withstand such pressure when it can be seen objectively to be going in the wrong direction? And are not Church authorities also human beings, with only finite knowledge, finite abilities to respond, and a finite readiness to give up old, apparently proven, ways in favor of new and untried ones? Do they not therefore need a certain amount of "pressure"?

There are several reasons why they require this pressure. Concrete decisions never spring from purely theoretical reasoning alone. Church authorities, as finite human beings, need a more than theoretical stimulus in order to feel existentially the strength of an argument and to make decisions with sufficient speed. Further, members of the Church, faced with the choice of several legitimate possibilities, are not just the passive objects of the wisdom of authority from above, but they may say in practice what they want. Finally, secret policy making behind locked doors, is no longer a practical possibility today. For all these reasons, one cannot say that public debate is inappropriate to the questions which Cardinal Suenens raised.

And even if the interview were, to some extent, "rushing into print," those who criticize this "rushing into print" must ask themselves if a more rapid solution to the problems the cardinal delineates would not have made his action unnecessary. The fact is that in Rome a lot of things happen too slowly. If the Church and ecclesial life are not to suffer for it, many things must be done according to the tempo of the present day, a tempo which the Church cannot herself determine in advance. If the Curial apparatus as it now exists is incapable of such rapid, carefully considered, and courageous decisions, then that is just one more example which supports Cardinal Suenens's demand for a reform of the Curia—which is still in abeyance although a beginning has been made—and his demand for decentralization and greater independence for the local Churches. The point is this: you cannot "deal with" the cardinal's interview by saying that such matters should not be discussed in public. The interview can only be "dealt with" by dealing with the issues which it raises."

PUBLIC OPINION IN THE CHURCH

"Public Opinion in the Church" was the title of the French theologian Marie-Dominique Chenu's article in *Le Monde* (6-21-69):

The basic issue is really the fact of releasing information to the press according to the common laws of public opinion. At the Council where he was one of the leaders, Cardinal Suenens had already expressed his diagnosis on several occasions and had asked for these structural reforms. What has been added here is the fact that these previously known and well-thought-out convictions have been made accessible to the "people of God," through a means extending far beyond the limited reach of seminars and conferences. It is in reference to this point that the reaction in certain milieux has been most lively in the face of the publication of this interview and the arousal of public opinion.

The Council, we know, had been especially concerned with the question of the role of public opinion in the contemporary world. But the decree as formulated and adopted at the beginning of the Council remained tightly bound to preconciliar mentality. Later, the Council laid the groundwork for a reconsideration of the problem: the Church is a people whose communion and relations are not diminished by the authority, no matter how exalted, guaranteed by it in faith.

We find ourselves now at the stage of putting these salutary principles into effect. The shock created by Cardinal Suenens' intervention manifests their full significance.

Going beyond the incidental aspects of this interview, we observe that the dispute turns basically on the issue of the existence of public opinion in the Church, on its legitimate function and its objective laws. Here we have need for a patient and clear-sighted reform of a regime in which closed doors and secrecy—the secrecy of the courts of the Old Regime—were the normal procedure of government. The rigorous discretion, even reserve, which the internal deliberation of authorities and their government expects from participants as well as reporters, is one thing. The blocking of all news through appropriate organs to the members of the community, is something else again. For lack of it, people are summarily charged with disrespectful and indiscreet criticism of authority.

And yet what is at stake is the very existence of the Christian community. What sociologists determine about the social nature of man, the theologian must apply analogically to the nature of the historical Church. There is even more reason in this case, because the Church is a collective subject of the Word of God, requiring communication, subject to subtle, ambiguous, and restrictive laws of opinion. For centuries, under the prevailing old regime with the authorities on one side and their subjects on the other, regulated and censored information had been the privilege of those governing.—Today, thanks to the socialization of the world, the field of communications has come to be a recognized entity. Hereafter, the internal law of all human groups is participation: participation, responsibility, conscience, liberty —all in relation to one another. Active participation is the condition for attaining freedom, the freedom of Christians in the

Church as well as of citizens in the state. Public information is no capricious epiphenomenon; it enters into the fabric of a community, realizing itself in a conscious and responsible exercise of the faith. Hence, it is a right, with all the richness contained in Pius XII's use of that word.

We can find no charter for this public opinion and its vital urgency for the Church and world more explicit than this declaration of Pius XII, whom few considered a liberal: "Public opinion is an attribute of any normal society composed of men who, conscious of their personal and social conduct, engage themselves unreservedly as members of their community. All in all, public opinion is everywhere the natural echo, the communal resonance of the present situation and events in the minds and judgments of these men. Wherever public opinion lacks expression and especially where such opinion is nonexistent, no matter what the reason for this silence or absence, the condition should be regarded as a vice, a weakness, a disease of the social life."

The pope continued: "We would like to add a word about public opinion within the Church (on matters that are open to discussion). Only those who either do not know the Church or do not know it well need be alarmed at this. For, after all, the Church is a living body; and it would be missing something from its life if public opinion were lacking through neglect on the part of either its pastors or its faithful" (Address to the World Press Conference, Rome, 1950).

Whatever opinion one holds about the various ideas of Cardinal Suenens, the value of the cardinal's intervention will be to have done justice and given effectiveness to the nature of the Church expressly defined as the people of God in a hierarchical community (*Le Monde*, 6-21-69).

Gregory Baum in the *Catholic World* of December 1969 wrote:

Catholics concerned with Church renewal were delighted when, a few months ago, they read the well-publicized interview of Cardinal Suenens. . . . All its issues relate to the immobility of the system versus the pastoral needs of the present day.

In a way, Cardinal Suenens said nothing new in his interview. He gave expression, clearly, courageously and with balance, to the convictions shared by vast numbers of Catholics and discussed many times by theologians in books and articles. Yet for many Catholics it was a sign of hope that a man so highly placed in the ecclesiastical hierarchy was free enough to discern what in fact goes on in the Church and find the words to express it in public. The interview was widely discussed and praised in Catholic publications all over the world. Unfortunately, many Catholics who a few years ago shared Cardinal Suenens convictions, have "turned off" the Church and all ecclesiastical talk, even the most progressive. These Catholics did not read the interview, and, if they had read it, they would hardly have shown any interest. These men have lost confidence that behind the flow of words about renewal there is the intention to change. But the Catholics concerned with renewal who have retained a modicum of confidence were delighted with the courageous analysis of the present situation made by Cardinal Suenens. . . .

He has been criticized for making his critical remarks public through the mass media. Suenens' opponents feel that criticism of the ecclesiastical government should remain secret, made behind closed doors to the proper authorities. Cardinal Suenens, the argument goes, has compromised his position by addressing himself to the public.

There is a grain of truth in this objection. In any society there are issues important to the government that ought to remain secret. Especially in a voluntary society, one built mainly on confidence and the common wish to remain together—and, sociologically speaking, the Church is a voluntary society—matters of conflict should be kept quiet. A society based on trust is greatly weakened by the abuse of authority. If conflicts arise is is usually better, for the sake of the common good, to work them out quietly among the people who are directly concerned with the issues.

If, however, the governmental system does not allow for the open discussion of these matters at the proper level, then it is necessary, for the sake of the common good, to inform the people of the issues and to persuade the government by the pressure of public opinion to deal with the conflict. This, I would say, is a general moral principle. If the rights of people are not protected by law, then the only power available to them is that of public pressure.

While the Catholic Church adopted the vocabulary of dialogue and praised consultation at Vatican II, it has not implemented these in its public life. The bishops cannot turn to Rome and ask that the issues which concern them be discussed by the pope with representatives of the world espicopate. Even at the synods and other meetings organized at Rome, the papal appointees keep a tight watch over the agenda. Pope Paul VI has avoided discussion with the bishops on such important questions as birth control and clerical celibacy. The policy of the modern papacy is to see the bishops of the world singly, at the so-called *ad limina visits*, but not to discuss issues with them as a group. According to the same tradition, one may add, the pope usually sees the cardinals in charge of the various Vatican offices singly and only rarely meets with them as a group. This practice, we note, differs greatly from the medieval custom when the pope made all important decisions in the consistory, *i.e.*, in the council of his cardinals. Under the influence of the Renaissance ideals of the absolute prince, the Vatican became a Renaissance court with governmental practices and—we may add—costumes tailored to the ideals of that period.

What is true of the highest level of ecclesiastical government is true of the lower levels. Bishops and episcopal conferences that seek honest conversation with priests and laity and are willing to make their decisions in the light of what they have learned in these conversations are still exceptions. Dialogue has often become an instrument of greater control. You invite the priests to speak their mind, you listen to them, you smile, and then you execute the decision you made long before the conversation began. Here dialogue is used to keep people happy and to create in them the illusion of greater freedom.

Because of the unwillingness of the Church's central administration to face up to the issues and to acknowledge the logic of episcopal collegiality, Cardinal Suenens decided to address himself to the Catholic people through the mass media. He revealed the problem, he explained what it meant, and he pointed out the direction in which the solution is available. In this sense he brilliantly exercised his office as teacher in the Church. The reason that Suenens' interview was a bit shocking was that we are not used to cardinals who speak honestly about what is happening in the Church. When a cardinal tells it like it is, we are amazed.

The same frustration with nondialogue in the hierarchy, we may add, is the reason why so many priests feel justified in addressing themselves to the public with their difficulties. Public opinion is the only power available to the man whose rights are not guaranteed by law. It is the public opinion in the Church that has in recent years been able to protect many theologians threatened by the central administration in Rome.

5

The Symposium at Chur

It seems to me that the time has come for the bishops to give up their staid routine in order to become involved in a program, however long it may take, which brings about that renewal which John XXIII so much desired, and which Paul VI is gradually trying to effect. Now this restructuring of the Church requires a much greater cooperation among the bishops than existed in the past. They are the real link between the pope and the faithful, and, therefore, between the pope and the priests. It is a time for courage.

The author of this appeal for courage was Father Brechet, a Swiss Jesuit. He wrote it July 11, 1969, just after the symposium of European bishops at Chur, Switzerland.

Like other observers, Father Brechet seems to have reached the conclusion that the bishops at Chur had not given sufficient proof of courage. Two months later on September 2, the Dutch bishops, in a letter to their priests, repeated what had become a common view:

We know that this symposium disappointed many. The reason was that a great number of Christians had hoped for too much. A reunion of this kind had no competence to make decisions. It was conceived rather as a meeting of bishops in which an exchange of information, experiences, ideas, and reflection in common, would be the principal objective. Seen in this way, we lived this reunion of European bishops as a useful experience. However, the way the symposium went disappointed us also. Its organization was not ideal, far from it, and what we also found unfortunate was that a direct meeting between the symposium of bishops and the priests present was considered impossible. Again, it appeared to us very clearly that certain wishes and certain trends, which exist among a great number of Christians in the Low Countries, found little response in the symposium.

The second symposium of European bishops met at Chur from July 7 to July 10 to consider the problems of the priests. At the other end of the town some one hundred protesting priests from various countries of Europe held a parallel symposium of their own and tried to obtain a hearing from their bishops. They wished to be heard and to be associated with them in their work. Between the two meeting places more than 200 journalists of the secular and religious world press were impatiently waiting. It was two months after the Suenens appeal for collegiality and coresponsibility and three months before the extraordinary synod of Rome. A hundred bishops meeting together could hardly fail to have something to say about the burning problems of the hour, beginning with the theme of their meeting: the crisis of the priesthood.

Divided on the attitude they should adopt towards the protesting priests, and not well prepared for this confrontation with world opinion which they had not expected, the bishops remained silent. The journalists had to wait until the final hour of the last day to hear a voice from the bishops deal with the problem of the priests with simplicity, in a personal and responsible way, and in a language clear to everybody. The closing address of Cardinal Suenens was followed carefully even by the protesting priests at this public session.

For Cardinal Suenens had come to Chur. He was welcomed, at least by the journalists and priests. It was his first public appearance since his interview with the ICI and this welcome was in a way a sort of referendum. Though well-disposed toward the cardinal, opinion was at the same time charged with a certain amount of more or less skeptical questioning. Would the cardinal stand up in public for his opinions among his equals and would he speak in the "logic of the interview"? Alfred Friendly suggested (*Washington Post*, 7-1-69): "What the conference at Chur may show is whether Suenens is, as the Rome newspaper *Il Messaggero* declared, 'a gulf apart from the great part of the Catholic hierarchy.'"

The meager information available permits us to know that Cardinal Suenens obtained the agreement of the majority of the bishops at the symposium that contact be made by some of them with the "rebel" priests. His suggestion was approved by a majority of 51-36 according to a reliable source. The problems of the priesthood were squarely faced in a letter from the theologian Hans Küng of Tübingen to the cardinal and to which the cardinal gave great prominence by reading it in public while delivering the closing address.

HANS KUNG'S LETTER TO CARDINAL SUENENS

Your interview, which has had an extremely positive response among us, your fellow-theologians, and among our priests all over the world gives me the courage to write to you even before the bishops' symposium in Chur.

I hesitated a long time about whether I should publish an analysis of the situation of the priest today for the symposium. In the end I thought it would be better if I addressed myself personally direct to you and, through you as intermediary, to your brothers in the episcopate assembled in Chur. I am sure that I am the interpreter of innumerable priests throughout the world, who have not the opportunity to speak directly to this very important symposium.

I have no intention of making concrete proposals to the bishops in this assembly. I only want to give my opinion about the present situation; perhaps you would give it due consideration in view of the fact that my forecasts before, during and after the Council give me a certain credit.

Taking into account the situation of our priests in the various countries of the world, one can make three observations:

(1) The crisis among the clergy is of extreme gravity. Many are convinced that free and frank dialogue is made difficult because of the way that the Church is governed at the moment.

(2) It is no longer possible to stop this process of reflection and questioning by using the methods of a former age. There is and there will be an ever-increasing number of priests leaving the ministry. Equally, there is and there will be a rapidly increasing number, not only in Western Europe and not only amongst the younger clergy, who want to make progress at any price.

(3) The real dilemma for a large number of the clergy seems to me to be this: *whether to carry on renewal with the bishops, or to carry it on without them and, as a consequence, against them.* This second solution would be disastrous. Even now it is not only the pope who is not being followed on some important questions by the clergy and laity, but the bishops as well. Moreover, there is an ever-increasing "credibility gap" between the bishops, on the one hand, and the priests and lay people on the other, and this is getting wider every day.

This, then, is what I dare to say in conclusion: I beg of you, your Eminence, to be our interpreter to the bishops assembled at Chur. Help our Church, and preserve it from these ever-increasing defections, from these psychological divisions, these arbitrary and badly-enlightened movements! Remember those crucial years at the beginning of the Reformation when the bishops, had they had the courage to shoulder their pastoral responsibilities, might perhaps have spared the Church the disasters which we now deplore!

Your pastoral choices are weighty with consequences for the future. Today, five years after the Council, it is not texts nor declarations concerning our priests that we are waiting for, but *pastoral decisions*—I refer especially to the problems of celibacy, of their professional status, and of their political and social involvement.

May the bishops, by their pastoral decisions, be a sign of hope for the clergy and for the whole people of God.

I know, Eminence, that these lines may appear audacious. But please believe that they are written by a theologian who is doing his best to serve the Church he loves.

Tübingen, 5 July, 1969.   *Hans Küng*

The closing address of Cardinal Suenens at the symposium of European Bishops at Chur on July 10, 1969 was a "well-balanced, wise and calm speech" according to *La Libre Belgique.* Joseph Schmitz van Vorst (*Frankfurter Allgemeine Zeitung*) praised the cardinal for carrying on "the struggle he began at the Council . . . against an image of a Church which lays down the law and decides, and another which submits obediently and in silence. An image of the Church according to which everything or almost everything is decided by the head and practically nothing by the members." John Hess of the *New York Times* agreed: "In a soft, humorous and down-to-earth manner Cardinal Suenens has shaken the establishment." In the words of a layman quoted by Henri Fesquet "he saved the symposium from mediocrity." Fesquet continues:

> Chur provided a rather unexpected spectacle, when the protesting priests, who for four days had confronted their bishops and denounced their outmoded attitudes, applauded the archbishop of Malines-Brussels with overwhelming enthusiasm, because they felt that, at last, their aspirations were understood. "He read our proposals," one of them said, meaning thereby that the cardinal had understood their deep concern. . . . By the same token he had rendered great service to the threatened unity of the Church. He became, in the eyes of the protesters, a worthy speaker, without losing his status among the bishops. He could serve as a conciliator when the time comes. On the other hand, his example was such as to incite his colleagues, tempted to harden their positions, to be more comprehensive. . . .

> For all these reasons, the Catholic hierarchy can be grateful to the Belgian Primate for having taken, by those recent initiatives, the place which is now his, and which, moreover, he assumes with incontestable ability. This is a trump card for the immedi-

ate and difficult future of the Roman Church and for her credibility in a world turned upside down and which more or less confusedly is looking to her for help (*Le Monde*, 4-15-69).

Not everyone interpreted the closing speech in the same way. Marcel Clement, in *L'Homme nouveau,* judged intolerable "the effrontery of this Church dignitary who questioned the commitment of the Vicar of Jesus Christ on the issue of sacerdotal celibacy."

THE PRIEST IN THE SERVICE OF THE PEOPLE OF GOD

The full text of Cardinal Suenens' address follows:
Dear Brothers in the Episcopate and in the Priesthood,
Dear People of God:

"At the end of these days of research devoted to the ministerial priesthood in a changing world and in a church in renewal, I have been asked to say what the priest should be in the service of God's people today.

"This will not be a presentation of conclusions drawn during these days, but rather a sharing with you, in my own name, of a few reflections on a vast subject, a topic of burning actuality and of multiple human and Christian repercussions for all the members of the people of God and, above all, for the priests themselves.

"Let us say, first of all, that this is not a matter of tracing the outline of what the priest—let alone the bishop—of tomorrow in the service of God's people will be or ought to be. To fix that image *a priori* would be to impede the life, to paralyze in advance the action of the Holy Spirit. I believe in God's originality, in the surprises of his hidden action and of his creative inspiration. I believe in the Holy Spirit at work yesterday, today and tomorrow.

"When Christ founded the Church and the priesthood that went with it, he did not specify in detail either its structures or its method of operation. There exists no image of the priest isolated from all context, *ne varietur* (unchangeable). The priest's place is within a network of relationships of every order: relationships with Christ, with the college of bishops, with other priests, with the people confided to his care. We must situate him in the midst of a presbyterium, which is itself bound to the college of bishops. Only a vision of synthesis can bring together the multiple facets, the various needs, the diverse appeals which the presbyterium must answer.

"This immediately lets us see in some fashion that in order to respond to the many necessities of a church diverse in its unity and one in its diversity, it is very probable that it will be multiple and various types of priests—and also of bishops —that will be indispensable tomorrow. And for the priest to be really adapted to the ministry which each community requires, we must dare to believe in the Holy Spirit and in the creativity he arouses in us. *Veni creator Spiritus . . . et renovabis faciem terrae* (Come, creator Spirit . . . and you will renew the face of the earth). We must believe in the multiform and always rejuvenating action of the Holy Spirit.

"It is impossible to understand the priest in isolation, out of context. It is, therefore of capital importance to situate the priest within the Church and to situate the Church itself in relation to the world. *Lumen Gentium* and *Gaudium et Spes* form an indissoluble whole. Let us try in a few words to situate the priest within the Church.

"What is this Church to which we are referring? The question is essential, for our image of the Church conditions the image we will form of the priest. For a great many years, the Church was identified with the hierarchy or so it appeared. Even now for some, the Holy Spirit is given first to the pope and through him to the bishops and through them to the priests who, in their turn, transmit his guidance to the faithful. This 'cascading' vision does not correspond to the theology of the Church. The Holy Spirit is given to the Church as such, and it is in the Church that each member benefits from the Spirit's action according to distinct and complementary charisms.

"The Church is not the hierarchy but the people of God, that is, the ensemble of all baptized. Is it necessary to repeat: the Pope and the bishops also make up an integral part of this people with their proper ministries belonging to the structure of the Church. Mgr. Moeller has called *Lumen Gentium's* inversion of chapters, which placed the chapter concerning the people of God before the one dedicated to the hierarchy in the service of this same people of God, a 'Copernican revolution.' This inversion also has its consequences when determining the images of the priest and of the bishop. From the fact that chapter 3 originally preceded chapter 2, the character of the bishop as situated in the heart of the people of God had not been sufficiently emphasized. Consider the rich words of St. Cyprian: *'scire debes episcopum in Ecclesia esse et Ecclesiam in episcopo'* (You should know that the bishop is in the Church and the Church in the bishop). This compenetration has far-reaching consequences.

"In the past, too, the "hierarchical" vision made definition of the layman difficult; he was considered like a noncleric, a nonreligious. Today the difficulty lies in defining the priest and his specific character in relation to the layman. This is due to a change of perspective which is in itself a good.

"Having thus briefly situated the priest in the Church, let us attempt to discover what our attitude should be toward the evolution which is now calling the priest's image into question.

"First of all, I think we must look this crisis in the face calmly and realistically. Let us not forget, either, to keep a sense of history as it teaches us the relativity of so many conceptions erroneously thought to be absolute because of a lack of historical perspective.

"If we could project on film the image of the priest throughout the ages, we would see paraded before us priests, bishops, even popes of extremely different types. Even the aspect of different clothes worn through the ages is significant and picturesque. What a difference between the presbyter of Jerusalem and the post-Constantinian priest, between the medieval and renaissance clergies, between the pre-Tridentine and post-Tridentine, pre-Vatican II and post-Vatican II priesthood.

"The image of the priest before Vatican II was character-ized by a tendency toward uniformity—sanctioned by the code of 1917—which sought to create a single style of piety, of priestly behavior, and of seminary formation. It is this 'standardized' image which we are now calling into question. How must we judge this ongoing mutation, realizing that it is itself tied up in the mutations of the world we live in?

"We will consider successively the moral, sociological and theological-pastoral planes. To start with the moral plane, we pass judgment all too easily on the young people of today, accusing them of lacking idealism and generosity.

"If indeed there is a questionable milieu of materialism and an unbridled eroticism in public life, young people are still capable, even today, of consecrating their lives to worthy causes. We must learn to recognize the positive values which attract the young: sincerity, a logic of life, a thirst for sim-plicity, authenticity, truth. We must examine ourselves to see what it is in our accidental and contingent structures that turns youth away; we must analyze their reasons for hesi-tating to commit themselves.

"The priest no longer wants to belong to a 'sociological class' which 'separates' him from the world. This is a fact. He wants to be with and in the world: he wants to be in the service of a Church which exists for the world. He knows that he lives in a world which is more and more secularized; and he wants to live in a critical solidarity with this world. When reacting against the 'clerical state' on the sociological plane, he by no means intends to renounce the essence of his priestly mission.

"The current which carries him toward the suppression of the 'clerical state' with its historical legacy of immunities and privileges joins with the movement which, on the temporal level, continues gradually to break up the social stratifications inherited from the old order and to do away with classes in society. On the other hand, in turning to the Gospel rather than to the world, the priest of today becomes increasingly mindful of the fact that the 'clerical state' does not date back to the origin of the Church.

"It is only since the fourth century that society has endowed clerics with a certain number of privileges, immunities, titles of honor, etc. . . . . It is only since the fifth century that the secular clergy adopted the monks' tonsure. In the sixth century, the law of celibacy was gradually introduced. In the eighth century, the introduction of the Roman liturgy into the northern countries led the clergy there to adopt Latin as their own first language, with its specific culture.

"On the theological and pastoral plane, it is the revelation of God, set forth in the Gospel message by the privileged testimony of the apostolic college which provides us with the ultimate criterion for evaluating the present situation.

"Without attempting an exhaustive description, we will give a few constitutive and essential elements, starting with those common to the priesthood of the People of God.

"The New Testament shows no 'sociological state' for the clergy. The term priest (*hiereus*) is reserved for Jewish or pagan priests. The New Testament clearly affirms that there is only one mediator, one master, one high priest: Christ himself. All Christians appear as one priestly and fraternal people. All should listen to the Word; offer a spiritual worship, be living offerings; obey the Spirit (*pneumatikoi—geistliche*); act in love; cooperate in coresponsibility. The ministerial priesthood is distinct from the general priesthood though directed toward the latter.

"At the heart of God's people, within the community, the priest, the bishop, like the rest and together with them, is above all one of the faithful. The ministerial priesthood, for the bishop as well as for the priest, is secondary to the status and mission of these persons as baptized. This status remains real and efficacious, even after ordination or consecration. Our ministry in no way replaces the many demands and normal requirements for a life of faith. The words of St. Augustine to his people are often quoted: 'With you, I am one of the faithful; for you, I am a bishop.'

"The priest, as well as the bishop, is part of and is identified with every man in the community of men united in the name of Jesus Christ. We can only look fruitfully toward our specific functions as priests if we have agreed to cooperate with all the people at the level of our common status as baptized faithful. Because of the failure to live out this first membership in the Christian community in close proximity to the faithful, the ministerial priesthood often appears distant and poorly adapted to the faithful.

"It is by reason of this insertion into the community of believers and also into the human condition, that many questions will arise, such as the possibility of the priest as a professional worker, to the extent that this would benefit the community.

"For reasons of his ministry and this service, the priest has received authority. The Vatican Council's Decree on the Priesthood explains this:

> In as much as it is connected with the episcopal order, the priestly office shares in the authority by which Christ Himself builds up, sanctifies, and rules his Body. Therefore, while it indeed presupposes the sacraments of Christian initiation, the sacerdotal office of priests is conferred by that special sacrament through which priests, by the anointing of the Holy Spirit, are marked with a special character and are so configured to Christ the Priest that they can act in the person of Christ the Head.

This spiritual authority requires him to be an authentic witness to the Gospel, to be a man of prayer, to strive to live completely the demands of the Good News. The priest is the leader of the community; he has the right to expect the cooperation of the others because he is at the service of all.

"This authority is fraternal, is spiritual because of the priest's fidelity to the Holy Spirit from whom he derives his role, and it is the authority of one responsible for the foundation, growth, and guidance of the community.

"Authority in the Church does not exist simply to maintain order. It must also insure that the faithful are constantly confronted with the Gospel message and that they find in it its principle of unity in the one same faith and the one same love. One important way of attaining this goal is to explicitate and encourage the inspiration alive within the community.

"The priest is called to enter into Christ's mission as related to his Father and to mankind. He cannot reduce his mission to its earthly dimension alone; the Church is not a spiritual Red Cross, nor the priest a social worker. He is one and the same time both a man of the second commandment—the test of authentic religion—and of the first, which imposes on man the awareness and adoration of God.

"These few reflections made in the name of two thousand years of Christian tradition, attempted only to indicate the direction in which the people of God will have to search, to discover in a renewed attentiveness to the prompting of the Spirit under the guarantee of the magisterium what the priesthood of tomorrow will be.

"This task of discerning and building, to which we are invited, can be accomplished by no one man: it is a task needing a Church for its accomplishment, a collegial task which concerns us all: a Church work, the work of the entire people of God, every man having his own charism; a Church work which must be open to a broad dialogue, in charity and with respect for all. Father Biot wrote:

If the Church is really and truly the people of God, all that constitutes its life in the world of men, all that makes up its mission and calling, all that there is to the structured instrument in the service of this life and mission, all this must be perceived, analyzed and studied by the whole people of God. Not that everything be entrusted to the arbitrariness of the anonymous and irresponsible mass, but rather that it be left to the action of the Holy Spirit who animates this mass, fashioning it into a people; and who, in this people and for it, enlightens those charged with strengthening the progressive understanding of the christian mystery as lived by this entire people of God on its way towards the Kingdom.

THE CARDINAL'S PRACTICAL PROPOSALS

"In the light of these principles and considerations, accordingly, let me summarize my practical proposals.

"1. First of all, one must accept as a fact that the rôle of the priest today is a problem, and his threefold commitment —social, professional and personal—should be open to examination.

"2. This examination must be faced, it must not be avoided, otherwise it will be done in an unsuitable way.

"It is clear (a) that the problem of celibacy, which is in the forefront of the public eye, should be placed in the overall context of the life of the priest and of the Church in the world; (b) that this problem is not necessarily linked up with the scarcity of vocations. The Protestant Churches of England have some 3,000 vacant places and yet they have a married clergy; (c) that discussion is of no value and pointless if it is not based on complete and living faith in Our Lord and in the Church; (d) that such an objective examination cannot be done under the pressure of partial surveys or of disturbing demonstrations; (e) that fidelity to the obligation of celibacy freely undertaken remains imperative.

"3. This study must be carried out in a positive way, because of the importance of the problem, but it is also necessary that it should be undertaken, at different levels, with all the members of the people of God—*en Eglise*, according to the expression of Cardinal Marty.

"(a) *At the level of the local Church*, it seems essential to me that the questions should be treated in a dialogue between bishops, priests and the community of the faithful. The means for doing this already exist: councils of priests, pastoral councils, etc., which should be brought into the dialogue since the priest is at the service of the whole community.

"(b) *At the level of the universal Church,* there are some problems which the local Churches can solve for themselves. There are other problems which, because of their repercussions, affect the whole Church—problems concerning the life of the priest fall into this category under some aspects.

"It is desirable, therefore, that the work of the local Churches in this field should be undertaken in common and discussed in a spirit of coresponsibility by the episcopal college in a way to be defined, and under the supreme authority of the visible head of the Church.

"The new international council of theologians of the Pontifical Commission would be a valuable instrument of such a study, together with experts of the various sciences, especially sociologists, who could bring light to bear on these problems.

Exchange of ideas, dialogue and research: all these things depend on the collaboration of the whole people of God; journalists, the 'makers of opinion,' have a very important rôle to play by giving objective, undramatized information, which alone can enable such a study to come to a successful conclusion.

"On a wholly personal basis, I propose the following main lines for research:

"1. The necessity of deepening the understanding of the evangelical value of a freely-chosen celibacy.

"2. It is also necessary, in my opinion, to revise, from many different aspects, the whole canonical legislation concerning dispensations from celibacy.

"3. There is need for a profound theological study about what constitute the essential elements of the priestly life and what are contingent to it, and to determine exactly the sacramental character of the priesthood.

"4. There is need to examine the possibility of admitting to the priesthood men who are already married, this to meet pastoral needs where vocations are scarce."

REACTIONS OF THE BISHOPS

Only a few of the reactions of the bishops are known. For example auxiliary bishop Butler of London wrote in the *Tablet:*

> The highlight of the symposium was Cardinal Suenens' address at the public closing meeting. This was in no sense an agreed resumé of the symposium. It simply gave the cardinal's own views on the flexibility of the Christian priesthood throughout history, on the present crisis, on the basic functions of the priest, and on the challenge presented to the whole People of God (and not only to the hierarchy) to reflect upon the future evolution of the role of the priest in a renewed Church. . . .

> Such a brief and bald account gives no idea of the impassioned oratory, the deep concern, and the high Christian hope, of this great religious leader. But I should add that, while Suenens had a tremendous reception from the general audience, there were among the bishops some who felt that he had taken unfair advantage of an occasion to express his own views (with little warning to them) when it would have been more appropriate if he had spoken in a less personal way. It is possible to sympathize with this reaction, and yet to hope that the speaker was voicing a point of view which quite certainly expresses the mind of one of the most important sectors of opinion in the Church today, a sector which is completely orthodox in its doctrine and theology but which has a vision of the meaning of Vatican II which many others (judging for instance from the correspondence columns) do not share and have never begun to understand.

Cardinal Pellegrino, archbishop of Turin, did not refer explicitly to the address of the archbishop of Malines, but his judgment of the symposium is nonetheless clear:

> We have lost too much time in Byzantinism, in subtlety and ill-founded fear. Now, after the Second Vatican Council which proposed a new style and a new spirit of existence, it is no longer

possible to carry on as before. Today when someone raises his voice to say we must go forward, many cry "scandal." But it is a "helpful scandal."

The Dutch bishops, in their September 2 letter agreed publicly with the Suenens analysis and program:

We hope that decentralization will be studied openly and in depth at Rome at the next episcopal synod and that it will take fruitful decisions for the Church. We wish to declare openly that the reflections developed on this subject by Cardinal Suenens in his exposition at the symposium of Chur, and earlier in his interview with *ICI*, have touched us profoundly. We intend to work with all our power in this direction.

6

The Logic of Vatican Council II

Philippe Muraille, author of this commentary, is a professor at the major seminary of the archdiocese of Malines-Brussels. He has written a number of studies of the theology of the Church.

To understand the stakes in the debate at this level, we must see the interview in the context of the ecclesiological trends current in Catholic circles. The Cardinal's proposal then presents itself as a new effort or, more exactly, as a clarification of what the Council wished to do and say.

Vatican II did not specify in all its juridical and functional aspects how to exercise collegially apostolic responsibility at all levels of life in the Church. The spirit which must animate institutions and relationships within the Church was more important to the Council than the letter of laws and regulations which too quickly become outmoded. This spirit appears clearly, according to Yves Congar, in the ecclesiological elaboration of *Lumen gentium*. Because the chapter on the people of God comes before that on the hierarchy, it shows that the Church is the common union of all believers in the one confession of the Lord. It also shows the differences of roles, situations and traditions.

From the theological point of view, the perspective was not the usual one of the Church's recent past. It had been more common to speak of hierarchy than of communion, of authority than of community of service.

This recovery of traditional and New Testament perspectives was to lead, on the practical level, to changes, becoming incorporated in the ways of doing things and of operating functionally. The Council, in fact, constituted a starting point and not a conclusion. It was not enough, therefore, to stop at explicit prescriptions: it was still necessary to state in a very concrete way what was the meanings of collegiality and of the unity of the people of God, with all bearing at different levels responsibility for presenting to the world of today the chance to live the faith in Jesus Christ. Hence, Cardinal Suenens proposed a program of coresponsibility which expresses clearly and functionally all that was a seed at the Council and was to come to life.

In practice, *Lumen gentium* implied a decentralization at all levels of decision-making or action in the Church; or, more exactly, a putting into practice of the full pastoral responsibility of the laity, priests, bishops and local churches in communion with the pope. It was not a question of abolishing but rather of recovering the full meaning of distinct roles in the Church. As Cardinal Suenens clearly indicated, a "logic of Vatican II" called for a functional program favoring the coresponsibility of all believers through their collaboration, and requiring a greater distinction between "decision making" and "decision taking."

Behind this suggestive and practical proposal for all relationships and for all communities in the Church there is, in reality, a theological vision which wishes to be faithful to the spirit of the Council. To the extent that this conception is adopted or rejected, conciliar reforms will be speeded up or delayed indefinitely: "The basic problem dividing us, consciously or otherwise, is one of theology; we are starting from differing visions of the Church especially in the matter of its necessary unity." In short, it is a question of knowing whether or not there is agreement on what the Council wished to do and say.

In many ways, the proposal of Cardinal Suenens appears in its broad sweep as a negative theology: to purify in order to affirm more clearly that unity does not mean uniformity, to define primacy so as not to confuse it with a monarchical power, to define coresponsibility which does not require that one of the two terms, head or body, be denied its role in decisions to be made or elaborated. Perhaps it is the negative form of this theology, even though often employed in the synthesis of St. Thomas Aquinas, which frightens many.

Every one agrees that there is a crisis in the Church, a crisis of authority, a crisis of unity and a crisis of credibility. Everyone wishes to heal it in the name of the Council. But there is no consensus when it comes to deducing a "logic of Vatican II."

The declaration of Cardinal Suenens constitutes in this regard a very revealing text on the theological trends prevailing today in the Catholic Church. As in the case of *Humanae Vitae*, two ecclesiologies, two ways of understanding the Church and its unity, are polarizing and confronting each other. Over and above the discussion on the institutions and structures to be kept or reformed, there are two conceptions of catholicity and of unity. In order to grasp what the debate involves at this depth it is useful to reread some of the commentaries provoked by the interview of Cardinal Suenens and to note, in passing, the motifs for agreement or disagreement.

AGREEMENT

For most, it is true, the position of Cardinal Suenens appears as a turning point concerning the way the theological options of the Council are to be understood; it makes more explicit what was said only imperfectly at Vatican II.

Among the most representative commentaries on what might be called a collegial position may be cited those of theologians like Rahner, Chenu, Congar, Küng and Lambert. They are cited at length below. Here I note only two reactions, those of Gerard Philips and Andrew Greeley.

Msgr. Philips played a very active role in the elaboration of *Lumen Gentium*. The way he views "the logic of Vatican II" proposed by the primate of Belgium is therefore important if one wishes to make a solid judgment.

"We would like to point out among other things", he writes, "the importance of the declaration of Cardinal Suenens on the unity of the Church in the logic of Vatican II, or, in other words, on this unity within *a harmonized diversity*. It seems to us, indeed, that the replies of the Cardinal, however remarkable they may be, run the risk which documents emanating from high authority have not escaped. Certain considerations contained in the proposal have a rather negative aspect which could conceal from the eyes of many the numerous constructive views given in the text." The author thus recommends examining carefully the content of the cardinal's statement rather than giving free rein to polemics. "Otherwise it would fail to achieve its objective of an adaptation that is more than ever desirable. The declaration does not aim to cause trouble, but rather to prevent it—it is an act of rare courage to which we pay homage" *Nouvelle Revue Théologique*, June-July 1969).

Father Greeley is interested in the functional and practical aspect of the coresponsibility proposed by the cardinal. To understand how opportune it is, we must see his program within the context of the present crisis in the Church, a crisis of credibility manifests itself particularly in a progressive falling away from the official Church.

In the *Catholic Voice* (7-2-69), he clarifies what is at issue in the proposed decentralization and coresponsibility: They should enable the Church to bridge the credibility gap that is so much discussed today. It is a question of putting into practice conciliar doctrine on the people of God and collegiality, so that the faithful are associated with a common witness; or, more exactly, so that the Church, as the cardinal pointed out, can be the work of Christ "with us all together."

This is a new perspective, but it does have the advantage of maintaining the Church in a state of participation (and, therefore, of permanent reform) in order to meet the demands of the Gospel of Christ and the appeals of the world. This is what the Jesuit weekly *America* emphasizes in its comment on the interview of Cardinal Suenens: "One of the chief merits . . . is that it evokes a renewed awareness of the continuing need for change." *Ecclesia semper reformanda.* Such would be the logic of Vatican II.

DISAGREEMENT

This is not the opinion of everyone. The other ecclesiological trend has been voiced by a minority no doubt, but one no less significant because of the authority it has.

In an article entitled "The Logic of the Council," Cardinal Felici said he did not see this logic in those "who criticize the work of the pope and would like to subject his authority as primate and supreme master in the Church to the control and approval of the bishops" (*Osservatore Romano,* 7-2-69). In actual fact, Cardinal Suenens does not oppose nor subject the authority of the pope to that of the bishops. On the contrary, he proposes a government for the Church which applies coresponsibility yet does not reduce the choice to one of the two terms: laity or hierarchy, bishops or pope.

Cardinal Daniélou similarly warned against "abusive interpretations" of the "logic" of Vatican II:

It is urgent that the work of Vatican II be interpreted with fidelity by showing the faithful what it truly is in the sense intended by the conciliar assembly, and what, on the contrary, is abusive interpretation. Let me explain: some have spoken of an opposition between the college of bishops and the bishop of Rome, the pope. Others have proposed as a solution of the problems which touch the priesthood a new view which is certainly not that of the Council (*Famiglia Mese,* Sept. 1969).

On another level we must likewise speak of the long supplement to *L'Homme nouveau* (6-15-69), in which its editor,

Marcel Clement, discusses and rejects the manner in which Cardinal Suenens "abusively" assimilated the logic of the Council to what could have been at best the logic of a majority: what makes law in a council, he holds, is not the majority, but unanimity on doctrine promulgated by the Sovereign Pontiff.

Two trends therefore are becoming clear. No doubt publicity always risks simplifying things and hardening the opposition by headlines such as: "Should the Church be a family or an army? a community of brothers or a bureaucratic organization?" But headlines aside, theological debate subsists.

Before drawing lessons from a discussion decisive for the future of the Church it is useful to see its import clearly. The issue in the Suenens interview is of a pastoral as well as of a theological order.

A PASTORAL QUESTION

How should we evaluate, from the pastoral side, the "decentralizing" tendency which sees first "local Churches" with their full apostolic responsibility exercised in communion with the Church of Rome and its head? It is a recognized fact that believers have more and more a tendency to detach themselves, consciously or unconsciously, from the institutional Church, to the extent that it does not include them in the major decisions which involve their witness, their liturgy, their ministry, and the theological expression of their faith in terms meaningful for the world of today. There is here a very serious pastoral problem to which, according to Cardinal Suenens, acceptance of coresponsibility can give an answer.

After *Humanae Vitae* and the encyclical on celibacy, it is clear that reciprocal "confidence" between believers and the official Church has become a major problem. One no longer recognizes in the method of decision making then adopted the vast project of collaboration proclaimed by the Council. What can be done to enable the Church to function as the people of God, and not as "a perfect society" administered by a hierarchy? What can be done to enable authority in the Church to be exercised in a common union, in the sacramental brotherhood and sacramental solidarity which are more essential than any difference of function? This question which takes seriously a concern of our times, is (as we have seen) particularly well understood and expressed by Father Greeley:

> The critical sentence in the Suenens interview, it seems to me, is the one that says, "Authority, if it is to be effective, must gain consent, and consent can only be gained where those involved have been able to take part—and their part is a very real one, though it requires careful definition."
>
> One need only to look at the two critical issues facing the Church on matters sexual to see the wisdom of the statement. The clergy of the world have not been consulted on closing the celibacy issue and, despite all pronouncements to the contrary, it has not been closed. Neither were the laity or clergy of the world consulted in a meaningful way on the birth control issue, and public opinion polls indicate that perhaps three fourths of both groups do not accept the decision.
>
> The sociologist and historian would both agree that the response to rapid change indicated by Cardinal Suenens is far more likely to be effective than the present heavy-handed attempts to "slow things down." In fact the practitioners of both disciplines would probably be willing to argue that a Church much like the one Cardinal Suenens describes will come into existence before the century is over. The only real question is how much senseless suffering and loss will have to occur first (*Catholic Voice*, 7-2-69).

A THEOLOGICAL PROBLEM

If the exercise of authority is a problem with pastoral overtones, the very conception of authority is an essentially theological problem and has not yet been solved.

There are two fundamentally different visions of the Church. These two visions determine the way one conceives the role of the pope in his relations with the whole episcopal college, that is, the relationship between the papacy and collegiality.

In a lecture in which he referred to the Suenens interview, Yves Congar examined closely what he calls *a very important unresolved ecclesiological problem*. This is how he sees the "monarchical position":

This position, held by certain members of the Curia, is one towards which it seems Paul VI leans, without expressly committing himself to it, as a result of his early formation and background. It holds that the bishop of Rome alone has supreme power over the universal Church as such. The pope communicates this power to all the bishops when assembled in Council. The Council, then, is only a sort of participation in the concern and the universal power of the pope over the whole church.

The argument in favor of this position is that the pope determines the agenda of the Council and, if he pleases, can withdraw a question from consideration. This is what Paul VI did at Vatican II to the questions of priestly celibacy and contraception. As it is he who sets the agenda and calls the Council, this assembly is simply a participation in the supreme power which determines its scope. This, in brief, is the monarchical position: one alone holds the total universal supreme power in which he permits others to participate when and as he wishes.

The "collegial position," on the other hand, to which Cardinal Suenens refers in his book on coresponsibility and in his declaration on the Church and its unity "in the logic of Vatican II," is described by Father Congar as follows:

The other position is the very contrary. It is held by men like Karl Rahner and my fellow Dominican, Edward Schillebeeckx, at Nijmegen. I myself lean very strongly towards this position but with a few reservations. It asserts that supreme power over the universal Church is always collegial, but that it can be exercised either collegially, or personally by the head of the College.

Having explained how this supreme authority can be exercised collegially over the universal Church, Father Congar continues:

> If we envisage the history of the Church, and particularly what happened with the Eastern Church, we see that this conflict has always existed. On the whole, the West has always had a tendency to develop the papacy towards a monarchical form. The Eastern Church has never and will never accept a monarchical authority which is absolutely foreign to its tradition, a tradition just as venerable and old, just as apostolic as the Western tradition, and just as clearly expressed by Fathers of the Church who are as important as those of the Latin Church.

To express the entire logic of collegiality, as Vatican II sought, it was necessary to contend with the texts of Vatican I which were thought out according to a logic of monarchy in which there is no reciprocity between the head and the body.

> Thus the pope always appears as *above* the Church and not *in* the Church. The whole problem lies there. It is a question of finding a formula and structures according to which the pope is truly *over*, since he is the head, . . . but he should be *above* in such a way that he is *within* the Church. The orthodox refuse to have the pope *above* because they want him within the Church. Now if the pope is *in* the Church, *in* the episcopate, *in* the college, will he not be one with the college, that is, will he not establish a certain reciprocity? For there is not only the movement which emanates from him by way of influence and authority towards the body, but a movement which emanates from the body towards him.

Father Congar points out that one can approach the problem from another angle and show that the pope is *in* the Church and not only *above* it, by observing the ecclesiological initiative of *Lumen Gentium*. Chapter 2 on the people of God precedes chapter 3 on the hierarchy. What can we conclude from this?

That Christian ontology, that is, the reality of Christian life is more profound and prior to any organizational structure. One must also place the powers of the pope and the bishops in this reality of communion in Christian life which is ultimately the people of God. Seen in this way, the pope is not *above* the Church, he is *in* the Church (La Croise, 9-19-69).

THE FUNCTION OF CRITICISM IN THE CHURCH

Certain reservations have been expressed, sometimes forcefully, about the proposal of Cardinal Suenens. We shall not go into the psychological reasons for them here, but only into the two motives of a more doctrinal character which prompt this resistance. They either center in an ecclesiology which claims that the pope is completely at the service of unity and the bishops nothing except through the pope—we shall return to this point later—or they disavow the role of criticism in the Church.

According to the second hypothesis, to speak of coresponsibility seems to be a way of bringing the Church up to date by speaking as everyone else does of codetermination, of democracy and of participation. It is true that the Church is not the world and that it should not be criticized in the name of the values of this world alone. The debate would be ruinous for the Church, if the word of men was to silence the word of God, in other words, if it did not take as its norm theology, the explanation of the word of God by the councils and tradition. Thus we must explain what we mean by criticism in the Church. True criticism is one based on theology, but there is a less true form based only on partial reference to the Gospel and the tradition of the Church.

The role of criticism is indispensable to the vitality of the Church. But when criticism is not based on serious theological grounds, that is, on attentive concern for the word of

God as expressed in Scripture and clarified in the tradition of the Catholic faith, it risks becoming blind to certain aspects of truth and makes any dialogue impossible. It confronts the Church with unfortunate choices between two terms of an alternative, either individual charism or hierarchical structure, or bishops and local churches, or the pope and the universal Church. It would be easy to multiply examples by rereading the history of the Church and the grievances formulated today in the "parallel" or "underground" churches. Neither term of these alternatives is true when one is asserted denial of the other. "There is today a certain way of invoking the idea of the people of God and of conceiving it which is not entirely correct," Father Congar has written. "At the present time the faithful often claim a freedom of decision or take the initiative by saying: 'We are the people of God,' as though the expression had the meaning of 'people' in the political order, that is, opposed to rulers, as though it designated a single undifferentiated mass, not a structured community."

The idea of "people of God" does not correspond to the idea of democracy. According to Cardinal Suenens:

> The vocabulary of a given time must be constantly corrected so that it does not prove false to the reality for which it stands. Having made this reservation, we can now say that the Second Vatican Council certainly was characterized by a move in the direction of "democratization" because of the accent it placed on the people of God, by the stress it laid on the hierarchy as a service. . . .

Reduced to one of these two terms, hierarchy or individual charisms, the Church is no longer wholly the Church of God or the Church of theology, but a thing of men. Theology therefore, in the last analysis, constitutes the norm, the rule which governs criticism in favor of "the whole truth."

It must be admitted, however, that criticism does not come

from just one side. There is indeed a way of exercising authority and the primacy in the Church which constitutes, at least in practice, an explicit or implicit challenge to the theological ideal defined at the Council in terms of collegiality and of community. A total centralization does not always permit free play to collegiality. To be in line with conciliar tradition one must both distinguish and affirm both terms of the alternative.

When criticism allows itself to be guided by purely rational principles, it confines itself within the limits of a certain rationalism and, as Paul Ricoeur has pointed out, "it deprives man of all depth and becomes for him a new principle of oppression." Man no longer has any norm other than an irreducible intellectual rigidity which is nothing but himself; the Christian faith then becomes nothing more than a cultural fact. It is no longer a response to this challenge of love and trust which is God.

The alliance of the critical spirit and the religious spirit is quite otherwise. The questioning it inspires accepts theology in advance, the word of God that all be one. It makes possible the word of men. It expresses itself, as Henri de Lubac says, in a "serious criticism, circumscribed in its object, made by competent and responsible men concerned with the just reforms or adaptations which have become necessary"; and, he adds, they "are inspired by love."

This is, consequently, the level at which the present debate must be presented, if we are to understand all its significance and all it holds of promise for the future of the Church in the wake of Vatican II.

COLLEGIALITY AND ITS IMPLICATIONS
ACCORDING TO VATICAN II

What does the collegiality desired by the Council really require? The answer of a collegial type of ecclesiology directs us towards a broad decentralization—in canon law, the form of worship, of witness, of ministry and of theology—which makes fully evident the whole apostolic responsibility of the bishops and the primacy of the pope in the service of catholicity.

On the theological level it raises the question of the definition of the relations between the pope and the episcopal college.

The conciliar texts give only the principles for a solution. When the Fathers described the relations which should exist between the primacy and collegiality, they often avoided speaking in terms of power, authority and jurisdiction and recommended communion, cooperation, collaboration in a spirit of concord and charity. This in fact is the heart of collegiality; this is the Christian wisdom which ought to rule its exercise. To grasp all the teaching of the Council one must reread what is said in chapter 3 of *Lumen Gentium* on the relationship between collegiality and primacy in connection with the preceding chapter on the people of God, this sacramental communion in Christ by which the pope is also *in* the Church and not only *above* the Church.

One then envisions a theology in harmony with the spirit of Vatican II which, as Cardinal Suenens said in his interview, "avoids presenting the role of the pope in such a way as to isolate him from the college of bishops whose leader he is. While we emphasize that the pope has a right to act or speak alone, the word 'alone' never means 'separately' or 'in isolation' . . . His role, in all its aspects, can only be understood in relation to the Church, in it and for it,—never apart from it or above it."

IN READING SCRIPTURE

The second principle to apply in theology is to confront the collegiality expressed in the Council with Scripture. Whatever be its authority for the living tradition of the faith, a council is always limited by the decisive authority which

is Scripture. What was not clearly elucidated or explained by
Vatican II, or by any other council, must be clarified in the
light of Scripture.

There is, therefore, a need to clarify what Vatican II did
not clearly state about local Churches, each of which is the
Body of Christ when they celebrate the Eucharist in the
communion of the Lord. If one accepts, with Scripture and
the Council, that the foundation of Christian life is the union
with Christ achieved sacramentally in the eucharistic mystery, then one must recognize—in agreement with a whole
theology both Catholic and dear to the Eastern tradition—
that attention should not be directed first toward the universal Church, but toward the places where communion
takes place, the *koinonia* with the Lord. The "legitimate
diversity," which is spoken of today, does not therefore pro-
ceed from a current fashion, but corresponds to a certain way
of seeing the Church take root in different places and in
different cultures where communion with Christ exists.

This perspective is more directly in harmony with Scripture than one which takes as its starting point the universal
Church conceived as a perfect, undifferentiated society. To
encounter men in their life, Christ speaks the human language of their culture and society, even in the sacred mystery of the Eucharist which unites them to all the Churches
which together form the universal church. This initial way of
regarding and living the Church, starting from its local and
eucharistic establishment, is in accord with Scripture as well
as with the point of view of mission or "aculturation" of the
faith, and with the Eastern tradition. As the Church of God
living the communion with Christ in a particular situation,
each local Church has full apostolic authority to announce
the faith in union with other local Churches and with this
privileged local Church whose head is Peter's successor.

The study of Holy Scripture also leads us to be more
specific about the meaning of the role and place of Peter
among the Twelve. He is simultaneously "singled out" and
a member of the college, but he is not outside the group of

Twelve. "Let us not say," Msgr. Philips points out a propos of a phrase in the Suenens interview, "that Christ confided his Church to Peter and the Eleven, but to Peter and the Twelve, for Simon is alway included in the group."

This would seem to imply that Peter and his successors can only stand out from or face the college to the extent that they are visibly *with* the college, in the college and in the Church. In this role, which has a strong theological basis, the pope questions the college and the Churches "in the name of the Lord" who is present in the Churches, to the extent that his questioning manifests, at least visibly by the way it has been conceived, his position at the center of the episcopal college which presides over the Churches.

This comes down to saying that the pope expresses himself all the more fully "in the name of the Lord" to the extent that he himself is in a position of reciprocity, of coresponsibility and of communion with the college which succeeds the Twelve.

READING THE DEMANDS OF THE TIMES

There is one last principle to recall when we interpret the will of a council or any other expression of tradition: the attention paid to the demands of the contemporary world to which the Gospel is to be preached.

Cardinal Suenens speaks of this clearly in his book on coresponsibility. It is his intention, he says, to interpret the Council by taking into consideration the urgent needs of the world, because the Church is willed by Christ "for the life of the world" (John 6:51). The proposal of coresponsibility is not expressed in political language but requires the language of an apostle and man of faith who faces up to the urgency of ecumenism, of the missions, and of the presence of the Church in the world.

The general assembly of the ecumenical Council of Churches recalled at Uppsala in 1968 that the situation of the millions of men who are seeking the hope the Gospel offers for today, requires that Churches which claim to be the Church of God renew themselves through diverse forms of witness, worship and ministry. To the extent that they present themselves, not as new Churches but as the Church of renewal, they will give witness to the reality of Christ "for the life of the world."

Today's values and demands and the present conjuncture constitute an essential "moment" for theological interpretation. We must learn how to read the signs of the times, not in order to conform to the world, but in order to discern everything which is an appeal of the spirit and which, for that reason, invites us to a "rereading" of the conciliar texts. This is the only way not to "annul" by a "tradition of men" the Word of God which is always in the process of becoming. A Christian should always be coresponsible for his time and for the vital questions it raises. The "monarchical" and "absolutist way" of understanding the Church no longer speaks to men of today.

We noted above the ecumenical aspect of the proposal for coresponsibility. But this aspect of the project, already stated or envisioned at the Council when collegiality was being discussed, raises again the pastoral and missionary demands that the Church ought to be present "for the life of the world."

From the missionary viewpoint, the Church is called today to give an account of its hope for the world. The Church cannot be, as Christ wished, "the covenant of the people and light of nations" (Is 42:6), if it does not witness visibly in its structures to a life in common, the life of this new man reconciled in Jesus Christ. The Gospel ought to come to men in their daily lives at their innermost depth where they reflect and decide to invoke the Lord who is other than men. The presence of Christ, manifested and lived in the Church, should above all lead to the reconciliation of men of all conditions: "all baptised in Christ, you have all clothed

yourselves in Christ and there are no more distinctions between Jew and Greek, slave and free, male and female, but
all of you are one in Christ Jesus" (Gal 3:27-28).

In the history of today's humanity in quest of itself, this
reality of grace given in Christ becomes a promise and a
need. It affirms the responsibility of each one while emphasizing that this responsibility ought to be lived in union
with Christ and, therefore, in union and reconciliation with
all men. It is a question of a grandeur which surpasses simple
democratic utopias in so far as it outlines today the new
humanity, the man fulfilled in God whom we seek.

It is perhaps useful to see clearly the movement which is
taking shape in a humanity which feels itself oppressed by
technology and its form of rationalism. Relationships of
responsibility ought to be multiplied so that this society will
respect man. Roger Mehl puts it this way:

> Little has been done in the area of a responsible society. Never-
> theless, the need for "involvement" of workers in the manage-
> ment of their companies is universally felt. Joint decision making
> by management and labor can soon become a reality. . . . In
> various countries, parent-teachers associations and associations
> of families are represented in official organizations for the man-
> agement of schools or the administration of public health. Plan-
> ning, which at one time was highly centralized, is organized on
> a regional basis, giving diverse groups of workers and producers
> the opportunity to be involved in decision making. One could
> multiply examples. All indicate the same trend: a decentraliza-
> tion of the power of decision. Even though the central authority
> has the final word, it does not decide everything by itself: con-
> sumer groups, often organized on their own initiative, are con-
> sulted. They know that their opinion counts and that their
> experience is not neglected.

The report of the second session of the conference of the
Church and Society department of the ecumenical Council of
Churches has made many useful suggestions on this matter.
Their thrust, like that of Pope John XXIII's encyclicals is to

restore the importance of "intermediate bodies." While a society dominated by technology tends to become hierarchical in a quasi-military way, a "responsible" society is one in which at all levels—local, regional, provincial—between the supreme authority and individuals one finds assemblies, groups, councils and commissions in direct contact with the interested parties (workers, consumers), representing them and, within the limits of their competence and experience, supplying the employers with suggestions, well-developed proposals and corrections.

One question immediately comes to mind: why refuse to the Church community what Christians and the papal encyclicals demand for a responsible secular society? In other words, do we really want, as Cardinal Suenens suggests, a responsible Church, coresponsible with Christ, and in the logic of Vatican II? Does one think that the Church ought to become a "responsible community," not starting with society as a model, but in the name of a model which the social doctrine of the Church calls for in society? The Church cannot be satisfied with urging the responsibility of all in the secular city without incorporating this same value into its own structures. The Church cannot exist authentically as a community of faith united in Christ unless it too expresses the wish to be a responsible society, one which distinguishes roles but gives to all its members, all groups, and all the Churches of which it is composed, the opportunity to participate in the decisions which will guide its future and formulate its faith.

The "whole" truth promised by Christ to his followers who turned towards the Kingdom is never a possession, still less a set of propositions reserved to a few or to a group. It is, on the contrary, a truth to be revealed by the whole ecclesiastical body confronted, in its internal dialogue, with the demands of the world. To reestablish "intermediate groups" is also to recognize differences in local Churches and their apostolic responsibility for all that concerns witness, forms of prayer and ministry. When this is done, the universal Church will appear as the work of God for which we all assume responsibility with our respective roles and spiritual gifts.

Admittedly, the institutional Church has up to now not achieved all the religious and social potentiality of baptism. It has been satisfied with advising Christians to live as responsible citizens in the world of men, without giving them the means to participate in the decisions which commit the Church of today and the future. From the end of the early Christian era up to now, the hold of universal ecclesiology has been so strong that it has overshadowed the eucharistic ecclesiology and the ecclesiology of the local Church. N. Afanassieff has pointed out that what has to be called the "system" of universal ecclesiology makes practically impossible the assertion of the local Church, in spite of the necessity of the local Church to meet the needs of missionary acculturation. From a universal perspective, the local Church can free itself only with difficulty. It must be understood according to the theology of the New Testament in which the local Church is the Church of God in all its fullness. To become a "responsible society," the Church should recognize these intermediate bodies which local Churches are, seeing them as centers for meetings and collaboration in decision making. This cannot be done without a profound understanding of the ecclesiological dimensions of the Eucharist which is always celebrated in a given place, a place which is also that of the communion of saints.

CONCLUSION

Will the Catholic Church continue to function on the basis of an exclusively secular model, one borrowed from an earlier time? Or will it be, not the center and the periphery, (which would give the impression that everything is rather at the periphery), but the unique Church of God which exists in various places in communion with Christ? Will this Church of God commit itself to being a responsible society, stressing the ideal of serving the secular city by reason of its baptismal profession of faith, or will it remain this "lonely crowd," this anonymous mass guided by decisions it understands less and less? Such are the stakes in this ecclesiological problem: is the pope exclusively *above* the college as the papalist hypothesis proposes, or is he both *in* and *above* the college, as the collegial hypothesis states? It remains an open question.

Confronted with the slowness of certain decisions urgently needed for ecumenical and missionary reasons, it was a simple act of charity to bring out into the open the divergencies of the theologies which confront each other. The word and the dialogue which lead to unity begin from a loyal recognition in the full light of day of the differences, tensions and alternatives. Today, the Eucharist or common union can become more real. When this occurs, the word which intervenes in the name of the novelty of God always prepares surprises and new starts.

Such is the task of today's theology faced with the challenge which comes from faith and which calls for more awareness of this relationship of reciprocity and for mutual recognition of the Church of God everywhere and that local Church whose bishop is Peter's successor. The grace of our time will be to have accepted the debate and to have recognized this event as a new step in the understanding of the mystery of the church as forseen by Vatican II.

•

• •

A Voice in the Wilderness

Gregory Baum summed up his views in the article in the *Catholic World* cited earlier:

What was the theological focus of Cardinal Suenens' remarks? According to the Belgian Cardinal, Vatican Council II was a turning point in the Church's history. A radical change has taken place in the Church's self-understanding. With a great number of Catholic theologians Cardinal Suenens believes that Vatican II has crystallized and promoted a radical shift in the awareness of what "Church," "Catholic Church," is all about. This shift has been variously described. How does the Cardinal describe it in his interview? Prior to the Council, he says, the Church saw herself above all as an hierarchical system, as a perfect society defined in terms of law. The hierarchy was the Church, and hence Catholics "belonged" to the Church.

The Council, according to Cardinal Suenens, has created in its participants a new experience of Church. Church is first of all a mystery of fellowship. Church takes place where people come together in the same faith, hope and love. Church, according to the conciliar teaching, is first of all the local community. The Church universal, including the entire body of the hierarchy, is constituted by the fellowship of the various local churches. People do not belong to the Church: they constitute it. Unity is not primarily a reality defined by law: it is, rather, the participation of all in the same life of Christ. The first meaning of Church, in other words, is not *hierarchy* but *fellowship*.

This shift demands the reinterpretation of all ecclesiastical concepts. Especially the role of authority and law, the function of the hierarchy and the role of the papacy in the Church must be reinterpreted in accordance with this new self-understanding. A key concept in this reinterpretation is, according to Suenens, the coresponsibility of all Catholics for the Church's life. Through baptism men do not simply enter the way of personal salvation: they enter a community of faith, in which they are summoned to assume responsibility. God guides the Church, Suenens keeps reminding us, not through the pope alone nor even through the hierarchy alone but through His presence in all the baptized Christians who are open to Him.

PRIMACY & COLLEGIALITY

In his interview, Cardinal Suenens applies the principle of coresponsibility above all to the pope's relationship to the world episcopate. Here the general principle has a special name: it is called collegiality. The dogmatic basis of collegiality, we recall, is not just the coresponsibility communicated through baptism but also and especially the coresponsibility communicated through episcopal consecration. Vatican II, as is well known, has laid down the doctrine of collegiality as one of its principal achievements. The bishops of the Church, we are told, are responsible with the pope for the teaching and policy-making in the Church universal. In the exercise of papal primacy this coresponsibility cannot be taken away from the bishops: for it is based, as much as papal primacy, on the Church's divine structure.

In the name of collegiality Cardinal Suenens has severely criticized the present system of ecclesiastical government, in particular the mode and methods by which authority is exercised by the Church's central administration. Here the cardinal has a few hard things to say. He accuses the central administration of unwillingness to recognize collegiality as proposed by Vatican II and of making the Church into an inflexible system insensitive to present needs and crushing the new life the Spirit creates among people. . . .

One accusation raised against Cardinal Suenens is grave. It has been suggested that he goes against the Catholic doctrine of papal primacy. It is true enough that the cardinal has brought up a delicate issue, one which Vatican I and II have carefully avoided: the limits of papal authority. But the cardinal's position is in no way contrary to the Church's defined teaching.

In his interview Suenens explains the doctrine of collegiality as laid down by Vatican II. The bishops of the Church, according to this doctrine, are not only responsible for their own local communities but also and especially for the teaching and policy-making in the Church universal. While Vatican II acknowledges the doctrine of papal primacy as spelled out by Vatican I, it joins to this the doctrine of episcopal collegiality which belongs to the divine structure of the Church and hence must be respected by the papacy. The pope may not use his supreme authority to exclude the world episcopate from its coresponsibility. It was "a serious omission" of Vatican II, according to Suenens, not to spell out how the teaching of episcopal collegiality modified the function of the papacy in the Church.

Collegiality is a dead word unless the pope changes the understanding of his own office. Vatican II proposes collegiality simply as an obligatory moral ideal. It is not yet a legal concept, but only a moral one. The pope is bound to respect the coresponsibility of the bishops, he cannot exclude them from participating in the highest government, he is never separated from them and always acts on their behalf, even if he makes decisions in canonical independence from them. The pope is part of the Church. He must exercise his supreme office while respecting the coresponsibility of all Christians and, in particular, the collegiality of the world episcopate.

But this is only a moral norm. If the pope does not consult the bishops and acts in total independence from them, his decisions are legitimate. He is within the law. He may sin gravely by disregarding collegiality, but his acts have legal force. If the pope refuses to act collegially and determines policy and teaching without taking into account the convictions of the episcopate, the bishops may lament, complain, and protest, but they have no legal claim against the pope. Legally—though not morally—the pope may act as an absolute monarch.

Cardinal Suenens raises the question whether it is possible to guarantee episcopal collegiality by some sort of legal norm. "Nothing was said (at Vatican II) of the consequences of collegiality for the pope in relationship to the other bishops." Then Suenens adds, "This is a serious omission, and it is causing us serious problems at the present time." Later he makes the following suggestion: "It follows from the logic of Vatican II (the doctrine of collegiality and the shift to general coresponsibility) that the individual Churches— through their bishops gathered in episcopal conferences

—should be consulted publicly and collectively, and enabled to collaborate in the documents that vitally affect the whole Church." Can such a rule be made into a legal norm?

While all Catholics agree that there are moral norms to papal authority—collegiality is just one of them—the question whether these moral norms can be translated into legal ones is controverted among theologians. Many conservative theologians would say that limits imposed by law are not reconcilable with the papal primacy as defined by Vatican I. From his public speeches this seems to be the view of Pope Paul VI himself.

Vatican I and II avoided the issue. In the explanations given to the Council fathers at Vatican I, prior to the vote on papal primacy, it was clearly said that the pope must use his primacy to build up the Church, not to ruin it, and that he cannot interfere in the ecclesiastical life of the single dioceses in such a way as to make it impossible for the bishops to exercise their ordinary function. Vatican I clearly recognized the limits of papal authority, but no attempt was made to spell it out in legal terms.

Vatican II was not willing to tackle the problem. By teaching episcopal collegiality it proposed a new ideal for the exercise of papal primacy, but it made no legal provisions that collegiality be respected. Vatican II repeated the teaching of Vatican I that the pope was at all times canonically free to decide whether to act singly by himself, or whether to act collegially with the bishops.

During the discussion, Pope Paul VI tried to enhance his own authority by a formula which would have moved the papacy farther away from any criticism in the Church. He proposed a modification to be inserted into the text, saying that the pope "was solely bound to God" in his responsibility. This modification reveals Pope Paul's own understanding of his office.

The papal modification was rejected by the responsible commission. The commission replied that the pope was bound not only to God, he was also bound to divine revelation, to

Catholic teaching, to the structure of the Church, to the principles of morality, etc. In other words, there are always some objective norms, however minimal, which express what obedience to God means in actual life. But the commission did not raise the question whether the papal acknowledgment of collegiality could be guaranteed in objective, legal manner.

Cardinal Suenens raises this question in his interview. Is it possible to express in canonical terms the limits of papal primacy, defined as full, supreme, and immediate ecclesiastical power? Would this contradict the plentitude of authority invested in the pope? The answer remains a controverted issue.

It seems to me quite clear, however, that if there are moral limits to papal primacy, then it should be possible to find some legal norms, however minimal, to protect these limits. Our whole understanding of society is based on this principle. There can be no moral obligation in society which is, in principle, beyond any kind of legal formulation. If there are moral limits to papal primacy—such as the collegiality of bishops or his conformity to Catholic teaching—then there must be some minimal canonical formulation of these. According to the Catholic tradition, in particular, law is an expression of morality. In other words, human morality is always sufficiently objective to find some suitable legal norm expressing and protecting it. It should, therefore, be possible to have papal primacy and episcopal collegiality guaranteed by some sort of constitutional law.

A famous example of this is the decree *Haec Sancta* of the Council of Constance, 1414-19. This Council found itself facing a Church in which three popes claimed to be legitimate heirs of the papacy. The Council decided to depose the three popes and appoint one in its own name. In the decree *Haec Sancta*, which was later ratified by the new pope, the Council of Constance declared that an ecumenical council can depose a pope in cases of emergency, if, for instance, he foments schism or promotes the destruction of the Church. We recall that the Council of Constance is as much an ecumenical council as Vatican I and II. (For a discussion of the most recent literature on the subject, see Francis Oakley, *Council Over Pope?* Herder & Herder, 1969.) We have here a clearly defined situation where papal primacy is limited by episcopal collegiality. The history of the Catholic Church assures us, therefore, that papal primacy is not intrinsically irreconcilable with canonical norms limiting its exercise.

Another objection raised against Cardinal Suenens' interview is, perhaps, the most difficult to which to reply. The cardinal is accused of stressing the independence of episcopal conferences so much that he seems to promote national Churches, foster nationalism in the Church, and thus prepare the dissolution of the Catholic Church into regional ecclesiastical bodies. This is what happened in the age of the Reformation and, in a different cultural context, among the Churches of the East. These Churches so identified themselves with the culture in which they lived and with the corresponding political institutions that the idea of a universal Church, under a single government, was no longer conceivable to them. But a Church beyond nationalism is without question the authentic Catholic ideal.

There can be no doubt that the Christian ideal is to have a Church beyond nationalism. In the past the Church has often failed here, not only the separate national Churches, we note, but also the Catholic Church in various countries. There is some evidence for saying, however, that today nationalism is no longer the universal temptation in the West. Nationalism is criticized within each nation. The exaggerated self-esteem and the grandiose political dreams proper to traditional nationalism are the objects of ridicule in wide circles in all nations. Who is more critical of Americans and American culture than Americans? National critique has today become self-criticism. People have begun to participate in many institutions, political, scientific, ecclesiastical, and commercial that extend beyond the nation. Since there is some evidence that the nation is being culturally transcended, the danger of strong episcopal conferences seems to be much less today than it was in the past. The danger threatening these conferences is, rather, that they represent only one segment of society, namely, the establishment.

The real cause of division among the peoples of the West is not nationalism but the diverse vision of society. Similarly, what divides the Church today is not the excessive attachment to national trends but the diverse attitude to authority and tradition. There is no tension between American and Brazilian Catholics because they belong to different nations and cultures. But there is tension if their views of authority and tradition are diverse. Progressive American Catholics have no quarrels with Brazilian Catholics who have opted for renewal and reform. The Catholic Church is no longer divided according to the inherited boundary lines, among which national frontiers were the most prominent; today the division occurs according to different principles and cuts right through the local communities and regional Churches. To promote the independence of episcopal conferences does not necessarily foster nationalism. It fosters ecclesiastical division only if these conferences give exclusive expression to the establishment and the interests of those who favor the status quo.

Is Cardinal Suenens a voice crying in the wilderness? There is much evidence for fearing that as long as the present administration remains in Rome, there will be no change.

7

Primacy and Collegiality

> *Gustave Thils, whose commentary follows, is professor of theology at Louvain and was a peritus at the Second Vatican Council. He is a specialist in ecclesiology and a member of the Pontifical Commission for Ecumenism.*

In his interview with *ICI,* Cardinal Suenens frankly faced the problem of the primacy of the pope and of episcopal collegiality—the relations between pope and bishops. His stand on this question produced a variety of reactions.

Predictably, the opponents criticize the interview for unduly reducing the role and the rights of the pope; while its proponents consider it both timely and necessary to recall collegiality and, above all, to put it into practice. Worthy of note is the voluminous and schematic character of the statements made by defenders of primacy, and the modesty, not to say timidity, of the supporters of episcopal collegiality.

DEFENSE AND ILLUSTRATION OF THE PAPACY

Supporters of papal primacy appeal to divine right. Marcel Clement, for example, asserts:

> In the Church, not only does authority come from the Lord, but *the form of government* has been determined by Him. It is Jesus himself who established Peter as supreme pastor, as His Vicar;

he was made the subject of full and supreme power. Thus, the Church, which is a true society, although not a political society, was established in divine right in the monarchical model. Since its foundation it has been, and until the parousia it should continue to be a monarchy; both this form of government and the authority which animates it are of divine right *(L'Homme Nouveau,* 6-15-69).

It seemed sufficient for Cardinal Browne, in an interview with Patrick Riley of NCWC, to reach for his Denzinger and read the article of *Pastor Aeternus* which declares that the juridical power of the pope is supreme, plenary, immediate and ordinary—a truly episcopal jurisdiction over the universal Church. Then he kept silence. These words, he seemed to say, need no comment.

Yet *Pastor Aeternus,* right at the start, indicates the purpose of papal primacy:

> That the episcopacy itself might be one and undivided, and *that the entire multitude of the faithful, through bishops closely connected with one another, might be preserved in the unity of faith and communion,* placing the blessed Peter over the other apostles, He established in him the perpetual principle and visible foundation of both unities (Denz. 1821).

This text also is capital, as the purpose of a power is one of the norms of its limitation. There are others as well, which will be mentioned later.

THE POPE "ALONE"

Another recurrent theme is that of the pope acting alone. *"Il Papa decide da solo!",* proclaimed Father R. Gagnebet in the *Osservatore Romano* (9-5-68). The article ended in an outburst of sentimental lyricism: "He alone (the pope) has the words of eternal life, he alone leads the faithful to the fullness of Christian life and toward the joys of heaven."

Marcel Clement, in the already mentioned *L'Homme Nouveau* article, summarizes Vatican II as follows: "Two subjects of power, or better stated, two modes of exercising the same, unique power: pope alone or pope united with bishops. The choice is the pope's."

Msgr. Gerard Philips, whose role in the Council was so important that he can interpret the texts with authority, sees things very differently. In a study devoted to a text regarded as among the least favorable to collegiality, the *Nota Praevia* to Chapter 3 of the Constitution *Lumen Gentium* (on the Church), he writes:

> The notion of collegiality is essential at many levels, but particularly at the highest level. . . . It follows, then, that the pope, primarily with regard to the bishops and proportionally with regard to the laity, is always first, but never alone. . . . Even though Simon Peter's temperament impels him to precipitate himself before the others, either to jump into the sea or to answer the Master's questions, he really is never acting alone, even when receiving promises not addressed as such to his brothers (cfr. Luke 22:31; John 21:15, ff.). It is also the vocation of his successors to be elected first, but not alone. . . . The pope is first, but not the pope alone: this is a program which even the dissident Churches are gradually beginning to recognize" *(IDO-C International,* 9-15-69).

THE INDEPENDENCE OF THE POPE

Different commentators felt obliged to recall the dependence of the college of bishops on the pope, and the pope's independence with regard to the college, as if the Cardinal's interview tended to support ideas which would imply the dependence of the pope upon the bishops.

Cardinal Daniélou, for example wrote: "If by collegiality is understood a modification in the structure of the Church which would limit the free exercise of the authority of the Sovereign Pontiff, and would place him in a position of dependence on the episcopal college, it is clear that such a conception is unacceptable" *(Le Figaro,* 7-12-69). Note the use of the conditional and the unexplained use of the term "dependence."

Cardinal Felici, who was Secretary of the Vatican Council and who is president of the commission for the interpretation of the conciliar texts, gave a similar explanation:

> Some, using a logic allegedly conciliar, and invoking a collegiality which the Council never understood in this sense, not content to criticize the work of the Pope, would seek to submit his activity as primate and supreme head of the Church to the control and approval of the bishops (*Le Monde*, 7-4-69).

These statements were published in *Osservatore Romano*. The whole discussion is over-simplified if only the terms "dependence-independence" are used. This question will be considered later. Meanwhile, one may wonder if it is the bishops who are really threatening the pope's independence. About the same time that *Osservatore Romano* published the statements of Cardinals Daniélou and Felici, Fr. Bruno Ribes, editor of *Etudes*, commenting on the appointment of the new Secretary of State, Cardinal Villot, wrote:

> What attitude will the Curia take? We are justified in asking this question, when we consider the reactions of certain cardinals: their statements, their premature disclosure of the nomination (hoping by this means to have it withdrawn), the untimely statements made to the Italian press, openly or—as one reporter put it—in the corridors (June 69).

Who, then, is really threatening the pope's independence?

POWER FROM ABOVE

Is the source of the errors attributed to the interview to be found in the exaggerated application of the democratic process within the Church? Cardinal Browne interpreted the interview as saying that the pope must act merely as the "representative" of the episcopal college. As he said to Patrick Riley of NCWC: "The title of the interview refers to 'the logic' of Vatican II. This implies that reference should first be made to the Council. But the Council never obliged the pope to act *merely as the representative of the college.*"

The reports on which Cardinal Browne based his judgment and his reactions evidently betrayed the spirit and the letter of the Suenens text. It says nothing whatsoever of that kind.

Several critics refer to the democratic spirit of the interview, for instance, Marcel Clement:

> Along with this priority of baptism goes its immediate corrollary, the priority of community. Each must live and insert his personal responsibility *into and with* that of all the faithful. Thus, Cardinal Suenens *necessarily* admits that the *three powers of* governing (legislative, executive, and judicial), of the magisterium, and of orders are *indifferently given* to all the people of God as a totality.

The italics refer to the statements which Clement presents as intimately linked. He continues:

> Such an error bears an explanation. It occurs when an attempt is made to "democratize" the Church by applying inadequately the social structures which are political in orientation (i.e., ordered toward the temporal common good) to a society which is prophetic (i.e., ordered to the pastoral care of souls and their eternal salvation) *(L'Homme Nouveau, 6-15-69)*.

This, however, overlooks the fact that the Suenens interview aimed at freeing the Church from inadequate social structures.

HESITANT MANIFESTATIONS OF COLLEGIALITY

"The task of the College of Bishops must be studied," Cardinal Alfrink declared (*Le Monde,* 6-24-69). "Yes, indeed," answered Karl Rahner in an interview with the Jesuit review *America* (6-28-69). "The abstract principle of collegiality was stated (in Vatican II), but what that principle would mean practically for the pope—how it should be worked out on the institutional level—is still quite unclear."

Meanwhile, *Present* (5-22-69) observed: "We are now several years removed from the Council and papal decisions are still conveyed by the *Motu Proprio* and the encyclical."

In brief, "the collegiality announced by Vatican II remains in swaddling clothes, without institutional guarantees, even in decisions of historical impact. Nonetheless, in view of the desiderata expressed by the episcopal conferences for the Synod, some progress has been made. The documents do confer one immediate and undeniable benefit. Nobody, not even the Curia's Cardinal Daniélou, will any longer be able to depict Belgium's Cardinal Leo Suenens as a lonely, eccentric, neo-modernist crusader. Most (if not all) of the ideas Suenens has been advocating in recent interviews get respectable backing in the compendium drawn up by the Synod's secretariat from the suggestions submitted by national hierarchies" (*NCR*, 9-10-69).

CONSULTATIVE OR DELIBERATIVE

At the Council, the bishops had asked for the right to be associated in some way in the governing of the universal Church. The Synod of Bishops was the response. A careful reading of official documents and papal discourses reveals the inadequacy of such a response in expressing the collegial task of the episcopacy. Instead, it constitutes a new organization intended to assist the pope in the fulfillment of his own mission, and having, moreover, only an advisory voice. Was this really what the bishops "of the majority" wanted? As it is, several bishops now are calling for a restructuring of the episcopal Synod.

Cardinal Alfrink told *ICI* (7-15-69): "It would be reducing and obscuring the importance of the Synod to believe that the Synod involved no more than listening to what had been decided, and proceeding to the execution of these decisions." The second Vatican Council, he explained, "had emphasized the importance of attributing to the mission of the bishops of the world, united with the pope, a theological and dogmatic value equal to that of the primacy of Peter."

Others, too, have been emphasizing this point. Uniate Archbishop Zoghby of Baalbek, Lebanon, asks: "Must we wait until the next Council to progress from a consultative Church to a collegial Church?" (*ICI*, 9-15-69).

"If the collegiality proclaimed in theory by the Council is not put into practice," writes Archbishop Baldassarri of Ravenna, "it is worthless" (*Sette Giorni*, July 1969). Auxiliary bishop Butler of Westminster wonders whether, at the present moment, prudence might not suggest a fuller implementation of the principle of collegiality than it did for the past century (*Tablet*, 9-20-69).

These demands coincide with those of Msgr. Philips in the previously mentioned study, a coincidence all the more striking because of its appearance outside the context of the Suenens debate. After having sketched a spiritual portrait of the Roman Pontiff as Eastern and Western Christians view him, the commentator on *Lumen Gentium* adds:

Such a perspective will become "credible" in the Western Church if the pope, first and head of all the bishops, successors of the apostles, gives (for instance) to the Synod of Bishops at the opportune time the authority to exercise real deliberative power in expression of their concern for all the Churches (*IDO-C International*, 9-15-69).

But if episcopal collegiality has not yet attained its due status, the reason might lie in the attitude of the bishops themselves. Indeed, writes Cardinal Koenig, Archbishop of Vienna:

To be effective, episcopal collegiality does not depend on what the bishops have the right to do, but on what they have the will to do. Thus effectiveness depends on their own initiative, on their own sense of responsibility, on their civic courage, if you will.

The bishops, as a college, will have the right to speak in the measure that they take the initiative (*Le Monde,* 9-11-69).

Cardinal Koenig called upon the bishops to take the initiative. The word "initiative" had been used in the commentary on *Lumen Gentium* by Msgr. Philips which appeared long before the Suenens interview. He stated that any truly collegial act of the episcopacy on the universal level always implies papal "consent." However, "neither the Constitution nor the *Nota Praevia* prescribes the precise manner in which the pope is to give his consent. Such juridical forms vary with the times. As it was said at the conclusion of the paragraph, it would be sufficient for the pope to approve or at least "to accept freely" the decisions of the bishops, whether in a body or dispersed. *It follows that the initiative for a collegial act need not originate with the Roman See.* The history of the early Councils further emphasizes this point" (*L'Eglise et son mystère au deuxième Concile du Vatican,* p. 295). These lines are an invitation to act.

Bishop Butler in the London *Tablet* (9-20-69) noted that "Vatican II has reaffirmed *both* this papal primacy *and* the supreme and full power over the universal Church of the episcopal college. It is now for theologians to propose a theoretical reconciliation of these two affirmations.

"The pope, of course, 'may' (in the practical sense) always freely exercise his supreme and full authority. But the question (and it is fundamental to our view of the Church) is whether this legal freedom, which cannot be questioned, carries with it a moral freedom." In short, there is quite a difference between juridical legality and moral prudence.

A final point is the notion of the Church and the place of the collegial "perspective" emphasized by Father Bouyer. If this is exaggerated in one direction or another, he says, "it would mean the end of the Catholic Church, as it devolves in its basic structures, from the apostolic Church, instituted by Christ himself *on the foundation of the Twelve, Peter being one of them* but having among all, and with respect to all, *an irreplaceable role" (France Catholique,* 6-27-69).

PRIMACY AND COLLEGIALITY

Discussion of the relationship between primacy and collegiality, between pope and bishops, is a delicate, complex and serious matter.

To view this relationship solely as an encounter of "powers," limiting the perspective to such juridical questions, would be to limit severely the content and, consequently, to falsify the concept of this relationship. In the domain of Church affairs an act may be valid, even necessary, and, nonetheless, be lacking in concern for the rights of others, be abusive in certain respects, be devoid of Christian spirit, be regrettable, on the whole, for the pastoral life of the Church.

One fact seems indisputable: the increasingly important role and place of the papacy in the Church since the eleventh century, and particularly since Vatican I. It has been a steady process of reinforcing, of accentuating, and of putting in increasing evidence the papal role. Indeed, Vatican II seemed to be the beginning of an era of better *balance;* in fact, it recalled the fundamental position of the college of bishops in the governing of the universal Church and the proper mission of the assembly of Christians in the Church community. This search for balance—which is truly in the logic of Vatican II—must necessarily bring about a better understanding of the papacy. It will not appear any more as the unique subject of all power, of all authority, of all truth, of all rights. This is simply a necessary and welcome return to the "whole truth," *integra veritas.*

In reality, the dogmatic declarations of Vatican I concerning infallibility and primacy have been constantly and continually exaggerated. A book devoted entirely to the subject would hardly suffice to indicate this in detail. Here are some remarks, which could be helpful in this study.

EXAGGERATION OF PAPAL INFALLIBILITY

With regard to the infallible magisterium of the pope, Vatican I had defined that when the Roman Pontiff makes a dogmatic judgment fulfilling all of the conditions outlined for an *ex cathedra* pronouncement, he enjoys the divine assistance promised to the successor of Peter; thus, the declaration he makes is free from error, infallible and unreformable. The "prerogative of infallibility," *the* dogma of Vatican I, is fulfilled in reality *reipsa et actu* (Mansi 52, 1213) whenever the Pope "defines," and only when he defines; *solummodo quando* insisted Msgr. Gasser, in the name of the Delegation of the Faith, before the final vote (Mansi 52, 1213). According to Vatican I, the pope has, therefore, permanently the possibility of rendering an infallible judgment; this prerogative, however, is only actualized when he defines in fact, *quando definitivo actu proclamat* (No. 25, *Lumen Gentium*). Even so, some of the faithful believe, if not theoretically at least in practice, that the pope is always infallible. This is a considerable exaggeration.

Msgr. Gasser—unlike others—does not speak of the pope "alone." When the pope defines, he explained, this magisterial act is dictated by him, not by the college of bishops. For validity, the act does not require—at least not in *strict and absolute* necessity—the consent of the bishops. It is this *strict and absolute* character which is the crux of the problem. For, Gasser continues, we may indeed speak of a *real opportuneness, even of a relative necessity* for the consent of the bishops (Mansi 52, 1213).

Msgr. Gasser's entire article should be read. Here is what the reporter for the Delegation of the Faith had to say concerning the source of the infallibility of the Church. It would be useful to compare it to the thesis of Marcel Clement, quoted above.

Is it the bishops? Is it the pope? No, Msgr. Gasser answers, it is the Lord. It was He who promised the assistance of the Spirit to the college of bishops.

"Of course," he explains, "*de fide* decrees, even those

promulgated by general councils, are infallible and definitive only after being confirmed by the pope. But the reason for this is not the one given sometimes—I regret to say—even in this aula, as if all infallibility was residing in the pope alone and from him communicated to the whole Church. *I fail to see how infallibility could be communicated!* The real reason why the bishops, even united in Council, are not infallible without being united with the pope in matters of faith and morals is this: Christ promised infallibility to the entire magisterium of the Church, that is, to the apostles united with Peter" (Mansi 52, 1216).

This was what was put to the Fathers of Vatican I before their vote.

In brief, as Dom Guéranger himself stated very clearly in his book *De la monarchie pontificale* (1870, pp. 125-126): "In the council, it is the Holy Spirit who presides over this concord; and the infallible doctrinal judgment declared by pope and bishops is one unique judgment, having one unique infallibility, the infallibility of the teaching Church. . . . In a Council, there is but one simultaneous judgment; the Spirit enlightens the entire body."

EXAGGERATION OF THE PRIMACY

Vatican I defined the *fact* of a primacy of jurisdiction, making it precise that it is full and supreme, ordinary and immediate, truly episcopal and universal. Setting out from there and speculating in the abstract as to the meaning which might be given these terms, a *theology* of primacy has been developed, proceeding from conclusion to conclusion with extraordinary exuberance. What is worse, this *theology* of primacy has for some replaced the *dogma* of primacy.

Now, primacy itself—as referred to in *Pastor Aeternus*, mentioned previously—has as its goal *the unity of faith and communion*. This is the purpose but also the limit of this prerogative. "*Societates sunt ut fines*," Cardinal Ottaviani explains clearly in his *Institutiones iuris publici ecclesiastici* (Vol. I, No. 21). Wherever the *unitas fidei et communionis*, reasonably understood, is not at stake, we are outside the realm of primacy. Of course, primacy can be far-reaching: every person, every institution, every doctrine may be affected, but only within the limits of *unitas fidei et communionis*. And even in such an instance, the question remains whether an exercise of this primacy, along *with* bishops— especially *with* all the bishops—might not be more judicious, more adequate, more Christian.

The exaggeration of primacy is due also to many other factors which we can only touch on here. Once having demonstrated that the pope *may* intervene in a *particular* instance, the theory is advanced that the pope *must* intervene in all similar instances. On the basis of the fact that the pope may make decisions *without* the expressed collaboration of the bishops, it is claimed, as an ideal that the pope decides alone! From the fact that the pope *may reserve for himself* some important problems, it is looked upon as normal that he reserves to himself *every* more or less delicate or thorny problem. From the fact that the pope had, at a certain period of history, in order to suppress abuses, *reserved to himself* the nomination of bishops, the thesis is held that he *alone* has the *proper* authority to name all bishops. Similar cases are numerous. In this domain, dogmatists go far beyond canonists, who are more realistic. They, the dogmatists, reason in the abstract, from an imperfectly defined major premise —for even the *plenitudo protestatis* is limited (*coarctari*) by divine and natural law (Mansi 52, 1108-1109). Thus, their conclusions go far beyond the limits of truth. *Latius hos* and fallacies abound herein.

TOWARDS AN IMPLEMENTATION OF COLLEGIALITY

Because papal prerogatives had taken over almost the entire theology of the primacy, the divine right prerogatives of the bishops on the universal level were given merely a symbolic and virtual existence. Since Vatican I, many were of the opinion that ecumenical councils would cease to exist. Why have a council, they said, if the pope can govern alone?

Thus, this solemn manifestation of the college of bishops seemed outdated. The college itself was virtually forgotten; many of the bishops at the Council—and not only those who had received their theological formation at Rome—had never heard of it. It was rather a diffused ecclesial consciousness, a profound sense of the mystery of the Church, as also the systematic, clumsy and, at times, disdainful opposition of the minority, that brought the Council Fathers to realize, so rapidly, that episcopal collegiality was of primary importance for the welfare of the universal Church.

Various decisions (synod, bishops in the Curia) seem, apparently, to favor the growth of collegiality. In fact, and to speak very honestly, they rather disfavor collegiality. On the one hand, they only grant the bishops a juridical role (Curia) or a purely consultative role (synod); and law, for curial theologians, is transformed easily into dogma. On the other hand, the role of the papacy is amplified: the pope now presides over new institutions issued from the Council and over which the episcopate has no real power.

There is a long—a very long—way still to go before the principle of collegiality written into Vatican II is put into practice, really and not just formally; effectively, not merely in speeches; loyally, and not through diplomacy; from concern of dogma, and not merely from a sociological necessity; in its own right, not as a casual advice.

Without a true and authentic acceptance of these pronouncements of Vatican II, our Church will not have the "credibility" which can and which should be obvious to other churches working for the restoration of unity.

•   •

The essay by Karl Rahner, S. J., quoted in Chapter 4, is especially relevant here:

The Demands of Reform

There has been lively discussion at all levels of the Church of the famous interview given by Cardinal Suenens. The pope himself commented on it indirectly. People feel that they have to take a position for or against. The pope has made it clear that objections raised against the holy see will be assessed humbly and with sincere objectivity. It appears, therefore, that one need have no doubt at all that the Synod will be able to realize something along the lines of Cardinal Suenens' aims, even if the Roman reaction to his interview has not been precisely friendly.

PUBLIC OPINION AS NECESSARY PRESSURE

It is quite impossible today to limit an episcopal synod to the rôle of giving advice only on those questions about which it has been explicitly consulted. Initiatives coming "from below" can only be of service to the pope in his own mission. This is especially true when "from below" includes representatives of the universal episcopate, which, with the pope as its head, holds after all the highest power in the Church. Further, a synod is certainly not the time to separate the pope from the rest of the episcopate and to emphasize his own special function.

Cardinal Suenens's interview made many important and highly desirable recommendations to the Synod and it can be considered as such an initiative "from below." It is inevitable, as always happens in such cases, that one will agree or disagree with this or that formulation or opinion. All aspirations and demands for reform in the Church and especially in the Roman Curia point to the need for a new synthesis, a new "balance" in the concrete application of contrasting ideas which together make up the real world and can never be transcended by a higher principle. That is why such a synthesis—between law and freedom, the unity of the Church in the papacy and the autonomy of the local Churches, and so on—is always historically conditioned. And so each synthesis is itself open to criticism and can be changed.

Courage as the surest way forward

A short article like this can obviously not answer all the important and detailed questions that the comprehensive interview of Cardinal Suenens raised. But before one decides whether one is for or against the interview, one should study it carefully. I am afraid that many admirers and many opponents of this statement have not read it carefully and that they arbitrarily read into it what suits them or what annoys them. In this way they fail to do justice to this carefully weighed document, which formulates its demands clearly and concretely without ever being theoretically one-sided and so in this sense "heretical." Everyone knows how difficult it is to do that. What usually emerges is an apparently wise and carefully balanced "on the one hand and on the other" line of reasoning which has no real dynamic for the future. Or else one tries to base justified practical demands on theoretical positions which lead to dogmatic error. Whoever feels that he thinks in a more balanced way than Suenens must ask himself whether his thoughts for a better future for the Church are capable of being made effective, or whether he is simply using his "balance" to dispense himself from really doing anything.

The difficulty in evaluating Cardinal Suenens' interview seems to me to be a question of whether there is still much time in the Church in which to make the necessary changes, or whether we already have "enough disquiets" in the Church. Naturally, put in this way, the question is posed in much too stark a fashion. It may be that there are some questions which it would be better to leave alone, at least for the time being. It depends, it should be clearly stated, on which questions they are. But there are very many pressing questions of great importance which can only be solved by very considerable changes in the constitution and the life of the Church. Such changes must of course preserve meaningful continuity with past history. But there is a very bad method, still widespread today, of only allowing changes when they are squeezed out of the authorities of the Church as the smallest possible concessions, and then they appear as tiny modifications of a previously ordained and sacrosanct pattern. This procedure today is damaging, it has fallen behind the actual practice of the Church and decreases its credibility. Real change is needed on many issues, not hushing-up tactics and small concessions laboriously won.

For example, one need only look at the Church's laws on marriage, above all on mixed marriages. The world is never free from compromises, but when a compromise is based on a false principle, then no possible progress can be achieved. Suenens is right, for example, to wonder with some anxiety what the new canon law of the Church will look like. Will it really be a "framework," which will leave room for the bishops of each nation to develop the particular characteristics of their own Churches? Or will the new Code—apart from a few "contemporary" modifications—be like the old Code, a detailed law for what is in practice a highly centralized administration? Will bishops in the future still have to ask Rome whether they may permit their faithful to receive Communion in the hand or not? Must Roman prelates and canonists with a juridical mentality administer a law on mixed marriages when they cannot be capable of assessing the situation in Germany, where one million two hundred thousand people are unlawfully married in the eyes of the Church?

The fundamental question is really whether much that is very important in the Church should change, in spite of all the uncertainty and unrest that it would cause, or whether, wearying of all this uncertainty and unrest, we should go back to a triumphalistic, monolithic system which belongs to the age before Vatican II. At the present time the Church certainly cannot stand still. Should she go backwards or forwards? Should she take a risk or should she embark on a work of restoration?

It should no longer be possible to deny that the only right way forward at the present moment is that of taking a risk when in doubt. The experiment of Vatican II can still fail. But if it fails, it will be because we lack the courage to carry on the experiment in the spirit of that Council. Suenens' interview flows from the conviction that today risk is the surest way and from the conviction that the experiment of Vatican II must be carried courageously forward. That is why his interview could provide a sort of programme for the Synod of Bishops, which, after all, has the task of realizing the fundamental programme of Vatican II in the spirit of Vatican II.

THE CHURCH AS AN OPEN SOCIETY

The basic problem raised by the debate on Cardinal Suenens' interview can be put in yet another way. Many people think sincerely that it is illegitimate to raise questions about issues on which the pope must finally decide. But when we realize that in a certain sense there never is a final word, not even in *ex cathedra* definitions, which are always open to subsequent interpretation, and when we leave aside the question we have already examined about the need for openness in discussion, then one must ask quite simply: because the pope has "the last word," must he therefore have also the last word but one? And the answer to this question is no. Furthermore, anyone who, as a responsible Christian sharing in the life of the Church, makes a contribution and speaks the "last word but one," cannot be said to be behaving in a manner disrespectful to the pope or to the papacy. This is true even when he says things that are contrary to the opinion of the pope. . . .

It is perfectly possible to be very holy and selfless and yet to make a faulty judgment about situations and therefore go wrong on subsequent decisions. In such matters, as every Catholic child knows, a pope is not infallible. Why then do so many people find it shocking and a matter for reproach when they hear someone say that on a particular question Rome has not made the right decision? Such a critic can have just as much faith in the primacy of the pope, and just as much respect for the pope, as others. St. Thomas Aquinas says of the conflict between Peter and Paul in Galatians 2:14:

> This incident gives an example first of all to ecclesiastical authorities: an example of humility, in that they should allow themselves to be criticized by subjects. Secondly, it gives an example to the subjects: an example of the zeal and sincerity they should have so that they are not afraid to rebuke their superiors, particularly when the matter is public and threatens danger to many.

It is quite clear that Paul did not ask Peter for permission to rebuke him. One can argue about whether the rebuke was justified or not. But one certainly cannot argue about whether one may or may not say something critical to the highest authorities in the Church, without first having been invited to do so.

The Church has a highest authority, but it is not a closed, totalitarian system in which everything is allowed and determined by a single immanent point. The Church is an open society. The first reason for this is that the formal code of law in the Church is only one element in the system and is itself subject to other factors, and so the system is never finally closed in a totalitarian way. The Holy Spirit has not obliged himself to ensure that all good impulses and tendencies in the Church flow from the Petrine office. Of course nobody asserts this theoretically, but in practice some people react so sensitively to differences of opinion as to make it seem that they really believe that theory. The Church is an open society in which original and spontaneous initiatives can spring from very different sources. They do not have to be previously calculated or planned for.

It follows that there is now more scope in the life of the Church for surprises and for conflicts than at a time at which the papacy practically, although not in theory, was considered as a center from which almost everything had to emanate and on which no one could exert influence without

being expressly invited to. Provided this plurality of opinions
and tendencies is grounded in real concern for the best possible fulfilment of the mission of the Church, then such conflicts will serve the Church better than the pretense that
there is complete agreement where there is not or admitting
only the abstract possibility of serious differences of opinion.
The Church would not be the Church of Christ if she could
not live with such conflicts. They are unavoidable, they can
be lived through, and they can be fruitful. There are certainly many Christians in the Church who view the coming
Synod of Bishops with anxious concern, precisely because
they love the Church. They are anxious because this new institution must gradually prove itself, something it has not so
far done. Cardinal Suenens' interview sketched out an
agenda for several such episcopal synods.

8

Church Institutions: A Critical Interpretation

Roger Aubert, who wrote this section, is Doctor of Theology and Professor of Church History at Louvain and editor of the Revue d'histoire ecclésiastique.

Several weeks before the Suenens interview, the London *Times* (4-5-69) editorially formulated the problem of institutions, a problem which is at the root of the growing malaise of much of the clergy and faithful:

The Council, without formally diminishing the authority of the papacy which its predecessor had defined, inscribed in its acts a complementary source of universal authority—namely, the college of bishops. Their collective authority was seen as coming not from papal delegation but from divine institution. At the level of doctrine this was clearly stated. But for the doctrine to have practical force, institutional arrangements are necessary to allow the collective voice of the bishops to be heard and to be decisive. Nothing has been done in that direction since the Council dispersed expect the weak innovation of an advisory Synod of Bishops. Exclusive reliance on centralism, which is the historic form of authority in the Roman Catholic Church, will not check the fragmentation which the pope so much deplores. The Vatican Council defined a co-equal and more hopeful principle of authority, but it has not yet been brought into play.

This text parallels strikingly a statement of Cardinal Pellegrino, Archbishop of Turin, one of the most noted figures of the Italian episcopate. His statement takes on added weight when one realizes its publication date, August 28, three months after the much-publicized and much-debated interview:

Concerning this interview, I try to understand it in the light of another extended interview which I had in Brussels (with the Cardinal) on January 17, during which these problems were debated at length. Except for an article by Father Rahner published in the German periodical *Publik* during the meeting at Chur—which struck me as the most profound interpretation—it seems that the press in general has not grasped the essential point of the interview: that the principle of collegiality proclaimed by the Council has not yet found practical and concrete application, capable of effectively influencing the life of the Church. The aim of the interview is to assure that the upcoming Synod, with the pope and the bishops in full agreement, find concrete ways of practicing this collegiality. This fundamental request seems clearly legitimate to my mind.

Other cardinals, as we know, have been less understanding. Without discussing those who judge it inadmissable even to think of publicly giving advice to the Sovereign Pontiff, let us note the reaction of Cardinal Léger, the former Archbishop of Montreal and a leader of progressive opinion during the Council. He expressed a fear that the decentralization of the Church proposed by Cardinal Suenens and the efforts to give a greater autonomy to local Churches might ultimately "reduce the role of the pope to that of a club president and the Church to an immense Rotary where people would come to exchange ideas and perhaps do a little bit of good."

These criticisms, and especially the misgivings of Cardinal Léger, inspired some interesting reflections in the American *Catholic Messenger* (7-3-69):

Cardinal Suenens, in the name of collegiality and coresponsibility in the Church, has "put it all together" in a dramatic public appeal for continued progress in decentralizing and defeudalizing the Church. Basically, he attempted to spell out the need for change in the way authority and unity are manifested in the Church and to indicate some of the practical changes this would require. . . . Reaction to Cardinal Suenens' statement has been depressing. . . . It seems appropriate that a man from North America should bring out, even if only implicitly, the issue of power hiding within this controversy. If we read Cardinal Léger correctly, he is saying: be careful with this talk of decentralization in the Church. Without the tight structure and rigorous discipline of the past, how will the Church be able to show an effective face of power to the world? How will the pope be able to function as an effective spokesman of millions? How will we be able to make legislators and premiers and presidents pay attention to us if we can no longer point to rigid lines of authority which enable the pope, in effect, to deliver millions of troops in solidarity on a given issue?

Cardinal Léger knows that structural discipline means political power. The critical question for effective action is this: How many troops can you deliver? And he also seems to recognize that the tried and true way to answer that question (with impressive numbers) is to impose the needed discipline from above.

Although we do not think the Church is in the world for the purpose of exercising power in the world's terms, in political terms, it has, nevertheless, functioned that way for a long time. Most of us are, in fact, accustomed to thinking of the Church as a power bloc. And we know that, in terms of power, Cardinal Léger is right: a clubby Church would have very little influence on the world.

What will happen if the Church gives up its highly structured, tightly disciplined institutional style of life and encourages a freedom-loving "evangelical" style which might be confused with Rotary clubs? Cardinal Suenens has not taken up this question directly—nor has anyone else that we know of. The Gospel does not even answer it: we are told there only to "Come, follow Me." The manner of the following is up to us in our time and place.

Alternatives to an institutional structure based on the political power model are not yet in sight. They will not be in sight until enough elements of the Church take the risk of striking out on new paths of Christ-following to build our experience of freedom in unity to the level where a new-found faith in evangelical freedom takes over the consciousness of the whole Church. We have an appalling lack of that faith at present. It is this that Cardinal Suenens is trying to push us toward.

This article seems to set up a total opposition, as if solidly organized structures were necessarily incompatible with the true spirit of the Gospel. Henri Fesquet, in *Le Monde* makes the necessary distinctions:

Do not the more perceptive Christians see beyond certain inevitable excesses of such a period of turmoil—perhaps more or less in a confused manner—but nevertheless see that it would be folly to remove the "institution" from the "event"? This is actually at the core of the question. What is necessary is that the institution serve the event and not be an obstacle to it. This, unfortunately, is far from being the situation today.

It is precisely from the perspective of a new synthesis between the institutional and the "prophetic" aspects of the Church's government that Hans Küng, professor of theology at Tübingen, has used Cardinal Suenens' program of reform to sketch an ideal portrait or (as sociologists would say) "model" of a pope responding to the still confused, but more and more precise aspirations of an ever increasing sector of Christianity today. Even if the contrast is exaggerated, as the author later agreed, the article is important both in itself and because of the reactions it triggered. Here is the central element of the article. The rest of this text will be found at the end of this chapter, beginning on page 197.

Such a pope would be imbued with an authentic and evangelical concept of the Church, rather than a juridical, formalistic, static and bureaucratic one. He would see the mystery of the Church in the light of the gospel, of the new covenant, not as a centralized administrative unit where bishops are mere delegates and executive assistants of the pope, but as a Church realized authentically in the local Churches (communities, cities, dioceses, countries all considered individually) which form one communion in the unique Church of God and who are linked in this manner to the Church of Rome as the focal point of their unity.

Such a pope would not consider the decentralization of powers as a dangerous prelude to possible schism. Far from blocking legitimate diversity, he would encourage it in the areas of spirituality, liturgy, theology, canon law and pastoral activity. His aim would not be to concentrate all authority on a single point, but to serve unpretentiously the immense diversity of the local Churches within the one Church; he would not suppress the pluralism of the diverse theologies by inquisitional methods of constraint as past ages had done, but would encourage their freedom and their service to the Church. He would not take jealous advantages of the plenipotential prerogatives in exercising an authority conceived according to the old order; he would exercise an authority of ministry in the spirit of the New Testament, taking into account the necessities of the present day: fraternal cooperation among equals, dialogue, consultation and collaboration between the bishops and the theologians of the Church universal, participation in decision-making by all concerned, and an invitation to coresponsibility.

In this way the pope would consider the papacy as a role within the Church: the pope would not be *above* or outside the Church, but *in* the Church, *with* the Church and *for* the Church. There would no longer be isolationism or triumphalism; the pope would no longer be separated from but united with the Church, a unity sought unceasingly and realized in a new way by him. In all important documents and grave decisions he would seek the collaboration of the bishops, the laity and the best theologians; and he would never repudiate them afterwards. If at some time he must act "alone," he must never act "apart," "separated" from the Church and the college of bishops, but in a spiritual communion and in an indissoluble solidarity with the Church universal. He would consider the assistance promised to Peter not as a personal inspiration but as the special help given within the deliberation and cooperation with the Church—a promise of the Spirit to the Church as a whole.

Thus, such a pope would be holding the reins on the administrative apparatus of the Curia, and would check its tendency toward hegemony. He would remove useless bureaucratic and administrative burdens from the center, and would concentrate a major effort on real internationalization and profound reform with the help of theologians, sociologists, business administrators, international organizations, and the like. He would encourage both an in-depth study of the system of nunciatures and a renewal of the curial system according to objective and public criteria, a renewal which would remove any suspicion of high-handedness. He would organize cooperation according to the principle of subsidiarity and would transform, with improvements, the system of *ad limina* visits, the bishops' personal five-year reports, as well as many other things.

Thus, the pope would oppose not justice, but "juridicism"; not law, but legalism; not order, but immobility; not authority, but authoritarianism; not unity, but uniformity. He would be a man chosen not by a college of cardinals dominated by one nationality, but by a body truly representative of the universal Church. The choice would be determined not by nationality but by merit. This man would renounce the powers which he holds through secondary and extrinsic titles (metropolitan of the ecclesiastical province of Rome, primate of Italy, patriarch of the West, sovereign of the Vatican City State); this man would concentrate on his pastoral task towards the universal Church and towards his own Roman diocese; this man would draw all toward him with his pastoral concern.

Thus, the pope would acquire a new concept of his role within the Church and within modern society. In agreement with the bishops he would exercise his ministry for the ecclesial community and its oneness in a new way; he would give new life to missionary endeavor of the Church in the world, pursuing efforts for peace, for disarmament, for the improvement of social conditions among races and peoples with much greater influence. Thus, both within the Christian *oikumene* and outside of it, he could give witness by his words and by his works to the voice of the Good Shepherd. In the spirit of the Gospel of Jesus Christ, he would be the leader and the inspiration of the post-conciliar reform; and Rome would become once again a place of encounter, of dialogue, and of loyal and friendly cooperation.

According to Cardinal Suenens—and he is not alone in this opinion—this is a picture of the papacy as it might be. Nothing he says is in contradiction with Vatican II. And if there be contradiction with Vatican I, it is because Vatican I needs to be corrected and completed in the light of the Gospel—the clear intention of Vatican II. In any case, the juridical categories of Vatican I do not suffice to define a way, upon the basis of scripture, in which the ministry of Peter can be considered, as a *service toward the universal church, a primacy of service* in the full biblical sense of the word—and this altogether independently of any historical or exegetical justification for the succession of the Roman bishop which is, for many, a secondary consideration. A primacy of service would be more than a "primacy of honor." This later is unforgivable in a servant church; by its passivity, it can be of service to no one. A primacy of service would also be more than a "primacy of jurisdiction." Considered from the viewpoint of power and authority, jurisdictional primacy creates an irreparable misunderstanding. Taken literally, it does not consider the essential service; taken in the biblical sense, the ministry of Peter can only be a pastoral primacy, pastoral service to the universal Church. As such, it is founded solidly in the New Testament, regardless of the question of succession. As such, it can be of great value to the whole of Christendom today. Once more, John XXIII showed clearly, although sketchily and in a pragmatic perspective, that this different pope is possible.

This text confirms what a systematic analysis of the religious and secular press reveals: one of the crucial points of the debate reopened by the intervention of Cardinal Suenens is the question of relations between the Holy See and the national episcopates and of the practical exercise of collegiality in the Church. Obviously, the interview focused on other problems as well, problems such as the relations between the bishop and his people which are very important for the *aggiornamento* of postconciliar ecclesiastical institutions. However, the newspapers seem to have predominantly emphasized the tension which has been developing since the Council between the center and the periphery. Four issues in particular have been receiving attention: the role of the Roman Curia; the role of the Sacred College of Cardinals, especially in regard to its election of the Sovereign Pontiff; the function of nuncios; and closely connected to it, the methods of selecting bishops. Although, actually, these are only different aspects of one fundamental problem, it has seemed preferable to consider them separately.

A. The Roman Curia

Cardinal Suenens has insisted upon the necessity of reforming the Curia, a reform which would call upon the advice of specialists in the fields of sociology, management, human relations, and even political science. In his criticism of the present operation of the Church's central organization, he was not calling individual men to account; he was rather denouncing a "system" which imprisons these men and which urgently needs to be changed.

The temptation in the Church today is to burden the Curia with all the sins of the people. For this reason many have joined in unreserved applause of the Cardinal's call for a radical reform. To cite one example which contains an interesting comparison:

On any number of occasions in political life we have seen a fellow whom we know and have confidence in named head of some government bureau: defense, economic affairs, education, etc. We have told ourselves that with "him," at least, things will soon change; yet nothing did change. Nothing changed because, even though this department head had power and had authority, he was a prisoner of the system and of the inertia built into the system. The same is true in the Church. It is the strong inertia of the Roman Curia which must be overcome if we are to give the pope free exercise of his authority once again (C. Paquot, *La Voix du Temps*, 6-8-69).

Others, while recognizing the vast need for continuing improvement, thought the cardinal had been too harsh. Antoine Wenger writes (*La Croix*, 5-29-69):

Among the institutions not considered in the Constitution on the Church was the Roman Curia. The cardinal considered it with his own severe criticism. Like all human institutions the Curia always needs to reform its ways and its spirit, to discover every day the meaning of service and the respect of persons, to work in a spirit of love and humility.

It is true that one meets certain persons in the Curia who exercise their functions with a will to power, believing themselves permanently charged with the authority which is only temporarily in their hands for the sake of service. There are those persons who hold back reforms and who more or less openly contradict the letter and spirit of Vatican II. If we take an inventory of Curial reforms, however, we will find the results quite encouraging. Future historians will stand astonished at the amount of reform brought about by Pope Paul in so short a time.

Basically, does not all of this come down to the psychological difference between the half-empty bottle and the half-full one? Or to use another comparison: the varying degree of optimism during a steep mountain climb depending on whether our attention is directed back on the distance covered, or forward on the distance still left to climb.

This is also what *Mundo Social* (7-15-69) published by the Spanish Jesuits has well noted:

In his declarations, Cardinal Suenens gives little attention to the progress already made by the Church in the area of collegiality, in the reform of the Curia, which has reached an acceptable level of internationalization in its highest offices, etc. . . . It is not that he denies the value of all these things, but his aim is to point out what remains to be done and to protest the prevailing spirit of the Curia which could stifle even the most hopeful initiatives. He shows how very little has been realized in the spectrum of conciliar achievements and that the foot dragging in achieving the reform of the Church is having disastrous results.

But some ask—and their reaction definitely deserves our attention—if it is not oversimplifying the problem to content ourselves with opposing "center" to "periphery." This is particularly the point of a layman from Uruguay, Hector Borrat, editor of a major Latin American Catholic magazine, *Vispera:*

First, the cardinal, following a pattern fairly current among critics of the Roman Curia, hits only at the "center," Rome. He establishes, however by contrast and without shading, the anonymous local Churches of the "periphery." He presents a confrontation between a visible Rome and a nebula of Churches which, though local, are not localized, between real and ideal. It should not be surprising, then, that the criticism is focused in a single direction, while the admiring praise flows forth toward the local Churches, because of their seemingly unique privilege of being situated outside the boundaries of the Vatican City State.

After much development, which will be discussed further on, and some examples of the assistance which the Roman center may furnish to the Church of the periphery in precisely this area of *aggiornamento* recommended by the Council, the article ends:

To emphasize only decentralization would be to neglect the great historical currents of the world which is, itself, traveling toward a gradual centralization for better or worse. To decentralize the Church while political and economic power is becoming centralized, is to make her dispersed and feeble, to decapitate her, to prevent unified action, and unified reaction against the ever more pressing pretentions of Caesar and his court of merchants and generals.

For us in Latin America, Catholic and ecumenical centralization is a matter concerning the life or death of our autonomous local Churches. To dissolve the bonds which unite us to the Roman "center" would be to surrender ourselves to the wealthy Churches of those nations which hold economic world power and enrich themselves by exploiting the richness of our human and natural resources.

The remarks of Stephen Dessain of the Birmingham Oratory also indicate the positive and beneficial role which can be played by the intervention of Roman authorities in the life of the local Churches:

> I heartily agree with so much of what Cardinal Suenens says that I hope I may say I am not altogether happy about some of the facts he adduces in support of his theses. He describes the way Roman authorities treated three of the heroes of his youth, Cardinal Mercier, Dom Lambert Beauduin, and Père Lebbe. It is true that, in the time of Pius X, Cardinal Mercier, like so many others, was suspected of Modernism, but earlier it was Leo XIII who gave him wholehearted and very much needed support when he was promoting a revivified scholasticism against the strong opposition of the conservatives of Louvain. And it was Leo XIII who sent a message to Cardinal Suenens' predecessor, I think through the nuncio, to the effect that "the persecution of Cardinal Mercier must stop completely."

There is a frank account of the trials of Dom Beauduin in the *Revue d'histoire ecclésiastique* (1966), according to which those ultimately responsible for them were certain of Dom Beauduin's Benedictine superiors in Belgium, the German Primate in Rome (of all Benedictines) and Cardinal Bourne. Then, did not the opposition to Père Lebbe come mostly from French missionary orders and from bishops in China drawn from those orders? Whereas it was the popes who supported his policies, Benedict XV with the encyclical *Maximum Illud* in 1919, and Pius XI, who consecrated in St. Peter's in 1926 the first six native Chinese Bishops, chosen by Père Lebbe himself.

The question is, therefore, more complex than it seems at first glance. It is undeniable—and Cardinal Suenens never sought to deny it—that, since the end of the Council, Paul VI has undertaken a series of reform measures, which have improved both the membership and the functioning of the Curia. It is no small credit, if one considers how difficult it is to reform a highly organized body, particularly if it is not a mere bureaucratic institution, but a "sacred administration" which is more or less unconsciously identified with the divine-right prerogatives of the Sovereign Pontiff. But it is also undeniable—and on this question the cardinal sought to sound an alarm, because he saw the situation from outside and realized its urgency—that there is a widespread impression that the essential reform is yet to be undertaken. This is not because of half-measures, often explained (as Abbé Laurentin has so subtly suggested) by the pope's own tactfulness in seeking "to reform without brutality, without violence, with respect for his closest neighbor—in this instance the Curia" (*Enjeu du deuxième synode*, p. 143). Rather, it is because the very place of the Curia in the Church needs to be fundamentally rethought.

The present state of the Curia is due in large measure to an historical evolution which cannot be held to have reached its ultimate and final conclusion. The immense increase in the number of problems Rome has reserved to itself since the Middle Ages and in the number of dioceses (fivefold within the past century) has resulted in a situation wherein the popes, increasingly unable to keep up with all the administrative problems, have relied on a bureaucracy which has developed steadily, and which inevitably has become identified with the pontiff himself. Thus, it has come to look on those activities of its offices as the normal exercise of papal primacy, whereas they are only a "personal privilege." The reform, initiated in 1967 and gradually implemented since then, has brought several interesting innovations which reduce the danger of the Curia's becoming a sociological entity closed in upon itself: the temporary nature of appointments to important positions, the new methods of information, the greater internationalization. But, on the other hand, this reform has resulted, through the very improvements it introduced in the operation of the Curia, in a further centralization of the Church's administration in the hands of the pope himself. This situation is not devoid of danger to his authority, as he becomes identified with every error committed in the Curia—the "Illich Questionnaire," for instance. But one may especially question the extent to which these reforms have corresponded to the spirit of Vatican II. During the Council, some had suggested that the Curia be reorganized as an "organism of collegiality," at the service of the college of bishops gathered around the successor of Peter and responsible, in union with him, for the Church universal.

Interesting, in this perspective, are the comments of Hector Borrat, who has already shown himself to be in anything but complete favor of the cardinal's suggestions:

> The college of bishops need a curia for the simple reason that it can only exercise direction of the universal Church when it itself is gathered in Rome. Once its members have returned to the diaspora—their usual residence—the college of bishops must be represented by a permanent institution in continuity with itself, collegial like itself, and, consequently, equally capable of carrying out the collegial government of the Church. There is nothing to prevent this organization from being the Curia, named not only by the successor of Peter, but by the bishops of the world, a curia which would truly reflect the catholicity of the Church. Like the synod, the Curia must become a sort of representation of the local Churches, by means of appointments which depend both on the pope and on the episcopal college united with him.

It is the task of the canon lawyers and the sociologists to frame laws from these suggestions and to propose concrete forms of actualizing this hope which, although still vague, seems to be a step in the proper direction.

B. *The College of Cardinals*

In his book, *Coresponsibility in the Church,* Cardinal Suenens raises the question of the relations between the pope and his two advisory bodies, the Synod of Bishops and the College of Cardinals. He remarks that this problem, though delicate and complex, interests the whole Church. According to present legislation, the College of Cardinals elects the pope and thus, indirectly at least, determines the general orientation of the Church's pastoral activity in the world.

The *New York Times* (3-30-69) commented as follows: "Leon-Joseph Cardinal Suenens, primate of Belgium, has suggested that the synod take over the task of electing popes, and he was recently backed by Bishop Alexander Carter, head of the Canadian Catholic Episcopal Conference. In an interview in the American Catholic weekly, *Ave Maria,* Bishop Carter declared: 'It is almost unbelievable that we will go on forever having people electing a pope who have not themselves been elected by their own peers.'"

The further treatment of the issue by the Archbishop of Malines-Brussels in his interview brought many additional reactions. Antoine Wenger, for example, writing in *La Croix* (5-30-69), apparently after talking to various persons in Rome, discussed it with a prudence that hid its positive aspects:

In his interview Cardinal Suenens again raised the question of election of the pope. He places this problem, commendably, within the realm of theology. He quotes in this context the thinking of Bishop Butler, member of the Theological Commission at the Council, which is that at the death of a pope, authority in the Church devolves upon the college of bishops as such. The cardinals' privilege of electing the pope is then only justified by reason of some sort of implicit delegation of this right by the world body of bishops. Cardinal Suenens wonders whether the election should not then fall upon the presidents of the conferences of bishops, since they are the collegial grouping, rather than upon the College of Cardinals, which merely forms an advisory council for a pope.

Paul VI, in his speech to the new cardinals, May 1, has reaffirmed that the election of the pope is the prerogative of the Sacred College. At the same time, though, he gave the College a more universal representation. However, the fact remains that in the future there will continue to be an ever greater number of aged cardinals retiring from their governing activities in the Church because of the age limits. This is a very real anomaly. Would it not, then, be possible to remedy this inconvenience by having those presidents of conferences, who are not themselves cardinals, come together with the college of cardinals for the election of a pope. It is good at this point not to lose sight of the fact that the pope is still bishop of Rome; that if the consent of the people is required in an episcopal election, this must also be the case for the Church of Rome, represented both symbolically and actually by the college of cardinals.

Much clearer and less reserved, however, was Bernard Häring, professor at the Alphonsianum in Rome, in approving Cardinal Suenens' suggestion that representatives of the episcopal body rather than the cardinals should elect the pope. This he said, would give the papacy "greater prestige," increasing its credibility. "If the cardinals, most of them old, one-third of them Italian, elect the next pope, papal prestige will diminish. If the episcopates around the world elect the best man, he will be one of vigor and will offer a totally different image. And if the bishops of a diocese are elected by clergy and laity, then the new pope, elected by these bishops, would represent the people of God."

A French theologian Louis Bouyer, in a long if rather confused article in *La France Catholique* (6-27-69), took a strong stand against the proposal to fuse the College of Cardinals with the episcopal synod. That would

... reduce the papacy, under the guise of making it more representative, to an emanation of the universal Church. ... In a word, the synod has shown itself to be a means of bringing together the collegiality of bishops with the primacy of the pope. This is an intermediate means between the necessarily extraordinary manifestation of collegiality, around and in union with the pope, which is the ecumenical council, and the ordinary exercise of collegiality, which is hardly organized and which tends to be ineffective because of the great number and dispersion of the episcopal sees.

On the other hand, the college of cardinals is a means of effectively and permanently bringing together the primacy of the pope with the exercise, ordinary or extraordinary, dispersed and therefore implicit or in council and therefore explicit, of the college of bishops.

One of these organizations is new in form but traditional in principle, namely, the gathering of bishops around the visible head of the college. The other is an organization now being renovated, and liable to further modification in the future, in its contacts with the entire episcopate and with the universal Church. It is a necessary organization if the unifying role of the pope is to be effective. The former serves the purpose of representing the members of the episcopal college to the presiding member of the college, the pope; the latter serves the function of representing the pope himself in his unique role of unifying the whole body of bishops, and indeed, of unifying the entire Church.

This twofold schema, nevertheless, seems to derive more from *a priori* speculation than from observation of facts, of the theological milieu which is the life of the Church in its centuries-long theological and historical development. Father Bouyer does not pretend, of course, as did some medieval theologians, that the cardinalate, highest degree of the ecclesiastical hierarchy, is of divine institution; he does recognize that "in many aspects it appears as an institution simply ecclesiastical, and therefore, reformable." But he judges that "in its essence, it corresponds to so fundamental a place in the life of the Church, that it is within the competency neither of the pope nor of an ecumenical council to alter it as presently suggested." Is this not to absolutize the cardinalate in a fashion not easily justified by history?

In fact, "cardinals" are mentioned from the beginning of the Middle Ages, but these were the pastors of major churches and deacons responsible for important administrative or charitable works, with the privilege of assisting the bishop in his cathedral on major feast days.

Meanwhile, the pope began to request the presence of neighboring bishops at his liturgical functions. These "suburban" bishops also participated in Roman synods, where questions dealing not only with the concerns of the diocese of Rome but those of the bishop of Rome as primate of Italy and patriarch of the West, and even as pastor of the church universal, were discussed. But this participation in the supra-diocesan tasks of the bishop of Rome was not limited to the "cardinal bishops"; any bishop passing through Rome during a synod took part on a level of equality. Thus, it seems that it was as bishops, and not as cardinals, that the suburban bishops had a role in the synods.

According to the famed historian of canon law, S. Kuttner, of the Pontifical Commission on the Science of History, and other recent historians, it was not until the Gregorian reform of the eleventh century that a progressive evolution trans-formed the essentially liturgical function of the Roman cardi-nals into the church's principal governing body. The pope's desire to avoid the rivalries of the great Roman families, and later the intervention of the German emperor in papal elec-tions, eventually brought Nicholas II in 1059 to reserve the election of the bishop of Rome to the cardinal bishops. They were joined at the end of the following century by the priest and deacon, cardinals of the Roman clergy. Thus it was that the Roman cardinals acquired a considerable increase not only of prestige but also of influence as direct assistants to the pope, whose centralizing influence in the life of the West-ern churches increased steadily from the time of Gregory VII. The importance of the cardinals was further strength-ened by the predominant role which some of them played in the politics of the Church as legates or negotiators of the Holy See in secular controversies which had brought pope and emperor into conflict.

One consequence of this evolution was the admittance to the Sacred College of an increasing number of non-Roman clergy. Until the end of the Middle Ages, it was usual for such outside members to establish themselves at Rome; but when the Council of Trent decreed that bishops must main-tain residence in their own dioceses, the presence of the foreign cardinals became problematical. Realizing the ad-vantages of having the universal Church represented in the Sacred College, the Trent Fathers expressed their wish that the pope continue to recruit cardinals from every nation, but no longer asking them to abandon their flocks. While the organization of the Roman congregation by Sixtus V (1586) was gradually reducing the importance of the consistory, the proportion of "foreign" cardinals continued to increase. A factor behind this increase was the interest of rulers in acquiring a right of supervision and a voice in papal elections. Eventually, there evolved an official right whereby the more important princes were allowed to submit to the pope a fixed number of national cardinals, called "crown cardinals," for election to the College.

Father Bouyer insists very emphatically that the pope is not, according to Catholic theology, a "super-bishop" who stands above and outside the rest of the bishops but rather the first of the bishops, that is to say, primarily the head of the local Church like other bishops. From this he concludes that it would be a kind of theological error to seek to confide the election of the pope to the college of bishops; rather, it must remain by right with the members of his local Church. But the rapid overview just given of the historical development shows just what sort of juridical fiction is involved in pretending that today's College of Cardinals is the local clergy of the Roman church.

It must be added, moreover, that involving the universal episcopate in the election of the successor of Peter would not, in any sense, eliminate the participation, even the predominance, of the sacred college in his election. A number of possibilities exist. One solution might be to restrict participation in the conclave to active cardinals (that is, to exclude those who have reached the age limit and those Roman cardinals who have no direct Curial responsibilities) but to include those bishops who by right belong to the synod but who are not cardinals. Another possibility is to give the episcopate its own voice in the election of cardinals, currently a purely personal prerogative of the pope. The idea suggested by Cardinal Suenens in his interview, that "the personal advice of the episcopal synod of the country concerned be taken into account," so that the creation of future cardinals would no longer seem to derive from the "good pleasure of the prince" was greeted by some with indignation. But if for centuries the popes had judged it quite right to allow secular rulers predominant voice in the appointment of certain cardinals, it does not seem at all improper that such a right be accorded to bishops representing diverse sections of the People of God.

These are merely suggestions: others are still possible. Here lie the research possibilities for the specialists. It is up to technical journals to take the lead on this issue and on others, as the daily and weekly press have done. One thing is certain: the expressed desire in the Church to see the meaning and the structure of the College of Cardinals seriously rethought in order to integrate this institution better into episcopal collegiality—while not restricting the supreme and universal authority of the papacy.

C. The Mission of Nuncios

The most criticized passage in the cardinal's interview is that relating to the nuncios. Thus, Father Wenger comments in *La Croix* (5-29-69): "The portrait of nuncios which Cardinal Suenens draws is anything but flattering. One is almost led to believe that it results from a particular situation under which the Archbishop of Brussels suffered. Nonetheless, the generalization is unjust."

Hector Borrat, who has been quoted above, takes on even more determinedly the defense of nuncios, this time appealing to examples from Latin America: "The nuncio is not always an obstacle: sometimes, it is he who fills the place, which conservatism, or fear, or simply the shepherd's political incapacity has left vacant" (ICI, 9-15-69).

There is no denying that this aspect should not be forgotten. The voices raised in Spain and Poland draw attention to the helpful role of a nuncio in stimulating a phlegmatic or timorous bishop and in pressing through certain pastoral or social ventures encouraged by Rome against the immobilism of a traditionalist milieu. Despite the truth of this, it has nonetheless been recognized that the Cardinal has put his finger on a real problem here, a problem that is not to be evaded. To remain with examples from Latin America, let us consider one such acknowledgment from the theologian and very popular public figure, Jorge Mejia (*Criterio*, 7-26-69):

> Where does this analysis lead us? Cardinal Suenens suggests that a local bishop, a member of the Conference, be more especially concerned about the relations with Rome. The same could be said for relations with the state, with the difference that this would normally be the duty of the president of the Conference.
>
> Does this imply abolishing the institution of the nunciatures? I would be the first to admit that this proposal is hardly practical. The Holy See has a good number of diplomatic personnel in its service, a training center in Rome (the Pontifical Academy), and a vast choice of candidates. All of this cannot end immediately. Others will say that the right of diplomatic immunity will always be useful and will permit unhampered communication between the bishops and Rome. Other advantages can also be pointed out; but there are many disadvantages as well among which the financial and economic is not the least important. But the most important is without a doubt the inherent ambiguity of the office of nuncio today, as implied by the Council.
>
> What is asked for, therefore, is that this reality be taken into account; that a reorientation of this ecclesiastical institution begin in the manner that the times and the documents indicate; that new solutions be looked for and applied, for example, lay envoys; but, above all, that a way be found to implement the recommendation of the Council, namely, "to define more rigorously" this function and office. The rest will follow.

After the above-quoted reservation Father Wenger also added: "We also believe that the evolution of relations between the Holy See and the States, especially the establishment of organizational ties between Rome and the episcopal conferences, will entail a profound change in the functions of nuncios."

The Council expressly requested that the function of the papal representatives be more clearly determined and, especially, that their role, properly ecclesial, be better set off. Yet

just a few weeks after the publication of Cardinal Suenens'
interview, there appeared from Rome a *motu proprio* on "the
functions of representatives of the Sovereign Pontiff" (*Sollicitudo omnium Ecclesiarum,* 6-24-69). Italian journalist, G.
Zizola presented it in the *Informations catholiques internationales* of July:

> The *motu proprio, Sollicitudo omnium Ecclesiarum,* which gives
> to nuncios primarily an ecclesial function and only secondarily
> a diplomatic function, is officially dated June 24. However, it
> was published in *L'Osservatore Romano* on June 23.
>
> Why such haste? According to some opinions, the pope wished
> to reply by this *motu proprio* to the issue as it was raised by
> Cardinal Suenens in his interview in the I.C.I., concerning the
> status and mission of the pontifical representatives, an issue
> which had particularly irritated the "political" milieu of the
> Roman Curia. Through the publication of this document Paul
> VI would have sought to allay the anxieties of the Curia, to
> grant, partially at least, certain requests for change, and to close
> definitely the debate concerning the much-contested legitimacy
> of this diplomatic apparatus of the Vatican.
>
> Reformation of the status of these papal representatives is at
> once characterized by the wish to preserve the traditional sys-
> tem and to renew it. It is a reform which is typically "Monti-
> nian." It was inconceivable that a pope, formed in the heart of
> Vatican diplomacy under Pius XII and who personally believes
> in the ever-present value of the diplomatic machine, could have
> gone along further than he did in the direction of Cardinal
> Suenens' theses. In a way the institution of the nunciature has
> been strengthened by this reversal of the classical functions.

Perhaps the publication of this document, which stresses
the fact that nuncios and apostolic delegates must not
supersede bishops, but must work in the authorized service
of the local Churches, was somewhat hurried along because
of the famous interview. But to the person who is familiar
with the plodding but careful pace taken in elaborating such
documents, it is evident that this one was not drawn up in

reply to the interview. Does it, however, in fact constitute a reply to the "desires" expressed by Cardinal Suenens?

A Belgian newspaper, *De Standaard* (6-25-69), the day following its publication, replied "no" most emphatically:

> There is no doubt whatever as to the author of this text: it was drawn up by the Curia without any deliberation with the bishops. To the Roman Curia this *motu proprio* was thought to be the best answer to the "rebel" Cardinal, the Archbishop of Malines. It is thought that this text will boomerang. It very evidently proves that Rome has not learned anything nor wishes to change anything. It does prove that Cardinal Suenens had in no way exaggerated the situation in his May 15 interview.

A little later, one of Germany's best canonists, Johannes Neumann of Tübingen University, penetratingly exposed the extent to which this *motu proprio*, despite a certain number of positive points, still remained outside the perspective that would be expected from a grounding in episcopal collegiality. The text of this article is found at the end of this section.

Basically, in the *motu proprio* on nuncios, as in the 1967 reform of the Curia, we are dealing with a series of real improvements that respond to the wants of the various sides, but improvements that have kept the old frame of reference and have not been sufficiently well restructured according to the theological principles put forth in the Constitution on the Church.

The nunciature in its present form dates back to the sixteenth century, a time when the pope was a sovereign of an Italian State and had important political interests to defend across the European board. It was also a time when the majority of religious questions had to be dealt with on the governmental plane, because of the close bond between throne and altar throughout Europe. It was normal that, under those conditions, the image of the nuncio was patterned after that of a diplomat (and for its model was chosen the world's best, the contemporary Venetian diplomacy). Moreover, direct communication between Rome and the various Churches of Christendom was slow and difficult, often complicated by strict government controls. The nuncio was the prelate who, because of his diplomatic function, would enjoy the greatest liberty of movement. Thus, we can understand how recourse to this diplomat could grow, and how he could become something of a natural intermediary between the Holy See and the local Churches, (his diplomatic immunity permitting him to transmit Roman instructions to bishops and first-hand information to Rome.)

With the loss of the Papal States, a great part of the nuncio's diplomatic activities lost its purpose. Besides, with ultramontanism making rampant progress throughout the nineteenth century, the essential functions of the nuncio were soon turned into those of a general agent of Roman centralization. This role continued to grow when the nomination of bishops, previously elected by chapters or designated by sovereigns, progressively, became centered in Rome. Finally, it is necessary to add a last consideration. Because of the current emphasis on the "Church of the Poor" and the desire to see the Church withdraw from the "Establishment" so as better to show itself a witness of the Gospel in the world, many are disturbed when the religious representative of the Holy Father to the clergy and faithful is a diplomat, with a life style definitely affected by this role regardless of the personal virtues of the man—even if he be a Roncalli.

The new *motu proprio's* concern to emphasize the ecclesial role of the nuncio, its insistence on this primary role over the secondary diplomatic functions, and the repeated recommendation to consider this ecclesial role as a service to the local Churches, all these indicate unquestionable headway on the way to the *aggiornamento* of the function. But two serious difficulties remain. First, there is the problem of deciding whether a complete dissociation of the two functions would not be better after all: a religious function for the local Churches and a diplomatic function for the governments. This latter, regardless of some opinions, does retain its usefulness especially in those situations where the Holy See seeks to offer its moral authority for the greater service of humanity, peace, social justice, the third world, etc. Next, and more important, regarding the religious function of the papal representatives which has become the essence of their activities over the past century, the new Roman document still gives the impression of having been inspired by a purely monarchical ecclesiology, rather than the ecclesiology of communion which is the true traditional conception revalorized by Vatican II. By insisting, as it does, that, through the official representative of the Holy See, nuncio or apostolic delegate, the pope normally exercises his primacy, it seems—whatever the real intentions of its authors—to consider the local Churches as subdivisions of that universal Church directed from above by the Holy See, enjoying no doubt a certain autonomy, but supervised by a type of parallel hierarchy as prime guarantee of the unity among the Churches and between the Churches and the Apostolic See.

This perspective, coming from the ecclesiological practice of the last century from the time of Pius IX to that of Pius XII, neglects the communion of the local Churches and the direct exchange between local Churches and Rome. Instead, due to the influential bias of papal legates, "central administration" was judged "safer." From the ecumenical point of view, especially in Eastern Church affairs, one need not dwell any longer on the extent to which this underlying conception could not but hide the real sense of episcopal collegiality as proclaimed in the conciliar texts. The fact that nuncios receive precedence over archbishops and bishops, even when the latter are in their own dioceses, again reinforces the unhappy picture: the nuncio having to appear as taking the place of the pope and, in a permanent and regular fashion, exercising in his name his "universal episcopate" in each of the Churches of Catholicism, while in reality he is only a liaison man between the pope and the other bishops.

However, there is much speculation as to whether this liaison man, who is definitely needed, should not rather be the president of the conference of bishops, entrusted with the task of presenting directly to the pope, on periodic visits facilitated greatly nowadays, the situation of the Church of his own country (and also the situation of the universal Church as that country sees it), and in turn receiving orientations directly from him without the double screening of the office of Congregations and the nunciature, with the real danger of having a high functionary's viewpoint presented as being that of the pope.

It is, nevertheless, important to keep in mind Hector Borrat's observations mentioned above. They warn us against idealizing the local Churches in contradistinction to the admitted excesses of centralization. History, time and again, confirms his remarks. Local churches are not always equal to the situation. An external control can sometimes be desirable for the greatest good of their religious growth. A stimulus from above can sometimes render some invaluable services. Roman weight can, in certain cases, help these Churches resist some more or less open governmental pressures opposing truly religious interests, or even help to arbitrate between conflicting tendencies in favor of a more open approach. These are well-known matters among historians, and it would not be difficult to cite examples from the news every day. Which is to say once again that broader studies with the collaboration of various disciplines will still be necessary in the years to come in order to try and determine in a more precise way the orientation Vatican II intended.

•

•   •

The Revision of the Statute on Nuncios

The excerpts below are taken from the commentary of Johannes Neumann of the University of Tübingen, on the *motu proprio Sollicitudo omnium ecclesiarum,* the statute on the Nuncios of June 24, 1969. This commentary appeared in *Orientierung* of Zurich September 15, 1969.

THE NECESSITY OF PAPAL ENVOYS

If one considers the Church as the people of God on pilgrimage, tested but sanctified by the Spirit, one will not deny that the bishop of Rome has the right to know what is happening in the various local churches throughout the world. To know this, the bishops of Rome have for a long time had recourse to the help of residential bishops as well as that of personal delegates. Since the sixteenth century, they established the central authority, the Roman Curia, primarily with a view which would extend toward worldwide activity. . . .

The way the envoys of the bishop of Rome presented themselves as "servant of the servants of God" to their brother bishops not only offended and humiliated many, it provoked disturbing complaints at synods and did a great deal of harm to the Church. . . .

That is why it is not surprising that at the Second Vatican Council likewise there were attacks against the papal envoys, and certain fathers even desired the suppression of the apostolic nuncios. Thus Archbishop Ritter demanded that the tasks of these envoys be taken over by the episcopal conferences themselves. In the name of the Polish episcopate, Bishop Klepacz asked that the president of each episcopal conference assume the function of apostolic nuncio, including the function of representing the Church to the government of his country.

However, the formulation and review of the pastoral function of bishops at the third session of the Council did not specifically take up the question of apostolic nuncios, for they are not directly concerned with the duties of bishops. So discussion of this matter was halted. But Bishop Gargitter made the point that it was the commission's wish that it be taken up in the spirit of the Council when the reform of the Curia was discussed.

ANTICIPATION OF THE SYNOD?

The fact that discussion of the role of the nuncios by the synod of bishops is not provided for, is simply a logical consequence of the idea of centralization determined solely by the principle of the immediate authority of the pope. The publication of new directives for the work of papal legates four months before the opening of the synod made it unmistakably clear that the Holy See has no intention of accepting any proposal whatsoever of the representatives of episcopal colleges on the question of envoys. It alone makes the decisions concerning them with full power and freedom, not only free from considerations of national interest, but also independent of consultation with the bishops. The legates of the Holy See are solely at the service of the pope; they have absolutely no function as regards information and coordination deriving from the College of Bishops or placed at their service, but are exclusively organs of the Sovereign Pontiff. Thus understood, the synod of bishops has no competence to deal with this question. That is why it was not necessary for the pope to become involved or even to ask its approval. . . .

If the bishops of the world accept this without discussion —and they seem to wish to do so—their inability to represent legitimately and with full powers the Churches entrusted to them, whether they be alone in their dioceses or assembled in episcopal conference, will be clearly shown in the decisive relations of the Church with the outside world, that is, with governments and society. Here then, relative to the evident *"nota explicativa praevia"* of the Acts of the Council, is an official commentary and proof that the Holy See attributes no legal significance to the "collegiality" of the bishops on which the third chapter of *Lumen Gentium* lays stress. . . .

THE NEW REGULATION

As long as the papal legate has the duties of obtaining objective information on ecclesiastical and politico-ecclesiastical relations, on the corresponding coordination of the tasks of the Church as well as a general function in the service of unity, and that *participation* in the concerns of the Churches to which he is sent, it is right that no serious objection be raised. Of course, canon law (c. 267) already contained the description of this ecclesiastical task in a more concise way.

But their competence has become greatly extended, since they must "watch over" the religious life and make a conscientious report to the pope (*advigilare debent in Ecclesiarum statum et Romanum Pontificem de eodem certiorum reddere*, c. 267 § 1 n.2). On the one hand, one can welcome the fact that the main functions of papal envoys, which were not previously specified, have now been clearly defined and without secrecy. On the other hand, however, these now defined tasks of the legates of the Sovereign Pontiff should prompt the bishops and bishop conferences to an examination of their validity in a way that is realistic and solidly grounded theologically, as well as responsible and Christian, and to devise remedies if they should be necessary. What the code now in force categorically asserts, in c. 329 § 2, that "the Sovereign Pontiff freely names the bishops," is now regulated in article VI, keeping in mind earlier customs: according to this regulation it is incumbent on the papal delegates to "gather information" about those who would be suitable as bishops or as ordinaries, on the same footing as bishops, and to propose the most "adequate" of the candidates to the competent authorities.

What had already been the practice, the consulting "with precautions" of religious as well as "prudent" laymen, is now raised to an official norm. Thus it is that where there still exist electoral bodies, their judgments are also relegated to officially limited areas. Above all, however, the present efforts of many of the faithful and religious—efforts which are by no means new—to be able to exert a certain proper and legitimate influence on the choice of candidates for the office of bishop are in this way indirectly rejected. The proposals of episcopal conferences on this subject must likewise pass first through the filter of the papal legate. In short, it is he who designates the one who pleases him. Moreover, the papal legate is not held to any procedure in these examinations; he can gather the information in any way he pleases. It is here that the bishops might ask themselves what is, in the last analysis, the function and significance of their conferences, if the representative of the Apostolic See has such broad powers of decision. As long as the "High Commissioner" of the pope has full, all-encompassing powers, any limitation on the term of office of the bishop, as it was proposed recently, would simply mean an effective increase of the influence of the central administration of the Curia at the expense of the personal responsibility of the bishop. Ultimately the extension of the power of the nuncio diminishes the prestige of episcopal conferences and legitimate electoral bodies, as well as the confidence of the faithful and clergy in their bishops.

If the Church is "the people united by the unity of the Father, Son and Holy Spirit," then one who has the confidence of his Church also enjoys that of the Bishop of Rome. As a matter of fact, now the reverse order has arisen: The one who pleases Rome—or, more accurately, its representative—is the one in whom the clergy and the people of this Church must place their confidence. But in a difficult period the solidarity of the governed and the governors is a preliminary condition for a healthy and fraternal relationship of confidence. In our time obedience can only be established on a basis of mutual confidence. When these norms were drawn up, the Holy See was no doubt guided by the centralizing and absolutist principle used up to the present in the Church, according to which, in critical moments, an unquestioning, obedient *official* is "safer" than a personally responsible *bishop*. The question today is obviously whether—apart from the operation of divine grace, which as we know also presupposes certain qualifications—the situation can be managed without the confidence of the faithful, the so-called laity and the clergy, in their Church leaders. However, the new regulations give the papal legate the right, unquestioned and inaccessible to objective verification, to declare a troublesome candidate "unworthy." And, inversely, even more than before, the man who will be promoted to the episcopate must try to be agreeable to the nuncio or to the delegate, which often means an absence of personal opinion and consequently of personal responsibility.

It is true that Article VIII provides—less clearly, however, than did c. 269 1—that the legates cannot infringe on the jurisdictional rights of the bishops. But they have to carefully follow the work and the decisions of episcopal conferences. And although they are not members of the conference by right, they are—at a minimum—supposed to not only participate in each first session, but also to follow the debates with the help of the agenda and the documents, and make a detailed report to the Holy See. Confronted with this juridical situation, it is no longer really possible to speak seriously of a responsibility peculiar to local Churches, however limited it be. The bishops, of course, still have responsibilities, but not the right to decide freely. Even now it often happens that one can speak with a relative openness at conferences, but one must pay scrupulous attention to the formulation of protocol. If even private gossip—on which the papal envoys live no less than other "diplomats"—is not to be prevented, then indeed the duty to make what is in fact a "pauper's oath" in regard to the papal legates makes clear how narrow the borders of the "ordinary and direct" pastoral authority has grown, authority which as such is a divine right (c. 334 and *Lumen gentium* n. 24-27).

That bishops direct their dioceses "under the authority of the pope as their proper ordinary and immediate pastors" (c. 334; Christus Dominus, 11) is simply a rhetorical flourish if the nuncio can at any moment intervene in the name of the "higher authority," not only in their debates, but also in their decisions.

Again, if, according to Article X the papal legate holds first place in the relations of the local Churches with the outside world, the bishops are practically relegated to the position of "chief pastor." The healthy relationship which states that the primary and immediate competence belongs to the bishops, while the papal envoy can only intervene when the forces and possibilities of their own hierarchies are exhausted, is now in fact reversed. It is true that the papal legate—this regulation is not therefore limited to the nuncio—must ask the bishops for their "judgments and counsels," but this very indication shows how little he is bound by their advice, and how little juridical value it has. In recent times, it has happened more than once that bishops still offered resistance against national interests while "through diplomatic channels" a "new course" had long since been taken. The bishops did so at their own risk and were often reproached for their stubbornness, while the Holy See showed itself "so" intelligent and its representative "so" pliable. These incidents have not only hurt the prestige of certain individual bishops, but also the *"ordo episcoporum"* as a whole. Perhaps this secondary effect was not altogether unintended.

By the publication of *Sollicitudo omnium ecclesiarum* what had previously been the "custom of the court" became now a codified norm. The mandate of the Council decree concerning the pastoral duties of bishops, that "the office of papal legates be more exactly defined" (Article 9), was carried out in a way that many bishops would not have been able to foresee as they discussed and voted on it at the Council. For the sake of formality, it is fulfilled by the limiting clause according to which the pastoral role peculiar to bishops must be taken into consideration. Theoretically, the office of the resident bishop is respected, because of its divine origin and special principle of law. But, in relation to the supreme authority of the pope, understood as immediate episcopal authority, the bishops were assigned in a clear and rational way, a domain which should be theologically inaccessible, and which conceals in its practical and juridical consequences still unforeseeable dangers. Of course, the episcopal function is formally recognized as such, with its original independence, but on the juridical level it is so limited that in reality the bishop is left with no independence nor responsibility of his own. The order of bishops remains as a state, because it is not possible to suppress it, but it is so bound to the primatial direction that the actual responsibility for the Church in a given region no longer resides in the particular bishops, but in the papal envoy who chooses them, supervises their work and indirectly directs them. The bishops are in the position of "functionaries" juridically, and bound by the directives they receive. . . .

It seems to be a rule of law that to the degree that the power of the central authority is strengthened the inner commitment of the individual is weakened. In matters of faith this could be a fatal development which the bishops cannot be indifferent to. They must wonder now, prior to the synod of bishops, whether they should not resist directly. Without doubt, the document in question is not a fulfillment of the wish expressed at the Council by the majority of the bishops, but the fruit of this curial position which believes it must "repair the damage" done by the Council. Were the efforts of the Council, the struggle for the principle of collegiality in vain? This seems to be the case.

And now, what do you propose to do, Fathers?

D. The Nomination of Bishops

If the question of nuncios demands a great deal of attention, it is because the nomination of bishops in the present system depends on them more and more. In this respect, the recent *motu proprio* changed nothing. Quite the contrary. After a nuncio has remained in a country for several years, the make-up of the episcopate in that country may have been profoundly modified through his influence for better or worse. Sometimes for the better, a fact too often ignored; but for the worse, too, or at least in a manner that fosters mediocrity or timorous conservatism.

It would not be difficult to find examples. The final decision is taken in Rome, of course; but too frequently this decision is based exclusively on the recommendations of the nunciature. Now, there is a great danger that conformity, real or supposed, to the preferences of the representative of the Holy See plays an important part in the manner in which candidates are proposed or turned aside. If the relations between Rome and the periphery did not pass solely through the channels of the nunciature, if the bishops of a country could regularly and normally have their opinions heard in Rome, the decisions of the pope when nominating bishops would be seen in a less polarized light—certainly a most desirable goal.

But the question of the nomination of bishops is much wider than that of the influence of nuncios or apostolic delegates. The Suenens interview also took up the frequently expressed wish of today's clergy and faithful, that the entire diocesan community take part in the choice of their future shepherd.

In allying himself to this aspiration, the cardinal might have merely been seeking to diminish the role of the pope in the Church, particularly in this domain, and to favor the independence of bishops with respect to the Holy See. This, at least, is the opinion of Louis Salleron, one of the mentors of today's French conservatives:

Cardinal Suenens' ideas are quite simple. They focus on the notion that the Church, as "people of God," is by that very fact a democracy. Consequently, authority proceeds from base to apex, and the pope, since there happens to be a pope, must execute the common will. We will certainly not find this thesis expressed summarily; yet, this is the thesis. Yes, it is this thesis that is presented in terms carefully calculated and articulated around the notion of collegiality. For the people of God is really nothing more than an alibi for the claims of the bishops against the Holy See. In other words, the notion of "people of God" has as its sole object the affirmation of the primacy of the college of bishops over the primacy of the pope (*Carrefour*, 7-9-69).

Two months before the interview, Father Wenger had expressed himself somewhat differently on the subject of "Authority in the Church" (*La Croix*, 3-25-69):

The Council gave a timely reminder that authority in the Church is first of all a service. The pope and bishops are now getting up new structures, and seeking a new spirit in the exercise of their authority.

The dissidents believe that such reforms are too timorous and too prudent. They would like authority in the Church in the world to become more democratic. Today, power derives no longer from birth, from wealth or from genius, but from the people. It is exercised in the people's name and with their participation.

The dissidents would like to transfer this theory to the Church. To this end, they recall that the Dogmatic Constitution on the Church, *Lumen Gentium,* places its statement on the people of God (Chapter II) ahead of its statement on the hierarchy (Chapter III). This structure, largely due to Cardinal Suenens, indicates the intention of the Holy Spirit. It shows that our fundamental character as the people of God, royal, priestly and prophetic, is more important than distinction, within this people, between various functions.

This does not mean, however, that hierarchical authority is merely a delegation of power by the people of God. It is a particular charism, permanent and institutional, which consists in the gift of the Holy Spirit by the imposition of hands. It is the Sacrament of Orders given in a universal manner to the pope, immediately and fully to the bishops as successors of the apostles, and, by them and in dependence upon them, to the priests.

This does not mean that the Church, in the exercise of authority, can learn nothing from the times. Notions such as democratization, participation, decentralization, structures of communication and coordination, and management must find their counterparts within the Church. Councils of priests and laymen are merely beginning. Their role and their importance in the Church must increase.

Father Barsotti, writing in *Osservatore Romano*, rejects any attempt at "democratization" in the Church with a phrase which, in his opinion, shuts off all debate: "The flock does not choose its shepherd." He forgets one thing: the faithful are not sheep! Let us not overwork rural analogies. Besides, it is quite evident that no one in the Church seeks to deny that authority, once designated in due manner, is invested by God with its proper charism.

Still more cogently, the American Catholic sociologist Andrew Greeley put his finger on the crux of the issue:

I have argued repeatedly that the present crisis in the Church is not one of schism, apostasy or infidelity, but of credibility, consensus and alienation. Large numbers of Catholics are not going to leave the Church, much less is anyone likely to start a new heretical Church.

Rather the danger is that Church leadership will continue to lose its credibility; a substantial segment of the Catholic population will withdraw consensus from the leadership and will remain within the Church but substantially alienated from the Church as an organized institution. It is within the context of that very real possibility that one must read the remarkable interview that Cardinal Suenens gave recently to the world press; the program of "coresponsibility" he describes is an obvious attempt to arrest the erosion of consensus which is going on within the Church. (*Catholic Voice*, 7-2-69)

This can be applied to pastoral and priests' councils, but also to the preliminary choice of that shepherd whose task it will be to direct and govern the People of God in their options and projects. Thus, a real, coresponsible participation of the diocesan community with the episcopal conference in the choice of its future bishops would seem desirable. This would not be just the revival of an ancient Church practice, a pseudo-archaeological concern which is too often idealized by those who have only a superficial knowledge of history. The ancient practice of episcopal elections by the clergy and the laity was far from being a perfect solution—often giving rise to rivalries between factions and to the establishment of "pressure groups" whose motives were less than praiseworthy. Rather, in seeking to preserve the true Catholic notion of hierarchical authority by restoring the "credibility" of those who hold this authority, we should search for a flexible solution. Such a solution would take into account the lessons of the past, which younger generations so naively tend to discount as having nothing to offer. It would allow all concerned—laity, priests, neighboring bishops—to have their say in the choice of a bishop. Finally, it would avoid the deceptions and abuses of former systems of election which, in large measure, had first been the cause of Rome's intervention in this area of capital importance for the life of the local church.

GENERAL CONCLUSIONS

Examination of the various reactions to the Suenens interview brings an awareness of the complexity of the problems raised, at least in the domain of renewal of Church institutions. Some suggested that it was merely necessary to call attention to this matter in order to dismiss the cardinal's proposals. Faced with the unrest in the Church caused by a strangling centralization, the Cardinal pleaded for a re-emphasis on the local Churches and made several appropriate suggestions. The role of the center can certainly be beneficial, and historians know better than anyone else that it has been so in a number of instances. In today's world, which is becoming increasingly one despite the renaissance of a cultural pluralism, there can be no question of eliminating the role of the center—whatever the theological considerations on the divine-right primacy of Peter's successor. What is clearer, though, is that this inevitable centralization should be considered, in the light of Vatican II, as being exercised in the name of the entire episcopal college under the leadership of the "first among bishops." It is this entire college which is coresponsible for the welfare of the universal Church.

This viewpoint, which attempts to reconcile the legitimate autonomy of the successors of the apostles (who are not merely the delegates of the pope) with the requirement of unity (which is the first responsiblity of the successor of Peter), would also have the advantage of better defining the normal role of the Roman Curia as that of assisting in the administration of a collegially exercised centralization. This would diminish the all too real danger of the Curia being substituted for the pope in the exercise of a primacy conceived in fact according to the model of the absolute monarchies of Post-Tridentine times. (Note that the influence of sociological factors on canonical and even theological systems of ecclesiology did not begin only yesterday). Putting Vatican bureaucracy "in its place"—and a very useful place at that— would restore to the pope the leadership of the college of bishops by virtue of the will of Christ, his own proper position, and thus increase his "credibility," which so often seems obscure these days. Must it again be stated that considering the Curia in this perspective does not demean the persons, who are most often paragons of good will, but the "system" which tends to make these persons prisoners, a system established and developed in a particular era to respond to particular needs with the methods available at that time; but a system which no longer corresponds to the status of the Church and the world today, and must consequently be completely rethought, not merely improved in particular areas. Such an evaluation does not imply, as is so often unjustly charged, that the system was wrong from the beginning.

The renewal of Church institutions, which was barely more than outlined by Vatican II, is one of the most urgent necessities of our times. But it can only come to term if all men of good will and from all skills come together to weigh carefully the data of the problems in the world, and then seek the appropriate solutions to these problems. Such solutions can never be perfect—*le mieux est l'ennemi du bien* as has taught the wisdom of the nations—but they will, at least, permit the great notions of collegiality and coresponsibility to find effective implementation in the present situation. This implementation will be faithful to what must remain unchanged in Catholic tradition and remain adaptable to the concrete religious society of the atomic era, an era much different from that of the "Ancient Regime," or of the 19th century, or even of the Thirties. Willingly or not, Church institutions will have to adapt to this society just as they have adapted to all previous societies, often with a fairly long and harmful delay which, in the present instance, we would like to see reduced to the minimum. In our times, when the pace of acceleration is faster than ever before, a ten-year delay could lead to even graver consequences.

• • •

Portrait of a Pope

The following extract of the essay by Hans Küng develops his reactions to the Suenens interview:

The courageous, clear, and balanced interview of Cardinal Suenens, has elicited a gratifying positive echo. To our surprise this echo arose both within the Church and outside it, not only in the Catholic Church of Western Europe and America but also in the Church of Eastern Europe. The reaction we had expected was, for the most part, limited to certain elements in the Curia and certain well-known pores of traditionalism. Everywhere else it was realized that, in this event, a man positively engaged in the Church's service was calling for reforms long-delayed and now vitally necessary for the Catholic Church. We need not mention that Cardinal Suenens did not publicly set out on this path until he had been forced to admit that no other route would lead to the goal. And after all, why should we prohibit him from doing what his more traditionalist colleagues such as Car-

dinals Ottaviani, Felici, and Daniélou had done before him—
and not always with as much concern for other persons? In
his article in the journal *Publik*, Karl Rahner explained with
a convincing and helpful clarity that public criticism can be
legitimate, if not sometimes necessary, even against the pope.
Cardinal Suenens, then, needs no defense of his perfectly
orthodox doctrine or conduct. His historic interview falls
into a long tradition of public criticism loyally and fraternally
addressed to the holy see as exercised in Paul's criticism to
Peter, that of Jerome to Damasus, of Bernard of Clairvaux
to Eugene III, of Bridget of Sweden to Gregory XI, of
Philip Neri to Clement VIII, and of other canonized saints
including Catherine of Siena, Bernadine of Siena, Thomas
More, and Robert Bellarmine. We should not wait on this
account for Cardinal Suenens' canonization by some future
pope—it is probable that in the future, true saints will come
to be recognized in the Church without the prolonged
Roman "procedures." Yet we are convinced that, with this
interview, the prelate has given the postconciliar Church a
sign bursting with hope and that no one has any longer the
right to despair of renewal in the Catholic Church or even in
the Church of Rome.

A SERVICE TO THE CHURCH

Differing from many bishops who, to the detriment of
their own authority as well as that of the Church, present an
image of a leaderless "Church of Silence," the Cardinal has
effectively responded, through his actions, to this crisis of
confidence which is everywhere beginning to make itself felt
with increasing and worrisome rapidity—a crisis of confidence not only between the pope and the Church, but also
between the bishops and the Church. This crisis, besides
driving the upholders of reform to pessimism, also favors the
appearance of movements led by unbalanced extremists on
both the right and the left. What must be noted with particular satisfaction, however, is that even after different negative
reactions from Rome, Cardinal Suenens did not soften his

criticism under the pretext of having been "misunderstood" as usually happens in ecclesiastical circles. On the contrary, he has stood by the entire text and reaffirmed it. Such tenacity—which requires steady nerves, strong faith, and a sense of humor—is too rarely found in the higher ranks of the Church to be denied public praise.

Cardinal Suenens has rendered a great service to the pope whose clear thinking and good will he has always rightly recognized. He is a better apologist for Peter's service in the Church than all these traditionalists who defend an outmoded form of this service along with their own positions of power in the Roman system. Who has rendered a greater service to the Pope? Those who, in the days of reformation, pleaded for a serious reform of the papacy in the renouncement of its medieval form, or those who, invoking Matthew 16:18 and canon law, militated in favor of the *status quo ante* of the medieval era? Who better counseled the pope in the nineteenth century? Those who, despite the threat of excommunication, asked for the voluntary surrender of the Papal States? or those who invoking Matthew 16:18 and canon law again, defended an historical state which was already out of date, although Rome had yet to come to this awareness? Who today better supports the Pope in his truly difficult task? Those who seek a radical reform of the papacy according to the Gospel of Jesus Christ, or those who, after Vatican II, wish to bring the Church and the papacy back to Vatican I or who at least consider reform of the papacy to be accomplished with the nomination of a few "progressive" cardinals (most of whom, until now, have been nothing but liberal tokens for a system still unchanged, and the rest of whom have been largely counter-balanced by the nomination of less "progressive" cardinals) and with the creation of a commission of theologians which, to a large extent, can be manipulated by an increasingly inquisitional "Congregation of the Faith" and whose effectiveness remains to be proved.

The pope and the few sincere friends of reform working within the Curia feel that we should allow them more time. The present age, however, is not one which allows an idea to wait centuries or even decades for acceptance. A great many people, both within and outside the Church, think that we have already been waiting too many centuries. There will be no exterior schism in spite of this situation.

It is only by reason of a lack of confidence in the highest leaders of the Church that we can come to a state—and we should avoid it at all costs—where the clergy as well as the people are less and less concerned with the exhortations and warnings and ultimately even the encyclicals and decrees of the pope. The encyclical, *Humanae Vitae,* is only one example which shows how, in this situation which can really only be altered by Rome, the pope is no longer followed by a great many of the circles in the Church. This is true not only among laymen, but also among the clergy; not only among the "lower" and younger clergy, but also among the bishops. Those episcopal conferences which have opted in favor of liberty of conscience have in their turn rendered a greater service to the pope than those bishops, especially in North America, who have tried to suspend priests disagreeing with the encyclical. It is these bishops themselves who are greatly responsible for the dozens, and soon hundreds of priests who either have abandoned or will abandon their service in the Church.

CHALLENGE OF THE SYNOD

Karl Rahner has rightly seen in Cardinal Suenens' interview a program for the synod of bishops and even for further episcopal synods. Rome, it is true, has other plans for this coming synod. After the encyclical *Humanae Vitae,* the current synod now must serve to strengthen the Roman system and—the analogy of the communist meeting in Moscow after Prague seems to fit—to support the bright illusion of a monolithic unity of the world's bishops. Prudently, though without reason yet, this synod has been termed as "extraordinary," with invitations going only to the presidents of the episcopal conferences. Hence, the small number of progressive presidents from Central European episcopal conferences will be at the mercy not only of the power-machine of a well-represented Curia, but also of a crushing majority of conference presidents from the Afro-Asian countries who, to all appearances, are very conservative. The Curia's secret document, prepared for the discussion and bearing the insidious and ambiguous title "Schema Elaborated from Reports of Bishops' Conferences," very definitely reveals its penchant for uniformity. Its culminating point comes with the following demand: "that the conferences of bishops, before publishing a declaration on important issues, seek at an opportune time the opinion of the Apostolic See" (*ut episcoporum conferentiae ante edendam declarationem de re gravi apostolicae sedis mentem opportuno tempore explorent*). Should this proposal pass, neither the pope nor the Curia will have to fear any future critical declarations such as the Central European episcopal conferences' statements concerning the encyclical on birth control. We can rightly wonder if the bishops will allow themselves to be silenced in this way instead of pressing for answers to the questions of greatest urgency in our times, particularly the question of priesthood and celibacy.

The program of Cardinal Suenens is a long-term one. Patience and unshakeable determination are needed for it to come about. But that it will come about in one form or another is as certain as the loss of the papal states. The one question is whether reform will once more come so late that we will have to pay for it with heavy losses. (*Le Monde*, 8-12-69).

9

Legalism and Christian Life

Philippe Delhaye, author of this chapter, is Dean of the Faculty of Theology of the University of Louvain, internationally renowned moralist and member of the International Pontifical Commission of Theology.

At first sight, it would seem that moral theology has no place in a debate on collegiality and coresponsibility. And yet it does have a very definite place. What is being considered here are particular notions of education and the moral life. Is it necessary to continue directing the attention of the faithful to canonical laws which originate in the Code and in the Roman Congregations—laws which forbid certain acts on pain of mortal or venial sins? Rather, are not Church laws simply a way of helping the Christian conscience seek out the values taught by the Gospel? This latter view still allows for the possibility of serious sin; but such sins would arise from attitudes, intentions or omissions which are entrenched and lasting.

In his book on *Coresponsibility in the Church* (p. 149), Cardinal Suenens has pointed out the antinomy between a true and false "philosophy of 'Christian' laws": "the interpretation of ecclesiastical laws; striving as it does to bring out their true sense and significance, can only transpire in the light of the Gospel message. It must take into account the dimension of history and open itself out to a positive and dynamic vision."

The cardinal went on to denounce the deviations of post-tridentine moral teaching:

During the last few centuries, theological manuals, the usual seminary teaching, and confessional practice have accentuated the negative aspect. Laws were presented as barriers; or as immutable commands relating to precise acts. Sufficient care was not taken to bring out the fundamental values which these laws contain and the virtues they imply. Then also, these laws were often promulgated under pain of mortal sin, and attention was concentrated on an isolated act to avoid (eating meat on Friday) or to perform (Mass on Sunday). Thus, in an increasing degree, all these various factors led inevitably to a formalism which was more or less profound, and always dangerous.

These same ideas were taken up again and concretized in Point IV of the interview where the cardinal gives a series of examples illustrating the defects of a purely legalistic morality.

CHARITY AND CANON LAW

Some journals were quick to point out the contrast between the statements of Cardinal Suenens in the May Interview, and those of Cardinal Felici, President of the Commission for the Reform of Canon Law, in the *Osservatore Romano* the same month.

Cardinal Felici asserts that Christians need precise laws in their lives; the preparatory work for the new code of canon law must be done secretly, because of its "technical nature"; and that it is for the pope alone to take a decision on the final draft of this commission:

It is for the pope alone to decide if and when and how it would be beneficial to seek the advice of the bishops, as also to ask the opinion of all or of some of the Congregations and Offices of the Holy See, and eventually of other persons and organizations.

Cardinal Felici concludes with a defense of law and authority.

On the other hand, at a congress held in Dreux (France), in September 1969, a hundred theologians stated that "moral teaching must be radically rethought."

Referring to this, *Le Monde* (9-26-69) writes:

The human sciences—and principally psychology, since Freud—have drawn out the essentially "relations" character of the human being, and the infinite complexity of these relations. This has tended to make *love* a central moral value and a motive force of every action, even in its breach. Revelation only further clarifies this principle: it makes *Love* the Absolute Being and ultimate incentive of the universe. The "tragic" character of the human condition becomes clear in the saving *Love* which is Christ. Would not the proper mark of the Christian be that hope which reaches beyond all despair?

AN EXAMPLE: THE BREVIARY

The fate of particular laws and their importance concern Bishop W. G. Wheeler of Leeds, England. He praises the interview as a whole and even compares Cardinal Suenens with Cardinal Mercier. Basically, he follows a middle of the road position, discussing at the same time the Curia's excessive legalism and its wisdom and pastoral meaning. He fears, however, that a radical abandonment of precise rules would lead to laxism. He writes:

There are perhaps also a number amongst us who might have fallen away little by little from the life of prayer, if we had not some objective norm by which to measure ourselves. When a priest decides that he is no longer bound by the Church's law to recite the Divine Office, for example, the People of God are deprived of something for which they are the poorer. And every bishop will tell you that when the Office goes, scripture reading will gradually go also and by then mental prayer has probably already gone. (*Ampleforth Journal*, Summer 1969).

This problem of the obligation of the breviary is definitely a current one. Note in passing that the teaching of the manuals is exactly as Cardinal Suenens described it: the omission of one "little hour" (prime, tierce, etc.) is considered a mortal sin. This thesis is presented in Archbishop Palazzini's *Dictionarium Morale et Canonicum* (Rome, 1965).

In summer 1969, the French Bishops gave some new directives concerning the obligation of the breviary in line with the ideas of Cardinal Suenens. First of all, the issue is no longer a matter for decision by the Roman Curia, but by the National Conference of Bishops. Secondly, this obligation is considered as a practical consequence of a theology of the priest—the man of ecclesial prayer. Thus a lesser law is brought to life again by the spirit and the deeper implications of its theology. Finally, some distinctions begin to appear: lauds and vespers are just the normal prayers for morning and evening; and nothing is prescribed for any of the midday hours or compline.

SOURCE AND SPIRIT OF MORAL LAWS

A certain opposition also makes itself felt regarding the source and the spirit of moral laws. For example, some readers of *L'Homme Nouveau* (Paris, 7-6-69) expressed the opinion in letters to the editor that the pope (with the Curia) should be the sole legislator. Others think, on the contrary, that papal and episcopal authorities should consult the laity.

In the *Catholic Messenger* (Davenport, 4-10-69), Father Dennis Geaney asserted that the reason why *Humanae Vitae* is not observed is that it was prepared without the co-operation of bishops, theologians and married couples. He continues:

If the authorities are too far separated from the people, they will find themselves so out of tune and turned off that they will be forced to retire and make way for others who are tuned in to the thinking of the people.

In the *Sunday Press* (Ireland, 5-18-69) Tom O'Mahony hails the vision of the people of God as reflected in the Suenens interview. He sees this vision as the only way to avoid legalism and to encourage maturity and responsibility among Catholics: "Some will even be scandalized. But time will surely prove that its vision foreshadows the Church of the 21st century."

The resolutions of the Birmingham Renewal Group remind us that moral duties must be joined to moral values: "The Church has gone too far in handing down various obligations ready-made for all members."

The Birmingham text offers no concrete examples, but two spring immediately to mind. First, the ineluctable law of Christian mortification was hidden from many people by the precept which forbade eating meat on Friday. Secondly, for the obligation of avoiding dangerous reading, canon law substituted, under pain of juridical sanctions, the index of forbidden books. The number of necessary dispensations became so great it appeared simpler just to abolish the law.

How then should we view ecclesiastical laws? The Birmingham group offers the following suggestion:

> The Church should certainly exercise her authority in giving her members guidance, making recommendations, laying down norms of behavior, issuing warnings about the danger of ignoring directives, and so on. But the teaching authority of the Church should concern itself with these things only in general terms, and in such a way as to safeguard and encourage the initiative of the individual conscience. The Christian, helped in this way by the community, and in a spirit of fraternity with the other members of the Church, will apply these framework-laws (loi cadres) to the circumstances of his own life. He will reflect conscientiously in order to help with the determination of the Church's teaching and in deciding what positions the Church should take in face of the problems life presents.

A good number of Christians have been so formed in the mentality of warring against self and against human values that they are perturbed at proposals for a more open morality which they presume to be an easier morality.

In the *Sunday Independent* (Ireland, 5-25-69) a writer charged the cardinal with wanting to do away with mortal sins because Our Lord said: "My yoke is sweet and my burden light." He points out that Our Lord stressed it would never be easy and that we must take up our cross daily and follow Him. There are, however, even some classical authors who see the danger of this rigorist and negative attitude. According to Gustave Thibon (*Libre Belgique,* 10-1-69), we also risk making morality repugnant. He writes:

> I willingly admit that there is an irritating way of moralizing. It is the way of certain narrow carping and prying minds who in their preaching emphasize that evils are lurking everywhere, thus reducing morality to its negative aspects: don't do this; watch out for that, etc. This "moralism" is only a mask for inability and inhibition—a blanket so heavy that it smothers rather than warms.

A CONCILIAR SESSION TOO SOON FORGOTTEN

In his book on coresponsibility, Cardinal Suenens stressed that his plea for a more Christian and humanistic view of morality was in direct line with the teaching of Vatican II. In this regard, he referred (p. 148) to one of the major discourses of Patriarch Maximos IV. The résumé of this conciliar session of October 1964 should be read. In his *Chronicle of the third session of Vatican II,* Antoine Wenger succeeds in capturing the poignancy of this discussion: Should the Church arouse men's consciences to the values of faith and love or use threats to regulate exterior actions? "Is the imposition of commandments a real service?"

Bishop Louis La Ravoire of Krishnagar, India, had asked for more discretion in the matter of moral obligations under the threats of damnation. He felt "that there is a disproportion between the aim of the precept and the pain under which it obliges, as in the case of assistance at Sunday Mass. Our religion is one of love, not of fear."

Patriarch Maximos had criticized the legalistic mentality in which the precepts of the Church are framed and presented. Father Wenger summarizes this speech:

Today we can no longer impose a law without also explaining its meaning and wisdom. Because of the evolution in thinking and the developed sense of responsibility among the faithful, the Church must revise its method of teaching morality and especially its commandments.

Ever since the sixteenth century, this teaching had been becoming more and more legalistic. Christian morality must have a Christo-centric character and must develop a sense of responsibility. It is not a matter of changing immutable dogmas, but rather of promoting the sanctification of the Christian people. Many of the Church's commandments, such as those concerning Sunday Mass, Friday abstinence, and the sacrament of penance, are no longer accepted today because of the manner in which they are presented.

And Patriarch Maximos suggested "creating a commission of theologians to accomplish this revision of moral teaching so that the Church can become a blazing light and not an extinguisher."

Bishop Méndez Arceo of Cuernavaca, Mexico, continued along this same line in discussing the subject of freedom. Father Wenger summarizes this discourse:

Christ freed us from the law. St. Paul suffered to insure this freedom; St. Thomas taught that a written law does not sanctify by itself. St. Augustine recognized that we must use moderation in our positive laws to facilitate conversions. Moral teaching must be reformed, along with the whole of seminary education on this matter.

THE LIBERATING VOICE OF THE POPE

Listening to Bishop Méndez Arceo and considering the obstacles in the path of the Declaration on Religious Freedom, some said: "Freedom in the Church, that will be for Vatican III. . . ." In the Suenens interview of May 15 they saw a first step in that direction. For that matter, Pope Paul's speech of July 9, 1969, on freedom, also reflects an anticipation of Vatican III.

The pope stressed the autonomy of conscience in ecclesial affairs. In "the personal realm," it is a question of recognizing "for every man, an elevated degree of autonomy ruled by conscience which is the immediate and unshakable norm (Rom 14-23) of the moral act, and which, consequently, needs all the more, the enlightenment of truth and the support of grace (Gal 5:1; Jn 8:36) for it to further determine itself today" (*Gaudium et Spes,* n° 16 and 17).

In ecclesial structures it will be important then to keep in mind "the principle of subsidiarity" (*Gaudium et Spes,* n° 86) which, continues the pope, "in a well—organized society strives to allow the individual and the subordinate organizations the greatest possible freedom, while making obligatory only what is necessary for the greater and more general good, impossible to attain through other means" (*Dign. Hum.* n° 7).

The apparent conflict between "exterior law and conscience" must be resolved. "The mentality fostered by the teachings of the Council," says the Pope, "encourages a greater exercise of liberty, more now than before, in the internal forum of conscience. This mentality tends to temper the influence of exterior law and to increase that of interior law, personal responsibility, and reflection on man's great duties."

This return to the interior aspect of morality also restores the primacy of charity:

> We know that the Gospel stresses the interiority of moral obligation and that it has given an incomparable, but often forgotten, synthesis of this in the greatest commandment of total love of God. It is from this love that our love of neighbor flows, a similar love which extends to all: parents, friends, foreigners, enemies, all those who are far away, in a word, to all humanity.

We can look forward to a new style of "governing souls." The pope gives a sketch of this new style:

> In the life of the Church and each of its members, we will enjoy a period of greater freedom, involving fewer legal obligations and fewer interior inhibitions. Formal discipline will be reduced; all arbitrary intolerance, all absolutism will be abolished; the positive law will be simplified, and the exercise of authority will be tempered; true Christian freedom will be promoted—a freedom so greatly appreciated by the first generation of Christians when they were freed from the Mosaic Law (Gal 5:1) and its complicated ritual prescriptions (*Documentation Catholique*, 8-3/17-69).

A DUTY TO DISOBEY

The case of Captain Matthias Defregger is well known. On June 7, 1944, a German soldier was killed by Italian partisans near the little village of Filetto di Camarda. The commander of the German division ordered Captain Defregger to shoot all the men of the village. The Captain transmitted the order to a lieutenant. Only nineteen men between the ages of seventeen and sixty-five could be found in the village. These men were killed and the village was burned.

After the war, Defregger became a priest and some years later he was consecrated a bishop in the Catholic Church. It has been only recently that his wartime role became known.

Along with the juridical aspects of this painful affair (prescription, extradition), there is a definite moral problem. Should the Captain have obeyed? Or, on the contrary, should not his conscience have rebelled against the order received? This is the question examined by Gregory Baum in the *St. Louis Review* (8-8-69:)

> Catholic teaching, to be sure, has always specified that a man may not obey when he is ordered to commit a sinful act. But

this rule was hardly ever applied: its place in the general teaching on authority was minimal.

Theoretically, we can easily enough set up principles for disobeying orders and rules; but in reality it is often difficult to apply them. Can the Defregger case be useful to the Catholic episcopacy even though it was obviously brought before the public eye to humiliate the Church? Here is Father Baum's opinion:

> One must hope that the Defregger case will be a warning to the bishops of the Catholic Church to speak the truth about authority and obedience. The Gospel proclaimed by the Church is to make men critical of the idolatry which threatens them from every side. The Gospel summons us to be critical even in regard to authority.

The Church has always declared with clarity and precision its stand on obedience and authority, but there could be particular occasions in which a very special way of acting would be required. Baum continues:

> We must teach the double message of the New Testament: on the one hand we hear that the obedience to legitimate authority is fidelity to God, and on the other we hear that disobedience may be necessary since it is better to obey God than man. The decision whether to obey or not to obey passes through personal conscience, and no power on this earth could ever dispense a man from making his own personal decision.

"SUB GRAVI" LAWS

In *De Maand*, (Sept. 1969), Victor Heylen studies another aspect of the controversy—that of obligations *sub gravi*—questioned by Cardinal Suenens in his intervention. Msgr. Heylen remarks that the familiar style of the interview—too little used in ecclesiastical circles—has its own laws, which must be taken into account in appreciating the answers which spring "from living pastoral experience rather than from theory":

The cardinal is alluding to a certain jurisprudence and morality which has become, to a great extent, foreign to the Christian thought of our era. He does not question the necessity of adapted universal legislation. . . . He is denouncing the dangerous and ever-growing gap between the "norms" of the Church and Christian life.

This clearly shows the need for a totally new approach to laws and their sanctions; and indeed, this is the task of the present revision of the Code of Canon Law. But will it succeed in changing the common way of thinking and acting? Msgr. Heylen observes:

Will not the second Vatican Council come to clash with those strong opinions which are fighting to survive or at least to die as slow a death as possible? Certainly, authority has rights which remain incontestable and uncontested; and the Church remains the source of eternal salvation. But divine authority, although absolute, is no longer absolutist or arbitrary; and the Church authority which invokes divine authority should take this into account. And Msgr. Heylen concludes "Divine law and the law of the Church proceeding from it should remain, above all, a grace from God."

The same issue of *De Maand* published an article in which I tried first of all to investigate the psychological grounds of the opposition between legalism and a morality of interiority:

When we speak of Christian freedom, engagement, and spontaneity in the moral life, we risk being accused of undermining the authority of laws. Why? Because, under the influence of various historical circumstances (purely legalistic mentality; political absolutism; repression of any emancipation, even legitimate), we have identified the moral life with obedience to juridical "norms." In the article "Conscience" of the *Dictionnaire de Spiritualité* (vol. 2, col. 1572), Fr. Carpentier, S. J., has described very well this legalistic conscience. It has a sense of order, of law, of principles; but it is incapable of developing the general tonality of charity. "Its greatest weakness," continued the Eigenhoven professor, "is its giving preference to written texts over human values, to legal justice over personal justice. It thus acquires a rigidity which will of necessity crush others by this very rigidity, this lack of flexibility, makes it incapable of combining common good and particular good."

This opposition of doctrines is what the interview describes in pastoral terms.

Where should we look for a solution to this opposition? In the distinction between the different kinds of law.

First of all, we must situate the major directives, the fundamental laws of the Gospel. Then would follow the more precise precepts. We will consider them only as concrete interpretations of the fundamental laws. We will only be able to understand their significance completely and to apply them correctly if we search in love for the spirit which animates them. . . .

The *De Maand* article concludes:

For St Paul "the law of Christ" (Gal 6:2), "the law of faith" (Rom 3:27), "faith that makes its power felt through love" (Gal 5:6)—this is the grace of the apostles' revelation of divine love. To men who accept this message and respond in faith, hope, and love, ecclesial authority provides, at once, directives for life and sacramental graces: "All authority in heaven and on earth has been given to me," the Lord Jesus said to his Apostles, "Go therefore, make disciples of all the nations; baptize them . . . teach them to observe all the commands I gave you. (Matt 28:18-20) In this perspective, the moral life of the Christian is first of all his divinization as translated by the fruits of the Spirit (Gal 5:16). Ecclesial authority, liturgical life, and moral life are all permanently joined in a dynamic contact with Christ, continued in his priesthood.

At this point, the more precise laws take their place in the Christian ethic. It is from the love of God poured into our hearts by the Holy Spirit (Rom 5:5) that we derive the laws of respect for life, truth, marriage, as St. Paul reminds us in Romans (15:8): "Avoid getting into debt except the debt of mutual love. If you love your fellowmen you have carried out your obligations."

Lower still in this hierarchy of laws are the precise precepts which apply in one epoch but not in another. This is the area of our present uneasiness, for we all know that many laws are out of date. In the eighth century, the Church forbade manual work on Sunday in order to obtain a day of rest for slaves and serfs. Today, many city-dwellers relax by carpentry and gardening, by performing "servile" work. Should we not revise this law, reformulate it, perhaps discard it? Rather than entering frantically into casuistry, should we not reconsider Christian conduct and ecclesial directives in the light of the great values we wish to preserve. Is this not also what St. Paul affirmed when he declared that the purpose of a law can only be love (1 Tim 1:5)?

10

Ecumenical Hopes

Everyone knows how lightly, and with what scandalous presumption, some people, even very highly placed ones, make statements questioning the teachings and the decisions of the pope, thinking that this serves the Church. We won't accept that kind of catholicism, and most of the people of our diocese won't accept it either.

Like us, our separated brethren want to be respected and loved, but they instinctively distrust Catholics who are not in agreement with the pope. Keeping one's distances from the pope would just mean delaying reconciliation. We mustn't fall into the trap of those who would divide us still further, the better to make us fight each other, and then finally destroy us one at a time.

Bishop François Charrière, of Lausanne, Geneva and Fribourg, condemned protest in these severe terms on the eve of Paul VI's June 10, 1969, visit to the International Labor Organization and the World Council of Churches, both in Geneva. Was he thus condemning Cardinal Suenens' interview? Although he did not mention it explicitly, he did explicitly mention the "presumptousness" which is "sometimes seen even in very high places."

So, for Bishop Charrière, and undoubtedly for others as well, Cardinal Suenens' spectacular declarations were more likely to harm than to advance the cause of Christian unity.

True, in this interview, the Archbishop of Malines-Brussels

does not develop his ecumenical preoccupations, perhaps because the questions asked did not give him the opportunity to do so; a few months later, when a Protestant asked the same questions, the ecumenical dimensions of his suggestions were evident in every line. Perhaps, too, because the cardinal found that the problem of the relations between the center and the periphery, between primacy and collegiality, is so evidently a major concern of ecumenism, he found it unnecessary to stress the point.

Cardinal Suenens is not only the successor of Cardinal Mercier to the see of Malines. He wishes also to carry on the role of his predecessor, who with Lord Halifax in the Conversations of Malines, became one of the first pioneers of the ecumenical movement. He maintains close and warm relations with Christian non-Catholic bishops and theologians. One of them, Dr. Jerald C. Brauer, dean of the Divinity School of the University of Chicago, former Council observer, member of the joint commission which carries on the official dialogue between the Luthern Church and the Catholic Church, asked him about the ecumenical implications of his interview. The interview with Dr. Brauer, as published in *NCR* (9-3-69), follows.

"TRACT FOR THE TIMES"

Cardinal Suenens, I just finished your new book Co-responsibility in the Church, *and I think it is a brilliant "Tract for the Times." It is of seminal importance for all people interested in Christianity and for all believers in the Christian community. Even those people concerned with the ethos and mores of modern life, though not themselves believers, should read and ponder this book. I have seen no document that develops the implications and new directions of Vatican II as clearly and persuasively as this book.*

I should like to ask you several questions that appear particularly important to me as a Christian of the Protestant tradition. Protestants still struggle with the problem of papal primacy, and particularly the problem of papal infallibility. Even Protestant reformers were prepared to understand primacy in a certain way. As a result of Vatican II, and the consequent dialogue, it appears to me that a good deal of progress has been made in discussing the primacy question, and it is possible for this to become more viable for both Protestant and Orthodox Christians. Do you think, Cardinal Suenens, that the fuller development of the reality, not the theory, but the reality of coresponsibility will enhance this ecumenical possibility?

Well yes, that's exactly why I emphasized coresponsibility in my book—first, because I thought it was true, but secondly, because I think it is the key for all ecumenical dialogue. We cannot make any advance in the ecumenical field if it is not very clear that the church is the whole people of God, living as Christians in full coresponsibility, each according to his charism. There is the charism of the pope and of the bishops; there is the charism of the theologians; there is the charism of the laity, all complementing each other in their own way. I think that it is essential for the future of the church, and the future of visible unity that all should work out of this fullness.

How could you apply this to the question of the primacy of the papacy?

The question of the primacy of the papacy, if it is seen in the light of coresponsibility, makes it possible to view the papacy not as something disconnected, not as something in lone grandeur over and against anything else, but rather it is seen as standing in the midst of the total people of God in the whole church. The heart is in the center and the head is connected with the body. I should say the pope is the voice of the church, not in the sense that he is *only* the voice, since at the same time he has to give the final authenticity in case there is some dogmatic or moral controversy. But that means that he is never outside the church, or never above the church. I think it is useless to continue theoretical discussions in juridical terms, asking for example: "How far can the pope go and decide all alone?" I agree with what Dr. Ramsey said in his book *Church and the Gospel:*

> For a primacy should depend upon and express the organic authority of the Body; and the discovery of its precise functions will come not by discussion of the Petrine claims in isolation but by the recovery everywhere of the Body's life, with its bishops, presbyters and people. In this Body Peter will find his due place, and ultimate reunion is hastened not by the pursuit of the papal controversy but by the quiet growth of the organic life of every part of Christendom.

It was exactly to foster that growth of organic life that Vatican II insisted so strongly on the collegiality of the bishops under the pope but with the pope at the same time. The big problem in the church today is to put that collegiality in full action. It doesn't mean that the pope is subjected to the college of the bishops, but it means that his visible union with the college of the bishops in the elaboration of major decisions is of first importance for the good exercise of his primacy. The collegial process in the spirit of Vatican II goes further than some private consultation of the bishops: it implies an exchange of views, a discussion, a sharing, a true dialogue. This alone can create a common mind and at the same time makes place for plurality where plurality is needed. This process of discussion is such an enrichment for all that it really appears as the most appropriate instrument of the Holy Spirit at work, bringing about that convergence and complementarity of views which creates harmony and unity.

Do you think that papal infallibility appears different if it is viewed in the light of an understanding of the nature of the church determined by coresponsibility?

Yes, I think so. It would do away with the image of an arbitrary, autocratic, despotic, doctrinal authority, exercised by one man. This popularized image doesn't correspond to the true teaching of the church in the matter, but we have to react to the "isolation" in which the pope appears also in this field. Vatican I, when defining the pope's infallibility was very careful to avoid such disconnection and said on purpose that the pope had the same infallibility as that which has been given to the church: *ea infallibilitate pollere, qua divinus Redemptor Ecclesiam suam in definienda doctrina de fide vel moribus instructam esse voluit.*

This means that the pope is infallible, under certain conditions, because of the infallibility of the church and not vice versa. By stressing this identity, Vatican I wished to indicate that the infallibility of the pope is not something different, apart from, or outside the infallibility of the church. When the term *ex cathedra* is used in connection with papal pronouncements, the same interpretation is to be given as for infallibility. The emphasis falls on the meaning of the total church and the pope standing in the midst and speaking out of the midst of that total church. It refers to the pope's role within the totality of the whole people of God. He speaks from within this total center. I said in my book that perhaps a word other than "infallibility" could be found in order to avoid difficulties. Perhaps we can try another way of saying what this concept intends. The essence of the idea is that Christ will always be faithful to His church and that His spirit of truth will remain with her and in her and that the essential message of the Gospel will be given to all generations.

In your book you make clear that there are two theological views of the church at tension today: one, more juridical, more legalistic, and the other one emphasizing coresponsibility and decentralization. Why did you opt for the latter view?

Well, because I am convinced that the latter view, stressing coresponsibility, is in the line of the Gospel, especially of the Acts of the Apostles. I opted for this "pluralistic view" because it appears to be at the same time a more spiritual and sacramental view of the church and also because it opens the way for a true ecumenical dialogue. If you start with the idea that the church is a communion of local churches, at once you have plurality and unity at the starting point. St. Paul speaks about the church of God which is in Corinth, the church of God which is in Ephesus. He doesn't speak about the church of Ephesus, the church of Corinth, but the church of God in each place. So when we speak about the church of God which is in New York, London or Brussels, already we have unity in plurality, and we have plurality at the same time. The universal church exists concretely only in local churches in the daily reality of time and space. If we see the church as a communion of churches, at once we will be open for plurality and we will not identify the church with a legalistic uniformity. The center is there from the beginning for the essentials as the center of unity in faith, but pluralism is organically integrated as well.

One of the things that interested me in your book was your concern for a Christian style of life in the midst of a rapidly secularizing world. When one approaches this issue from the perspective of coresponsibility, a certain style of Christian life and action follows.

Yes, such a perspective would bring more freedom for personal responsibility and development. Too much legalism brought about a too detailed set of moral rules, often imposed under pain of mortal sin. It brought about a too rigid and authoritarian relationship between those in authority and those who had to obey. The idea of coresponsibility was already at work on every page of my books, *The Gospel To Every Creature*, and *The Nun in the World*. I am still trying to develop these ideas today. Nowadays there is a shift in our understanding of authority. We realize that those in authority, in and outside the church, need the entire community in order to exercise their function. They need the cooperation of all in the process of decision making. The entire image of authority is changing, which doesn't mean that authority is no longer necessary. No, it is just more respectful of the individual person. The leader is no longer the man who has all the answers, but the leader is the man who succeeds in creating the environment in which dialogue, research and constructive criticism are possible and in which the answers emerge by the gradual process of consent. I think that is the future direction of the church—all parts moving together *through, with* and *under* authority.

Your book Coresponsibility in the Church *really is this move towards such a church of the future. Does this not emerge naturally out of Vatican II? And open the way for a Vatican III? Is it not inevitable that the more coresponsibility is really actualized in the life of the church, the more councils there will be?*

One council in the past decided that a council should take place every twenty years, but such a rhythm wasn't taken into account. We may of course expect in the future a Vatican III. But much more thinking and research beforehand is needed in many fields, especially in the theological one, if it is to be really fruitful. I hope that we will not have a hiatus similar to that which marked the distance between Vatican I and II. If coresponsibility becomes more fully actualized in the life of the Christian community then the church will be much more alert to the necessity of sharing concerns and clarifying issues and constant renewal will be at work in the church. This will be done by the development of parochial, diocesan, national, regional and continental councils. Thus a Vatican III would really be an expression of the whole church.

What do you see as the next specific steps to be taken to achieve new levels of coresponsibility in the church? Without coresponsibility, I don't see how renewal can continue or how the new ecumenical reality can deepen and grow.

We must just start from where we are and move forward. What Vatican II set up we must develop fully in all directions. I think the key for the future is our loyalty in accepting coresponsibility at every level and putting it fully in action. At the highest level it means that the way collegiality will work out between the pope and the bishops will be an issue of utmost importance. The synod of the bishops in Rome in October will deal with that relationship. Will the synod bring about a still more accentuated centralization of the church or will it be a step towards decentralization? This will be the big question.

Vatican II stressed the need for more decentralization, for adaptation of the ecclesiastical life to the needs of the people in the local churches. But in the center a strong tendency still prevails to emphasize the primacy of the pope in such a way as to leave little room for practical collegiality of the bishops. The battle is still going on in Rome on the theological level, by stressing the absolute monarchical interpretation of papal power and, on the practical level, by reserving many decisions that affect the daily lives of the faithful, thus undermining the authority of the local bishops or the bishops' conferences. The danger of the present centralized system of government is that authority will lose its credit. People will not take sides for or against papal authority. They will simply ignore it. Those who are promoting decentralization are convinced that they are the most faithful to a real primacy of service. If collegiality is fully put into practice it will be of benefit for the church and for the pope because it would enforce his position in the right direction and not at all weaken it as many curialists think.

To remain on the highest level still, I see also as very important the new International Pontifical Commission of thirty theologians, created recently at the suggestion of the first synod in 1967. The majority of the members of this commission are known as first class theologians. When the synod asked for such a commission the intention was to put at the disposal of the pope the most qualified theologians of the world—united in the same faith, but belonging to different schools of thought—to help in the study and the preparation of more important documents, before they would be given to the bishops' conferences for further discussion. Such a group of theologians will be a big help too, I think, in preventing misinterpretations. Since they come from different cultural backgrounds they are well equipped for avoiding misunderstandings due to the fact that some terms have quite different meanings in different cultures.

I remember that when the Encyclical *Populorum Progressio* came out, there was some trouble in America because some words were used in the encyclical in a western European sense—the word "socialism" for instance. So, positively and negatively speaking, that commission seems to me to be rich in possibilities for the future.

This coresponsibility in the center about which you speak, how do you see it at work in the local churches?

I am glad that you use the words "local churches," for we have to think also in terms of the local people of God with their bishop. I am struck by the words of St. Cyprian: "Remember that the bishop is in the church and the church is in the bishop." The practical consequences of this are important. It means that we bishops are to be seen, too, in close communion with our priests, our theologians, our religious, and our laity and that we have to put into practice that permanent and open dialogue intended by Vatican II. Already some institutions have been created. We must develop and extend these and use them to the fullest. We have to be open to our priests, especially in our presbyterial council. I am not afraid of such a dialogue, even if it is not always comfortable. We have to listen to our theologians, but at the same time, theologians have to be in close touch with the life of the faithful, with the *sensus fidelium* at work in the church.

For example, just see what happened when lay people, very good Catholics, started thinking about marriage and life in marriage out of the center of their faith. They went to the theologians and said, "what you are expressing is not what we are experiencing," and they obliged the theologians to rethink all those aspects of marriage. This set loose a basic reexamination by theologians. What we have said in Vatican II about marriage is largely the fruit of that dialogue between laity and theologians, laity and priests and bishops. So to teach, one must constantly learn. Finally, we have to be open to competency in every line and in every area, otherwise there will be a credibility gap on all sides and grave misunderstanding and even unfortunate distrust will emerge.

Cardinal Suenens, you have just sketched out some of your hopes for the future development of coresponsibility at all points in the life of the church. What would you consider as the main obstacles in achieving that goal?

I would consider that the major impediments today are twofold. First, the lack of real, deep, evangelical faith. Secondly, the lack of courage in the implementation of that faith. We need men of faith, which means men totally committed to Christ, having met Him in a personal encounter and who, therefore, are ready to give their life to make Him better known and served and loved throughout the world; men who are translating the Gospel into their own daily lives, thus showing that Christianity is a message of good news for mankind. And we need men of courage to accept the heavy price to pay for following the logic of the Gospel. What courage is needed to remove from inside the church all that is not evangelical, all that is too human in the heavy heritage of the past, all that dust accumulated through the centuries! We need courage to walk on the waters, facing the difficult and even the impossible so we may demonstrate that more often than people think, "the difficult is what can be done at once and the impossible is what requires a bit more time!" Courage is nothing more than daily fidelity to the Holy Spirit at work, pushing us to speak and to act when silence, compromise and immobilism would be so comfortable and easy . . . courage just to be true to the Gospel and to believe that truth means liberty and justice and that we must promote, by every means in our power, that same liberty and justice where they are wanting.

This is very much in the spirit of Pope John when he said, "Let's just throw open the windows and let the air come in and let's see what happens."

Yes, yes, yes. If you make possible a draft of air there is a danger that you might catch a cold, but if you close the windows there is a much greater danger of suffocation.

Yes. If one doesn't have faith, one cannot risk.

That's it exactly. And faith means hope, otherwise, it's not faith. And hope means going ahead. We have to be impatient because the Christian future of our people is at stake. You Americans say: "Time is money." May we not say: "Time is souls!"

Let us concentrate further on the impediments to achieving greater coresponsibility in the life of the Church. To a Protestant, it appears that the curia itself is a major impediment to further progress towards coresponsibility. As I read your works, I have not seen you attacking the curia, or particular people within it, but I have noted your raising basic questions as to the adequacy of the curia as an instrument in the life of the church today. Is that a correct statement?

Yes. I analyze the curia. I do not criticize the persons in charge. It is my judgment that the administrative patterns of the curia, after three, four, five centuries of use must be drastically reformed to meet the different needs of society today. These patterns must take into consideration contemporary internationalization, the presence of the church on five continents, and the rapid pace of life. The church is confronted with all that is happening all over the world. She is deeply involved at all local levels. This must be faced realistically.

The first thing needed is a basic study of the whole administration apparatus of the papacy today and especially the role of the curia. What is its exact function? Is the curia only an instrument for the pope or is the curia at the direct disposal of the pope with the bishops. The answer one gives to that question has vast consequences both for the total church and for the curia itself. I think that we must see this in its theological depth. It is not simply an administrative issue. But now, after that, you can ask the question: "How is it to be done?" I don't know. I just say, well, we cannot do it alone. To discuss this issue we need the best experts on "organization on a large scale," the best sociologists, the best men in projecting the future of society and what the world will be in the year 2000, and the best theologians. The question is how can the central administrative structure be organized so that it can be truly faithful to its essential task—respecting at the same time the divine and the human components of the church.

Many Protestants and Orthodox respond warmly to such an analysis. I assume that it is because of your view of the church, that in all your writings, you press for a genuine pluralism, a rich diversity, within the circle of truth, all under the guidance of the Holy Spirit. To what extent, Cardinal Suenens, do you find various contemporary nontheological analysis of man, of society and of history, upholding this same view? For example, the contemporary biological view of man views man as an organic process and not as a given static form.

This is very much to the point. The church's view of herself has always been in close relation to man's total way of thinking about life at a given epoch in history. This did not undercut revelation, it meant that revelation was explained to man in terms that he could comprehend. For example, Paul took a Stoic concept, and a Greek concept, the *logos,* to interpret the meaning of Christ to a Hellenistic world. Aquinas depended heavily on Aristotle's analysis of nature to make sense of creation and revelation to medieval man.

What we now see in the philosophical field and in the scientific field is an organic, interdependent view of reality. In all areas of analysis, reality is seen to be indeterminate, an organic process with all dimensions interdependent and interacting as a totality. Without such a view man would not have been able to plan to enter space. This too is a form of coresponsibility. This does not mean that theology is dependent on this view of reality, but it's a sort of confirmation of this way of viewing the reality of the church. This confirmation makes it more understandable to modern man as the *logos* was to Hellenistic man.

Also in our view of races, nations, and continents, we are very conscious today of a process of continuity, of contingency, and diversity of people and nations. We are discovering now what we have long been. When the church went to different countries to preach the Gospel, we often confused our national cultural forms with the Gospel. And we brought all sorts of cultural forms in the name of the Gospel—Latin, the style or the architecture of churches, certain pagan holidays that we baptized, and so on. We put up ugly churches sometimes in countries where there was a lovely native style. Now we are beginning to see all the variety that is possible—*ecclesia circumdata varietate.* This is a reality of the church today.

The same shifts have occurred in sociology and in philosophy. We know that the same values can be lived in different formulations and in different ways. That is one way that a genuine pluralism operates. This is what we have now—a pluralism in the life of the church at all points reflecting the different stages and phases of history. We know that we must express even dogmatic formulations at a given moment of time in the face of a particular heresy and in terms that make sense to the people of that time. After a while, circumstances being changed, we have to express the same fundamental truth in other words. The truth does not change but its form frequently does. The history of the church demonstrates that the truth is the same yesterday, today, and tomorrow but the forms are the forms of yesterday, today, and tomorrow. We are searching for today's forms which will not violate the eternal truth but be adequate to it for today.

You have been criticized for having spoken out in public on a number of these issues. Why did you feel that you had to speak out in public?

I think a public discussion of church problems is very normal today—the more so when discussion is going on everywhere in the world. We are not accustomed in the church to dealing publicly with public opinion because we are still not fully aware that the church is the whole people of God. Since every Christian is coresponsible for the whole church he has a right to be informed of the problems which vitally concern the church. That right has been fully recognized by Pope Pius XII and by Vatican II. The council made an appeal to all its members to express themselves openly, even if it needed a lot of courage. This applies to bishops too! We are too often accused of being a church of silence and of fear. The liberty of the children of God is a reality of our faith—let us not forget it. That liberty of speaking involves liberty in formulating criticism. This, too, is normal, when it is done in a constructive, positive way. It is not disloyal to be critical in regard to any authority here on earth. Authority has to be open to feed-back: its prestige will be enhanced by such readiness for discussion. The final word to be spoken by any qualified authority will have more weight when the preceding words took the form of critical dialogue. This is true at all levels in the church and especially today. I, too, as a bishop, am part of a system and have to revise the exercise of my authority by daily confrontation with those around me. We need each other to obey together the Lord who is our only Master and the Gospel which is the supreme law and the final value of every tradition.

This is really a call to Christians of all denominations to be coresponsible and to perform their respective functions in mutual dependence. You can see that's why I call your book a "Tract for the Times."

I thank you for that expression so full of ecumenical meaning.

• •
•

Collegiality and Ecumenism

Even before the *ICI* interview, Cardinal Suenens had insisted on the ecumenical significance of this debate. In an article entitled "The Bishop—a Catholic View," published in *Concilium: Ecumenism:* No. 5 (April 1969), he wrote:

Everyone knows—and His Holiness Pope Paul VI has openly stated—that the major obstacle to ecumenical understanding is the dogma of the primacy of the pope, as defined by Vatican I. The main objection to this primacy is the assertion that in practice it eliminates episcopal collegiality or reduces it below the vital minimum. Vatican II— first by its mere existence and then by its actions and texts—has highlighted the inalienable role of the episcopal body with and under Peter. But a Council text— no matter how important—is after all only a text; it lives solely through its translation into the concrete, its *Sitz im Leben.* The Orthodox, Anglican and Protestant world is particularly interested in seeing the manner in which the bishops will translate this collegial attitude into actions.

At the close of the Council, Dr. Albert C. Outler, who had attended the Council as observer of the Methodist Church, wrote in an American magazine that the test of our ecumenical sincerity will be the implementation of episcopal collegiality at the very heart of the Church . . .

This is true especially of the bishop who is coresponsible with the pope for the life of the Church. An episcopal coresponsibility that is lived and carried to its logical and concrete consequences is, in today's Church, an eminently ecumenical service. If we desire to eliminate the "major obstacle" from the road that leads to visible unity, the primacy of the pope—which is contested by no Catholic—must appear within the balanced and complementary framework proclaimed by the Council. But how can this common concern be translated into life? A Council is doubtless a spectacular expression of this coresponsibility: its mere existence has led to the disappearance of a good many fears or prejudices, and its actions have contributed strongly to marking out the path towards ecumenism. But a Council is rare, and Vatican III is not yet on the horizon. Hence, the question arises for the present: What can be done by the bishop on the level of the universal Church? He can fully assume his proper responsibility in the institutions which Vatican II has created . . .

Everything that accentuates and improves the dialogue between the "center" and "periphery" is of capital importance. It is in putting into practice the pluralism of particular Churches that the central unity stands out better and is deepened: uniformity is not synonymous with true unity, no more than conformism is the test of obedience. We must live the communion of local Churches at the highest level, in the heart of the Catholic Church. In so doing, we will pave the way for the visible communion of the Christian Churches at the heart of the one Church which is the very hope of ecumenism. . . .

However, this kind of ecumenism is not taking place only in Rome; it is going on at the heart of every local Church, which is not merely a part of the universal Church but the very Church of Christ present under another mode. The Council has emphasized the coresponsibility of all the members of the people of God: this emphasis is eminently ecumenical. The Orthodox world attaches the greatest importance to this communion of all in the bosom of the people of God. The *sobornost* is a living reality at the heart of Orthodoxy. On its side, the Protestant world has placed the accent on the priesthood of all the baptized and on the active role of each of the faithful. Despite the differences which still remain on these points among the Churches —less in what is affirmed than in what is denied—a convergence is taking shape in attitudes and deeds. The bishop, more than anyone else, is called to put into practice in the daily life of his own Church the active and converging collaboration of all: priests, deacons, religious, laity. . . .

Much is said about the present crisis of authority and it is real; but we believe the manner of exercising authority is more of a crisis. Formerly, authority appeared above all as a juridical power of command; today, authority is conceived chiefly as a service rendered to the community by making the effort of all converge towards the common end.

If the bishop appears as the isolated head of his presbyterium and his people, he retards not only the evolution taking place within the heart of the Church, but also hinders the progress of ecumenism. On the level of both the universal and the local Church, the image of authority experienced will be a decisive factor in the harmony of the Churches.

We need merely think of a John XXIII who simply by his manner of exercising authority caused ecumenism to take great strides, laying to rest a good many prejudices. Paul VI, "pilgrim on the move" to Jerusalem or to Constantinople, evokes other images which themselves give cause for hope and prophetism.

It has been said that ideas are stronger than armies; nowadays, in the century of the visual, images can have a nuclear force. Each bishop is called upon at his level to shatter a certain conventional image of the bishop of yesterday and substitute the rejuvenated image of the post-conciliar bishop. We are emerging from a long era of juridicism, legalism, and at times even—it must be admitted—"talmudism." The absolute monarch type of authority is in the process of disappearing and giving way to a new type of authority based on multiple and diversified collaboration rooted in the whole.

Of course, we must not substitute for a juridicism "from superior to inferior" another juridicism "from inferior to superior"; the latter would be as harmful as the former and betray true co-responsibility by abusively expressing it in terms of parliamentarianism. The Christian variety of "participation" is too much a reality of faith to be reduced to our single human schemas and sociological categories. Ecclesial communion must be respected in all its complexity and complementarity: the bishop has the vital task of situating himself at its heart and animating it.

In promoting this active communion in theological faith, hope and charity at the heart of his own Church, the bishop fulfills the primordial requirements of Vatican II. In so doing, he responds to what "the Spirit says to the Churches" in the hour of ecumenism.

An Orthodox Commentary

It is well known that the Greek Catholic Church, which sprang from Orthodoxy, is agonizingly conscious of the need to restore unity between Rome and Constantinople. Bishop Zoghby, the Greek Catholic Archbishop of Baalbok, Lebanon, also testified to the ecumenical importance of the interview:

We can continue to keep up charitable relations with the Orthodox Churches, but it is absolutely out of the question to speak of Christian unity until a genuinely collegial system replaces the strictly advisory system within the Catholic Church.

In the West, however, the advisory system in the Church has made progress since Vatican I. It is a first step. Although the texts of Vatican II are not yet sufficient for episcopal collegiality to develop normally, they could serve as the basis for a real participation of the bishops in the government of the Church. Will we have to wait for the next Council to make a real move from this advisory system to a really collegial Church? It seems so. Then and only then will the Catholic church have eliminated the centuries-old virus that provokes division and schism, and ecumenism will be able to move from the level of brotherly love to that of dialogue. (I.C.I. 9-15-69)

PROTESTANTS REACT

This same vision of the situation and the problem has inspired a number of non-Catholics and non-Catholic publications to react to Cardinal Suenens' interview in a much less negative way than did Bishop Charrière, and sometimes in a very positive way.

"A Protestant believer could agree with a great deal of Suenens' criticism," says the newspaper *Trouw*, of the Netherlands. "One big difference remains however: the Cardinal does not question the position of the pope as patriarch of the West. Trying precisely to enlarge the limits of the regional structure which surrounds the man and the function, he intends obviously to give a broader meaning to the papacy. However, if that is to facilitate and clarify dialogue with other churches (not only with Protestants of the West, but also with the oriental churches) we would, again from the Protestant side, be happy with this vision of Suenens."

"A Courageous Voice" is the title of Jean-Claude Odier's article in *Paix et Liberté* (5-30-69), the Belgian Protestant weekly:

Without doubt, though a Protestant, I must warmly salute the statements made by the Archbishop of Malines–Brussels, not because they settle all arguments between Catholics and Protestants (we are far from this) but because it is part of our role to encourage any effort—whatever its source—which seeks a greater authenticity of life and of service in the name of the Gospel.

The statements that the Primate of Belgium gave to *Informations catholiques internationales* make a dent in the traditional Protestant complaint, that Catholicism is much too much the business of the Vatican and of the Vatican alone. We are pleased to note a clear desire to give local Churches their proper importance and thus to give bishops their own importance in relation to the pope. Let me quote this sentence: "We must avoid presenting the role of the pope in a way which would isolate him from the college of bishops whose chief he is." It is a fact that, for the Protestant commentator, the more the Catholic Church takes a collegial direction, the less the unacceptable idea of authority resting on the Sovereign Pontiff alone will be evident. For those of us who are used to not having any spiritual authority other than Christ alone, and to considering ministers and qualified laymen as the people in charge of running the Church, the meaning of collegiality seems to be the basis of ecclesiology. . . .

Obviously, we have serious reservations when the Archbishop of Malines-Brussels reminds us that a pope must make the Church of Rome "Mater et Magistra" 'the mother and the guide of all the Churches in the world.' Even pushed to its highest point, collegiality could never permit a "supernatural prestige" to be attributed to a particular local Church, and consequently to the bishop of Rome. One can think of real collegiality only if each member of a governing group has the same power or rather the same function. But this is a Protestant speaking, and the statements of the Cardinal are intended mainly for the Roman Church itself, let us not forget.

In any case it is very courageous of the Primate of Belgium to speak of "a true and Christian conception of unity which includes legitimate diversity, and an incorrect conception of this unity which prohibits or excludes legitimate diversity."

In conclusion, Jean-Claude Odier writes:

Certainly, in giving this interview, a prophetic voice has made itself heard within a Catholic Church which has unfortunately lived too long within the confines of hardened legalism and an institutional structure which finds it difficult to adapt to day-today events. A spirit of liberalization—of bishops in relation to the pope, of local churches in relation to the Church of Rome, of priests and lay people in relation to bishops—will certainly permit a greater ecumenical openness and the full discovery of Christ, without embellishments, as Head of the Church, of which every Christian is a member.

Georges Richard–Mollard, a correspondent for religious affairs who is very much aware of the problems of the Catholic Church, commented equally positively in the French Protestant weekly *Réforme* (7-5-69):

This spectacular declaration of the Primate of Belgium, on the eve of the second session of the episcopal synod in Rome, a declaration which summarizes so much other research and evangelical action, can provoke only one reaction: a genuine ecumenical *acknowledgement* of the irrepressible action of the Holy Spirit—an action brought about by the living word of God, which the technico-scientific revolution of our time obliges us to rediscover together as the only possible recourse. . . .

Never mind the insinuations and rumors that you hear about Suenens since he has spoken—this is nothing new in ecclesiastical circles whenever "the Lord God is the first to be served." What is of extreme importance for the universal Church is the fact, almost without precedent, that one of the highest dignitaries in the Roman Catholic Church, and not just a courageous theologian, a cleric under suspicion, or an obscure layman, has spoken so clearly. It would be good if the member bodies of the World Council of Churches, these Churches which are catholic, too, but not Roman, would take *for themselves* most of these declarations, and not be satisfied with listening kindly to criticism presented by someone such as James Baldwin, at Uppsala, without themselves changing in any way, without taking seriously the demands of the Gospel in our time.

The interview will undoubtedly be a milestone in the increasingly rapid movement of all the Churches toward a stricter obedience to the Lord, of a world that hungers and thirsts for justice and truth. Suenens, suspected and under attack, has already said that his declarations have brought him a great amount of mail from fallen-away Christians, who found their confidence in the Church renewed.

As for myself, I would like to quote on this occasion what I wrote during Vatican II, more in hope than because there was any good reason to think so. Telling of the long struggle that had led up to collegiality, I said: "I dare to hope that by a process of escalation in reverse, infallibility will little by little climb down the steps of the pontifical throne, and find itself in the totality of the People of God that was given the main place in *Lumen Gentium*." I wonder if this "rocky road, full of dust, failure and weariness" of which Suenens speaks at the end of his statement, is not the only road obedience can take.

THE NECESSARY CONVERSION

Hébert Roux, pastor of the Reformed Church of France, an observer at the Council, and one of those who, on the Protestant side, remains one of the strongest poles of ecumenical dialogue and research, developed a broader subject. He speaks of Cardinal Suenens' interview in an article introducing readers of *Réforme* (10-2-69) to the second episcopal synod at Rome:

Without going back in detail over what one could call the Suenens "case," which has seen many complementary developments during these last few months, in the form of declarations and talks, and which has given rise to so many hostile reactions, one should be attentive to a *fact* (which by the way is not without precedent, since there has been the Lercaro "case," the Dom Helder Camara "case," . . . and a few others). The same thing always happens whenever an authorized voice speaks out to stress publicly a certain number of essential issues of Church doctrine, issues given their rightful importance by Vatican II. The Cardinal draws the logical consequences which answer the deep needs of Christian people concerning church renewal, suggesting reforms that are desirable in the style of government of the Church in order to preserve unity in diversity. As soon as such a voice speaks out, you immediately hear other equally authorized voices in opposition, and they go so far as to denounce and even to discredit the interpretations given of the conciliar *aggiornamento*, trying to present them as suspect of deviationism. If we leave aside, as we should, any criticism or reservations we may have concerning the method or the form the Cardinal used to make his thinking known, there remains the fact that as far as content goes, the emotion stirred up by some of his statements or propositions in governmental spheres and particularly among those who will undoubtedly constitute the majority of the Roman Synod, gives an idea of the difficulties the Roman Church is up against when it is a question of moving from intentions to actions, of translating the principles lately proclaimed by the Council into facts and into the concrete life of the whole body of the Church.

One wonders if the 'logical implications of Vatican II' advocated by Cardinal Suenens do not run up against another centuries-old internal type of development, and if the former will be strong enough by itself to replace the latter. Above all we must wonder if the questions which were asked and which have not as yet received answers—about the reality of the local Church as the gathering together of the people of God and as a communion; about coresponsibility at all levels of Church life, the reform of canon law and the spirit of the Gospel, the pope and the Curia; and still other questions which have not been raised in a dogmatic way but existentially and pastorally —we wonder if these questions can receive any kind of solution, if the one question which precedes and underlies the others is not asked and clearly answered: *can Rome get out of the blind alley where the post-conciliar crises close it in more and more, in any way other than through a deep and decisive theological and ecclesial "conversion"?* This term must be given its full meaning, its biblical sense of turning around, of transformation, of changing the direction not only of one's way of thinking but also of one's way of living and moving; this is the meaning Jesus used when he said to Peter (already!), "And you will be the one, when you will be converted (when you have returned to me), to strengthen your brother!"

Let me give one last example to reaffirm the need many clerics and lay people in the Catholic Church feel for this theological conversion; they are working for it too. I am taking it from a recent article by Yves Congar in *La Croix* (9-19-69) on the relation between papal and episcopal power. There is here, he says, "*a very important ecclesiological problem which has not been solved,*" even if "in practice, things keep moving more or less. . . ." He shows very frankly that, starting with the texts of Vatican II, one can validly defend two opposing theses: one, monarchical, according to which the pope alone possesses supreme power *over* the entire Church, and another, that of episcopal collegiality, according to which the body of bishops exercises supreme power in union with the Pope who, *in* the Church, is its head. Now if the Pope is in the Church, a member of the body of bishops as its head, he couldn't be above it. To solve this paradox, says Father Congar, "*the pope would have to be above in such a way as to be within.*" From the legal point of view, there is no answer; it can only be settled *by going beyond legalism,* and the entire perspective and coherence of the thinking of Vatican II supposes this. As a matter of fact this thinking shows a profound change in the conception of the Church itself, according to which "*the reality of Christian life is deeper and prior to any organizational structure.*" But anyone can see that here, unquestionably, is a demand to reverse this centuries-old type of development of the Western Church, a development always in a monarchical direction, strengthening its legal, centralizing powers! The practical question concerning the relations of authority between the pope and the bishops implies in reality "*a great number of unsettled theological questions, which need studies that don't exist yet. . . .*" Above and beyond what Cardinal Suenens and many others ask, it seems to me that this is, honestly expressed, the basic requirement of this theological and ecclesial conversion which must extend to all fields of life and action, of doctrinal reflexion and of witness. It must do so in all Churches, under pain of decomposition and hardening. This basic requirement is that the ordering of the Church by the Word and in the Holy Spirit for accomplishing its service and its mission, is prior to and determines the order by which it should be governed.

11

The Second Synod: A Turning Point

The revue *Concilium* of April 1969 published these lines of Cardinal Suenens, stressing the importance of preparation for the synods:

Episcopal coresponsibility must enter into play even in the preparations for the Synod. Well before the opening of a synod, there should be a real exchange between the "center" and the "periphery." Not merely concerning the agenda, but also concerning the working mechanism of the Synod, for the future avoidance of tiresome monologues and to the profit of true dialogue. How then can we refrain from hoping that experts in discussion techniques can help to draw a maximum efficiency from these meetings that are so rich in potentialities? . . .

Experts could play a very important role in the synodal commissions which I believe are indispensable for ensuring effective work; the setting up of these commissions through the established system was too haphazard. I could go on at length listing the improvements to be desired in the procedure for debates, voting, etc. As a matter of fact, episcopal conferences have been invited to suggest improvements in view of later Synods. But here it is sufficient merely to indicate the eminently ecumenical interest of a more active collaboration on the part of episcopal conferences in the labors of the Synod. . . .

For a dialogue to be effective and fruitful there must be debate on preliminary and basic questions. It is useless to discuss questions of details after options have already been taken if the very presuppositions of a problem have not previously been examined with complete freedom. If such examinations appear radical in certain cases, they will seem all the more necessary: the success of common efforts is obtained only at this price. The experience of the preparatory commissions for the Council shows to what extent there can be a shift from the juridical preoccupations of a Congregation to the pastoral concerns of bishops actively engaged in pastoral life. Compare, for example, the primitive schema prepared by the congregation and submitted to the preparatory commission of bishops and the text voted on: there is a world of difference between the two.

Doubtless, all of this directly concerns only a certain number of bishops called to Rome by designation of their colleagues or direct nomination. But through these intermediaries each bishop can collaborate in emphasizing collegial responsibility. Everyone must tell himself that the Council is not yet completed and in one sense is only beginning. Life is more eloquent than declarations and everyone knows—following Zeno—that nothing demonstrates movement better than progress.

While the material for this report was being assembled and analyzed, in an attempt to provide a diagnosis of the crisis in the Church, the second Synod of Bishops was held at Rome from October 11 to October 28, 1969. For more than two weeks, 146 patriarchs, cardinals, archbishops and bishops also tried to diagnose the situation and come up with a remedy. It is, accordingly, appropriate to examine the extent to which—contrary to the fears earlier entertained by many —the vision of the Synod and that of Cardinal Suenens coincided.

Karl Rahner had earlier commented that the Suenens interview offered material not just for one synod, but for several. And indeed it was commonly agreed that the 1969 synod could not ignore the challenge issued by the Belgian primate.

"The Suenens vision of the Church is so vast that it will seem to many a preview of Vatican III," Muriel Bowen had written in the London *Sunday Times* (5-25-69). "The extraordinary Synod of Bishops which the pope has convoked for Rome next October promises to be a very lively one. A deep silence has been maintained regarding the agenda. But even if the agenda does not permit discussion of the Suenens proposals in the *aula,* they will certainly be the major subject of discussion in the corridors."

Actually, the synod's theme and agenda not only allowed but called for open and official discussion of the Suenens proposals. The meeting dealt with two related items, the relations between episcopal conferences and the Holy See, and the relations of episcopal conferences with each other. In other words, the pope asked the synod to help him bring Vatican I and Vatican II into theological, pastoral and juridical harmony, to relate primacy to collegiality, pluralism to unity.

Canadian theologian Bernard Lambert formulated the issues in even more penetrating and vital language:

> This was the question. The synod having been summoned to deal with the crisis in the Church, what principal direction would it give to that crisis? For some, especially for Cardinal Daniélou, it was a crisis of institutions and authority. What was needed was to reinforce institutional structures, to reassert the rights and powers of authority, especially of papal authority, and to suppress—to whatever extent might be necessary—any initiative not coming from above.
>
> For others the crisis was primarily one of faith, but also one of confidence in authority. What was most essential, in order to overcome it was to set free the forces of spiritual regeneration in the Church, to harness the capabilities for religious responsibility, to give rein to local and special traditions.
>
> We are here talking about two totally different ways of ruling the Church.

Few thought, when the synod opened, that the Suenens way had the slightest chance of being adopted. What Gregory Baum said on October 17 was what many were thinking:

We have to remember that collegiality was not formulated (by the Council) as a legal concept, but as a moral and sacramental principle. .... If the pope does not recognize the coresponsibility of the bishops, he is not breaking any law. .... If the pope does not let the bishops exercise their collegial responsibility, they can lament, complain and protest, but they have no legal remedy against the central administration.

The question now is to find some legal norms binding all Christians, including the pope, norms which protect and guarantee collegiality in the Church. If the moral force of Vatican II is not enough, if teaching alone does not assure the participation of the bishops and their churches in the supreme government of the Church, would it be possible to find legal norms which would assure the taking of measures in favor of collegiality? The synod will have to debate these questions. It is evident that the central administration wishes at any price to preserve its supreme power.

As the synod is almost completely in the hands of the central administration, its members prepare the texts, they set up the agenda, determine the rules of discussion, etc. It is most unlikely that, at present, the limit of papal power in a collegial Church will be stated in legal terms.

The known reactions of the Curia to the Suenens interview, the spirit and the letter of the *motu proprio* of June 24 on the nuncios, the theology implicit in the doctrinal schema prepared at Rome for the synod could not augur well for the attitude of the central administration of the Church vis-á-vis the "logic of Vatican II."

The hesitant and timorous embarrassment of the European bishops at Chur, the reputation for conservatism of the bishops of the Third World, the massive silence of the world episcopate after the Suenens interview, the very composition of the synod to which only the presidents of episcopal conferences were summoned, the secrecy with which the work of the synod was to be conducted all gave reason to believe that this synodal assembly could not attempt anything more than rubber-stamp the diagnosis and the treatment the

Roman Curia might provide. The wind was blowing towards pessimism.

But the wind changed. Of course, the Curia fought and sometimes fiercely. For example, it exercised considerable pressure on Msgr. William Onclin to tone down his report on the wishes of bishops regarding relationships between episcopal conferences and the Holy See. But its efforts took on rather the character of a quasi-desperate rearguard action covering a retreat. "An almost hysterical reaction," as the very keen observer, Francis Xavier Murphy, wrote in the London *Tablet*.

In fact, because this strategy had to be unveiled four months too soon because of the Suenens initiative, it backfired to some extent at the synod. The May 15 interview, wrote Donald Campion, editor of *America*, permitted "the problems to be treated at the synod to be discussed and diffused throughout the Church. The synod did not take place under a cloud of mystery, and the Catholic in the street was psychologically prepared for the debate. The interview likewise helped to persuade a great number that it was possible to speak frankly and to criticize the structures of the Church without disrespect for persons. Its success is also due to the fact that it provoked the explosive reaction of very conservative groups in Rome, and thus these reactions had time to dissipate before the opening of the synod."

William R. Mackaye commented (*Washington Post*, 10-19-69):

According to a Vatican observer as experienced as Bernard Häring, the anti-Suenens campaign directed by Cardinal Daniélou, had the opposite effect. . . .

From the very first day of the synod it was clearly apparent that an important part of the Curia had understood completely that the interview of Cardinal Suenens was not an isolated point of view, but represented that of numerous residential bishops in the world.

Even before the synod opened, Rome was able to learn the real feelings of the world episcopate because of the reactions to the doctrinal schema. And those reactions had an impact. The report of Cardinal Seper was noticeably different from the schema. It is solidly based on an ecclesiology of communion. It affirms that "unity should not impinge on legitimate diversity," adding the obvious corollary that "the latter should not be favored to the detriment of unity." It takes a stand on the fundamental problem:

> When the pope acts alone, he does not separate himself nor place himself outside the episcopal college. He acts with the power which comes to him from Christ as his direct and immediate vicar. This by no means implies that the primatial function can be exercised according to subjective and arbitrary norms. Quite the contrary, it ought to be exercised according to objective norms based on revelation, tradition and the divine constitution of the Church, as adapted to the changing needs of the times.

This opening statement was still, in the eyes of several, too vague and too uncertain. Cardinal Suenens said so calmly and frankly in the presence of the pope. (See full text, pp. 254-8.)

Nor was Cardinal Suenens alone. One intervention followed another on the Seper report. "Against all expectations, the point of view defended a long time by Cardinal Suenens was expressed—no doubt with nuances—by a number of those who intervened in the presence of the pope himself" (Jean Tordeur, in *Le Soir*, 10-18-69).

The synthesis of this doctrinal debate by Father Anton is unequivocal. There was unanimity or quasi-unanimity among the Fathers in favor of an ecclesiology of communion, in order to affirm the coherence between the primacy defined at Vatican I and the collegiality proclaimed by Vatican II to say that collegiality and primacy should not be opposed, that collegiality ought not to be only affective, but also effective, that the actual, historical, sociological and ecumenical reasons demand a beginning of collegiality. The majority, moreover, if it wants the pope to be free, does not want an absolute monarchy. Most want a more frequent exercise of explicit collegiality. For some, the organs of collegiality should have a deliberative voice, and not merely a consultative one.

When the synod came to vote on whether the report of Cardinal Seper should be accepted "as the basis for a further study in depth of the problem," there were 72 *placet*, 63 *placet juxta modum* (yes with reservation for amendments), 1 *non placet*, 2 abstentions and 5 null votes. The "further study in depth" was entrusted to the international theological commission recently created by the pope. The majority of the amendments dealt with the nature and modalities of this theological study.

The study introduced by a report of Cardinal Marty, of the more concrete aspects of the relations between episcopal conferences and the Holy See was to leave no doubt about the desires and expectations of the bishops of the world. Research here was carried out by linguistic groups. Cardinal Suenens was elected president of the French-speaking group to which he had been assigned. The wishes formulated in the group were expressed unanimously, including the one which the news and commentaries of the Roman press showed was the most to be feared: "that studies be undertaken of the modalities according to which the synod could share more effectively in papal elections." But it was in his own name, not in that of his group, that Cardinal Suenens intervened in plenary session to ask that the statute on nuncios be reviewed "in a more balanced theological perspective."

The synthesis elaborated by Msgr. Onclin on the research of the working groups shows clearly that all agree in affirming the primacy and freedom of Peter; in asking that the principle of subsidiarity be theologically studied in depth and applied in the Church in an analogous way; in seeking to establish closer relations and a better organized exchange of information between the Holy See and the episcopal conferences, and to create a central organism (which could be an expanded synod secretariat), in the service of collegiality; and in thinking that the synod is the best way to express collegiality. Most wanted the synod to meet every two years. Some wanted it to be a deliberative body. All hoped that the pope would attend it in person.

Voting confirmed overwhelmingly these recommendations of the episcopal college. Of the 143 voting: 130 favored a revision of the structures of the synod so that the "concern for collegiality" of the bishops for the universal Church be translated better in deeds; 119 favored a strengthening of the synod secretariat so as to make of it a permanent instrument by introducing into it a certain number of bishops designated by the synodal assembly; 126 wanted this Secretariat to be an instrument of coordination with the Holy See; 125 wanted the synod to be convoked in general assembly every two years; 128 wanted episcopal conferences (or the Eastern synods) to have the right to propose questions for the agenda of the synod; 110 hoped that the pope, while remaining free, would welcome the collaboration of the episcopal conferences for the study of the most important questions, and for the preparation of declarations and decisions concerning the preservation of the unity of faith and discipline in the whole Church; 126 favored the participation of episcopal conferences (or Eastern synods) in the activities of the dicasteries of the curia; 126 asked that the bishop or delegate of a region be listened to when questions concerning the internal life of a diocese or of a province were involved (Henry Fesquet, *Le Monde,* 10-30-69).

The synod discussed more rapidly, but in the same spirit, the third point of its agenda: the relations of mutual responsibility and solidarity of the episcopal conferences with each other.

The frankness with which all points of view were expressed, the method of dividing discussion groups according to languages, and the dropping of the rule of secrecy permitted extensive, rapid and open information: the Church and the world could have the impression that the bishops were living the ecclesiology of communion they had requested. Not only communion with each other, but with the universal Church, whose most urgent preoccupations were expressed, notably by Cardinal Marty, who asked that they be put on the agenda of the next synod. As also with the Roman Curia: the meetings with the congregation for the clergy during which the priests who accompanied the bishops were able to speak with complete liberty and frankness mark a historic date in the government of the Church. And perhaps the most striking of all was the communion with the Pope.

Paul VI decided on attending in person the working sessions of the synod. In his opening address, Oct. 11, he set the tone for the common search, and affirmed the "duty" to "give greater fullness and effectiveness to the collegial character of the episcopate" by expressing collegiality in terms of charity and of coresponsibility, and by defining the two dominant lines according to which the "post-conciliar progress of ecclesiastical communion" should be guided.

This balanced address appeared to Antoine Wenger to be "both an examination of conscience and a declaration of intentions." René Laurentin noted that "never had the pope spoken of 'collegiality' with so much insistence and clearness. This word, which he had not used when founding the synod, and which he had subsequently used in a very reserved and indirect manner up to last year, occurred thirteen times in this address, more than in all his preceding acts together, it seems to me." As for coresponsibility, "that word was chosen as subtitle on page 2 of the *Osservatore romano*, Oct. 11. It is clear that this official journal, anxious above all to express the intentions of the pope without ever going beyond them, would not have permitted itself such a choice without being sure of the intentions of the Sovereign Pontiff. This cuts short the absurd suggestions, widely diffused before the synod, according to which the thesis of coresponsibility launched by Cardinal Suenens was an attack on the pope." (*Figaro*, 10-13-69).

The closing address confirmed further the pope's openness:

> We feel obligated to assure you that it will be our concern, a pleasure rather than a mere duty, to study attentively the follow-up to be accorded to these expressions of public opinion, that is to say, to the votes which you, venerable brothers, have cast this morning and given to the presidency of the synod.

The synod will be convoked regularly every two years; its secretariat will be fully staffed, with the help of "bishops representing the episcopate scattered over the world," who will be able to contribute to the establishment of the agenda.

THE ELEVATOR TO THE THIRD FLOOR

"We shall, no doubt, recognize in the future", Jean Tordeur wrote in *Le Soir* of Brussels, "that this meeting constituted the revival of Vatican II, and that it was 'extraordinary' for the climate in which it unfolded, for the results it achieved, and for the seeds it has sown, but also for a not negligible part in avoiding pitfalls."

These pitfalls include one to which secular as well as ecclesial opinion was particularly sensitive, the risk of taking the means for the end, of reducing to rules of law the relationships of communion, and of concentrating on the organization of the Church at a time when its mission in the world is what is at stake.

"If we western Catholics are not careful" Professor Gerard Philips of Louvain told a press conference at Rome, "we shall soon have emptied of their meaning the concept of communion and of collegiality we have just discovered thanks to Vatican II. We shall soon, following our almost innate leaning toward juridicism, have transformed the communion of charity into a code of canon laws which threaten to smother and extinguish it. And our last state will be worse than the first."

In a similar vein, the Syrian Melkite patriarch Maximos V said: "Here we have tended to become too involved in patriarchialism, episcopalianism and papalism. A profound discouragement would overcome the faithful if we did not affirm more clearly that collegial structures have only one goal: to give better witness to Jesus Christ." Or, as Pope Paul put it: "It is a question of giving to the charity which animates the Church a more intensive, more ordered and more effective activity."

No one thinks that the synod solved all the problems of the Church's internal life and its relations with the world. But such was not its objective. It had to solve the question "upon which depends the solution of all the other problems of the Church" (Paul VI).

It was a kind of key. The key turned in the right direction; it could have been turned in the wrong one, or remained stuck. But a door unlocked is not yet an open door. "If it took time to get the motor started," Bernard Lambert wrote, repeating an expression of Cardinal Suenens, "it was to go a longer road and to go faster. . . . But it is urgent now to see how the motor is working."

Did the synod attain its goals on the level of principles and on the practical level? Two cardinals answered this question asked by the Catholic Italian daily *L'Avvenire* (10-30-69): Cardinal Daniélou said:

I think that the synod attained its goals, both on the level of principle and that of practice. On the level of principle, the important point is this: it appeared that we must not see in the primacy of the pope and the collegiality of the bishops two antagonistic realities, but on the contrary two complementary realities, each of which must be strengthened. First of all, Roman primacy came out of the synod reinforced because it was unanimously proclaimed by the Fathers, collegiality also came out strengthened, as the bishops became more conscious of their responsibility toward the universal Church.

On the practical level there appeared the need to establish more trusting and more efficient relations between the Holy See and the episcopal conferences. It is absolutely necessary to provide the means for assuring this cooperation, which is becoming ever more indispensable, while avoiding, nevertheless, the creation of new structures to obtain it. We must seek rather to make the present structures more effective, particularly by giving them more modern means (transmission of documents, exchange of information and personal contacts).

Cardinal Suenens was more nuanced:

The purpose of the synod was to study the relations between Rome and the local Churches. This purpose has been achieved in the sense that a certain number of important problems were raised. If you ask whether all the issues have been raised, I will answer no. There is still need for other synods in the future. Let's compare the synod to an elevator. I would say we have reached the third floor. Anyone who looks from below can say: "Look, it is up to the third floor. That's progress." But anyone looking at it from the tenth floor will say: "It is still only at the third floor." I believe, therefore, that an important evolution can still take place. On the level of principles, the evolution will consist of stating more clearly what is understood by a theology of local churches and of collegiality in particular; on the practical level, to set up the synod which has become permanent.

In a press conference at Rome after the close of the synod, Bishop Alexander Carter, president of the episcopal conference of Canada, likewise looked to the future:

We must attach great importance to the intervention of Cardinal Marty, supported by Cardinal Koenig, asking that the next synod have as its objective the special problems of priests, the special problems of married people, and the special problems of the Third World, such as hunger and underdevelopment.

•

•   •

The synod, then does not close this dossier; but since it is the "Suenens dossier," it can be closed with a quotation from the American sociologist Andrew Greeley.

If *Time* asked me to name the most representative personality of the sixties, the choice would be easy. I nominate Leon-Joseph Suenens, the man who did not give up. This has been a bad decade. After the brilliant hopes of the beginning, the sixties end in tragedies and deteriorations. Pope John XXIII is dead, the Kennedy brothers are dead, Cardinal Meyer is dead, Martin Luther King is dead, the *secular city* is dead, the credibility of the leadership of our republic is dead, the hope generated by the first session of the Council is almost dead, and countless innocent blacks, yellows and whites are dead.

The temptation to give up is, therefore, very great in such circumstances. Priests have given up, religious have given up, bishops have given up, college presidents have given up, political leaders have given up, many young hippies and drug addicts have given up . . . One can understand it. So many things have turned sour, so many dreams have been smashed, so many hopes deceived.

The Roman Curia, the military and industrial complex and the Kremlin are all still there and at work, completely untouched by the splendid efforts undertaken on all sides: the Peace Corps, the McCarthy campaign or Vatican II. Those who held power did not wish to give it up, or even to consider such a possibility. Thus, there wasn't much else to do except wait and see.

American civil society and the Church in America must still discover someone able to play the role that Cardinal Suenens has played in the universal Church. We have not yet found in our ranks the man who refuses to give up. We have, however, a great need of one.

Many responsible persons in the Church have the same ideas as Cardinal Suenens. In fact, the synod showed that an overwhelming majority of bishops were in agreement with the ideas he expressed in his now famous interview.

But the important point is that Cardinal Suenens was the man who stood up and spoke, the man who endured the violent counter attack of the reactionary members of the Curia (The French were even worse than the Italians). He had to experience the feelings of isolation when he saw himself attacked by a number of cardinals who questioned, in scarcely veiled terms, his loyalty to the Church. Many men of the Church thought that this interview was inopportune and that the chance he might have had to become the next pope had suddenly vanished. It was even insinuated that he might be asked to resign as archbishop of Malines-Brussels.

Hardly a few months have passed, and now the ideas of Cardinal Suenens have been inserted in the final recommendations of the synod of bishops. Few people of our times have seen what seemed to be a defeat turn so quickly into a victory. His interview was not, naturally, the only cause of the remarkable unfolding of the synod, but it was an important center of a symbolic rallying and it served to prepare minds in view of the synod.

Without his refusal to give up, the synod could not have known the overwhelming success it had.

We need men of courage, of tenacity and of hope; honest, intelligent and full of humor; men who take calculated risks instead of settling for narcissistic lamentations; but such men are rare.

Documents

Cardinal Suenens made two notable interventions at the synod.

The first on Oct. 14 in the presence of the pope on the doctrinal schema and the *relatio* which Cardinal Seper made on it. This is the complete text of this intervention.

ON THE DOCTRINAL SCHEMA

All of us in this assembly agree to affirm with the same fidelity that the Church is directed by the College of bishops with Peter and under his authority.

We do not disagree among ourselves either as regards the primacy which places us under Peter nor as regards collegiality which unites us with Peter. But our differences come to light on the way to understand the exercise of primacy according to the will of Christ. Now this question comes up in fact both as to the adequate juridical expression of the function of primacy and as to a fruitful exercise of it, adapted to the sensitiveness of the contemporary world. Our dissent, likewise, bears on the working out of collegiality so that it be the true and effective expression of a veritable coresponsibility and not only the fruit of a vague collegial feeling.

There are some who insist so strongly on the role of the primacy that they easily come to present the papacy as an absolute monarchy of the Old Regime type in which everything depended on the sovereign good pleasure of the monarch. A similar unilateral insistence leads in practice to the negation of collegiality. The *"sub Petro"* eclipses the *"cum Petro."* In such a perspective the danger is serious, and the hopes raised by Vatican II vanish.

We must recognize frankly that there is an uneasiness in the

Church on this subject. The fact, patent to all, is public and discussed among the people of God. Did not Cardinal Heenan recently write an excellent article in the *Sunday Times* on the necessity for a public expression of its thought in the Church?

We must, therefore, with serenity and clarity become aware of the tension in the bosom of a common faith between the tendency called monarchical and the tendency called collegial. At the bottom of this tension there are two different theologies of the Church. There is also a difference of mentality and of sensibility to the signs of the times in a world in which participation in the making of decisions (decision-making not decision taking) is seen more and more as a normal exercise of coresponsibility and as a *sine qua non* condition of the good use of any authority.

In the study of these questions we must absolutely avoid mutual suspicions or excommunication. Nobody has a right to present himself as being the sole defender of the pope: we all profess the same deference and fidelity. But we should have the courage to recognize clearly our disagreements if we do not wish to get bogged down in ambiguity.

When I read the Schema submitted for the discussion of the synod I cannot help but observe that the underlying theology in the text so exalts the primacy that the bishops appear to be reduced, in practice, almost to the role of assistants to the pontifical throne. This is serious, the more so that such a theology, which could be characterized as tending toward absolute monarchy, is in fact the one practically reflected daily in the articles of the *Osservatore Romano,* thereby creating the impression that only this theology is orthodox.

That is why I rejoice that the *Relatio,* appended to the text of the Schema, integrates much better and explains the function of the hierarchical ministry within the global reality of the communion of the People of God (ecclesiology of communion). But the *Relatio* itself confines itself to generalities. It is content to state the problems and does not add any new element for the elaboration of the synthesis between the primacy and collegiality. Moreover, collegiality does not receive its legitimate role, while the role of the primacy is again unilaterally stressed. That is why the *Relatio* itself is not yet satisfactory and I cannot approve it without reservations.

Among other things I wish to emphasize especially the two following points.

1. The reality and the importance of the local church.

It is essential to shed light on the nature and the importance of the local Church. The bishop is the proper pastor of the people entrusted to him and with whom he is in intimate communion.

The relations between the Sovereign Pontiff and the bishops cannot be understood exactly without an adequate preliminary determination of the link between the universal Church and the local churches. Likewise such a determination is equally indispensable if we wish to define in a valid way the nature and limits of the unity necessary to the Church while respecting legitimate differences.

2. The exact and harmonious relationship between the primacy and collegiality.

No doubt the *Relatio* (p. 18) rightly recognizes that the Sovereign Pontiff cannot act in an arbitrary way in the exercise of his power and that he is obliged to respect objective norms. However:

1) The exercise of the responsibility incumbent on the bishops for the universal Church is unduly restricted. In fact, the Sovereign Pontiff appears in it too much like the only one who bears responsibility for the whole Church, and the coresponsibility of the bishops seems to be limited to the help they may bring to the Sovereign Pontiff in the fulfillment of a function which is his alone. This limitation is the more serious as the faithful are already too often inclined to share these views restricting the function of the bishops to the government of their particular church.

2) What is affirmed about the origin of the power of the bishops is frankly equivocal. The *Relatio* (pp. 13-14) mentions an approbation of a social order coming from the hierarchical authority, which would be required in order that the power of a consecrated bishop be made fit to be exercised effectively. Now, the preliminary note to the Constitution *Lumen Gentium* in no way teaches the necessity for such an "approbation" of the power itself of the bishop. It simply mentions the necessity of an ulterior canonical or juridical determination in order that the existing power can be exercised. That is quite a different thing. Moreover, how could one

admit that a power given by Christ need have a human approbation.

3) The collaboration of the bishops in the course of history to the government of the universal Church is reduced to recourse to the Holy See. This certainly does not conform to historical truth *(Relatio* pp. 18-19).

4) The strictly collegial status of the bishops outside of Councils is only referred to in order to emphasize exclusively the role of the Sovereign Pontiff *(Relatio* p. 19).

5) The Schema (p. 10) affirmed that the Successor of Peter was constituted the visible principle of coordination and direction of all activity in the Church. This affirmation is contrary not only to the doctrine of Vatican II, but even to that of Vatican I, and it would ruin all true ecumenism.

CONCLUSION

Of course we wish in no way to deny whatever progress has been achieved in associating the bishops in the government of the universal Church. However, our anxiety remains great because experience shows us that although principles are often affirmed, they are much less often applied. One example among many other possible ones will suffice: think of the two decrees concerning admission to the religious life and to the contemplative life; neither the bishops nor the members of the Commission for the Reform of the Code were consulted.

It results clearly from all this that the doctrinal problems raised by the object of the deliberations of the synod are numerous and complex. It is quite evident that we cannot solve them in a few days. Making my own the proposal of Cardinal Doepfner, I am asking the Synod to send these problems to the International Commission of Theologians for study and examination. And I would add that our Eastern brothers take part in this work; their ecclesiology indeed, which was classic in the early Church for centuries, can teach us a great deal on communion and collegiality.

Of course, we cannot expect a rapid solution, but we can make progress in the search for even provisional practical solutions.

Texts with a perfect theological and juridical correctness are obviously necessary, but let us place more confidence in the vivifying action of the Holy Spirit, principle and source of unity in the Church.

Let us believe in the Holy Spirit, who, in each of us according to his role, is actively present both in the Sovereign Pontiff and the bishops and the faithful.

Let us believe in the Holy Spirit who speaks to us through the signs of the times.

.

.   .

In his second intervention, Cardinal Suenens wished to formulate a "few remarks on the subject of the motu proprio Sollicitudo omnium ecclesiarum" *of June 24, 1969, which reformed the statute of the nuncios. We give here the essential part of this communication:*

ON THE STATUTE OF THE NUNCIOS

I would like to express one wish: that the doctrinal commission which will have to study the precise relations between primacy and collegiality not remain solely on the level of principles, but that it clarify also with the light of an adequate theology, certain pastoral problems so that there be a theological link between the first part and the second part of our work.

I am thinking particularly of the theological study that needs to be made on the function of the nuncios—*ut sic*—for that raises in the concrete the whole problem of the relations between Rome and episcopal conferences, the very object of our debates. There is need, in a better balanced theological perspective, to look over the statute as it appears in the *motu proprio Sollicitudo omnium Ecclesiarum.*

On the theological level this raises quite a few problems.

a) The document begins by recalling affirmations of a dogmatic order (quotations from Vatican II), develops them and then shows their application through the establishment of a purely ecclesiastical network. There is nowhere indicated the passage from one level—that of dogma and theology—to another level, that of an ecclesiastical organization.

Thus, one passes from unquestionable dogmatic truths to an application of content and form, of a purely ecclesiastical order without making any distinction. The most flagrant example of the passage can be found in the use of the terms *legatus* and *legatio.*

This document speaks of the mission of the pope, as universal shepherd, by mentioning the terms *"pro Christi legatione* (a.A.S; LXI, p. 473). These terms refer to a certain theological reality. Again, the only place where *Lumen Gentium* speaks of *legatus* is the passage devoted to the bishops *"episcopi Ecclesiae particulares ut vicarii et legati Christi regunt* (LG n. 27): the word *legatus* indicates there, too, a reality of a fundamental ecclesiological order, of a sacramental order. It is oriented in the line of the bishops, heads of local churches, in communion with the other local churches and with the See of Peter.

Now, in the *motu proprio,* the word *legatus* frequently appears in an entirely different context: that of papal legates, that of nuncios. The transition between the mission of the pope *pro Christi legatione* and his role as sending *his* legates is astounding.

b) We regret that the "presence of the pope" in local churches is envisaged as bound primarily to the presence of the nuncios, his legates.

There is nowhere mention of this presence of the pope in local churches which occurs first of all at a deeper level: notably by the eucharistic celebration, by the communion of local churches with each other and with the See of Peter, by their participation in universal concerns. It is from this central theological reality that one must start.

The underlying idea of the document seems to be that the local churches are sort of administrative departments, possessed of course with a certain autonomy, but which have to be supervised, and they are supervised better by this centralized network, by this "parallel hierarchy" (for the nuncios are bishops) than by normal and daily exchanges and the *regimen Ecclesiarum* of the Churches with each other and with the See of Peter.

It seems, therefore, to neglect the communion of local churches with each other, sacramentally and juridically coresponsible and opt rather for a series of more or less autonomous departments which are centralized by the "safer" subterfuge of papal legates.

From the ecumenical point of view, especially in relation to the Orthodox church, this conception and this document only increase the difficulties. The reactions of the central committee of the Ecumenical Commission of the Churches have shown that collegiality understood in this way veils, in their eyes, the true communion of the local churches with each other.